They Should
Have Served
That
Cup of Coffee

edited by
Dick Cluster

South End Press
Boston

Library of Congress No.: 78-68476
ISBN 089608-082-x paper
ISBN 089608-083-8 cloth

cover design by Nick Thorkelson

Printed at Maple Press Co., York, Pa., USA
Typesetting and layout by the collective at
South End Press
Box 68, Astor Station
Boston. MA, 02123

Acknowledgements

Many, many people contributed time, advice, suggestions, and emotional support to make this book possible. Special thanks go to the authors of essays and subjects of interviews, and to Nancy Falk, Jackie Shearer, Jack Malinowski, Lydia Sargent, and Michael Albert. Bill Thompson, who made several important suggestions, died before the book was completed; *Slice the Dreammaker's Throat,* a collection of his poems, which will be available from South End Press, and testifies to the struggle to which he devoted his life.

I would also like to thank Gregory Falk Cluster and Shana Kuhn Siegal for the companionship and the particular children's vision of love and trust which they provided during much of the writing.

Contents

On February 1, 1960, four Black freshmen from North Carolina Agricultural and Technical College walked up to the lunch counter of the Woolworth's five-and-ten in the city of Greensboro, sat down, and demanded service. For five days they and others who joined them sat there while Woolworth's refused to serve them a hamburger, a coke, even a cup of coffee—because of their race. On the sixth day, the store owners announced that they were temporarily closing down.

Anyone who thought the new "sit-in" movement would die then and there was totally mistaken. It grew and it deepened. In the decade and more that followed, Blacks won the right to sit down and drink coffee in any restaurant. But more important, movements for much more radical goals emerged among Black people, white people, and other peoples, among students and soldiers, among women, and altogether among millions of Americans. The following pages are memories of those movements.

OLD MOLE

direct from*cuba....

As everyone knows, with the press blackout finally ended, 600 Americans have just left from Canada to break the US travel ban and cut sugar cane in Cuba. Right now they are arriving in Havana, together with 60 comrades travelling by plane through Mexico. They are the second contingent of the Venceremos Brigade. The following article, by a Mole staff member who has just returned from her work as part of the first contingent, is intended to provide a general overview of the experience of the Brigade. Articles on specific aspects of the Brigade and of life in Cuba will follow in future issues, and we welcome letters explaining what you might want to know.

by Gene Bishop

As the Cuban ships *Luis Arcos Bergnes* docked in St. John, New Brunswick, February 12, carrying 214 Americans who had been in Cuba cutting sugar cane, a Cuban woman on board ran up on deck. "Snow," she said, sticking out her hand, and then pointed to a cop on the pier. "Pigs," she said and ran back downstairs, "I can go home now, I've seen them both. Snow and pigs."

For us Northamericans, however, snow and pigs meant a different thing – we were home now. The reporters on the dock began baiting us, the Cubans said goodbye and reminded us that it was in the United States that they had the "really, big machetes."

Our comrades from the second group boarded the cattle-boat-turned-passenger-ship, and we boarded buses to return to the States. As our welcome, customs officials in Calais, Maine, took from us everything made in Cuba – from our Venceremos Brigade T-shirts to the many books and posters and magazines and Newspapers. "Coke is the One" said the first billboard.

A little over two months before we had landed in Jose Mari International airport in Havana, and had boarded buses for Campamento Brigada Venceremos, near the small town of Aguacate, about an hour and a half southeast of Havana. *Venceremos* means "We will Win." "Vietnam Vencera" said the first billboard – Vietnam will win. We all cheered – in a different sense we felt we were home in Cuba.

We had gone to Cuba to work. Always before, Northamericans who had gone to Cuba, had gone to see the revolution. We went to learn about it by being part of it. And we really worked. Rep. Richard Ichord, head of the House Internal Securities Committee said last week that "Americans who go to Cuba spend so much time in rallies and speeches with Communist publicity purposes that they have only a few hours left for the cane fields." We wish he could have seen our blisters.

We started in to work right away. The Northamericans – along with 60 Cuban men and women who were part of the Brigade – were divided into 7 smaller cane cutting brigades of about 40 people each. We were each given machetes and we walked out for our first lesson in the canefields. It was given by Reinaldo Castro, the Cuban national work hero – he cuts so much sugar cane that they jokingly call him the "human combine."

Then we tried it ourselves – grab the tall cane with one hand, slice the machete through on an angle halfway down the stalk, then off with the leaves. Finally, the remaining half has to be cut less than an inch from the ground, or the cane won't grow back next year.

At first, we weren't human combines, and we learned slowly. The Cuban discouraged the women from cutting, saying they would be more productive in the operation of piling the cane, in *(continued on page 14)*

The editor (right) with Cuban cane cutting partner, Juan Mari Mass, 1970.

Mass Movements Made the Decade:
An Introduction

The first person I remember talking about "The Sixties" was my junior high principal. He was speaking to a school assembly sometime soon after the Christmas vacation of 1959-1960. "We had the Fighting Forties and the Fabulous Fifties," he told a bored audience of Black and white teenagers in Baltimore, Maryland, "I hope that the decade we're beginning now will be remembered as the 'Serene Sixties.' "

The Serene Sixties sure sounded like a dull decade to grow up in, but I had no reason to believe it wouldn't happen that way. Neither the principal nor anybody in the audience knew what was about to happen 300 miles away in North Carolina, nor what was already happening 10,000 miles away in Vietnam. No one suspected that junior high school students like ourselves would boycott classes and be arrested in demonstrations.

Fourteen years later, I wasn't particularly surprised when junior high school students in Somerville, Massachusetts, where I now live, decided to walk out of school to protest the extension of the school year; in 1960 it would have been unbelievable. It would have been equally unbelievable if someone had told me that, as the result of the emergence of something called a Women's Liberation Movement, girls would one day take shop and boys would take home ec.

To say that "they should have served that cup of coffee" in Greensboro is to say that their refusal to serve it set off a chain reaction that the defenders of segregation in the South and the defenders of things-as-they-were everywhere in the U.S. would have given a great deal to prevent. The value of law-and-order, the truth of "American democracy," the legitimacy of private business, the rightness of "normal" sex roles and sexual relations...all came up for questioning. Despite the recent growth of a right-wing movement which is intent upon reasserting all these traditions, they are still very much being questioned today.

After an era when even *looking* different had been tacitly forbidden, simply growing hair became an act of personal rebellion, an expression of racial or anti-establishment identity, part of a search for alternative ways to live. In music, in clothing, in living arrangements, in the choice of drugs (marijuana, alcohol...some form has always been available), it was a time of feverish experimentation, all of which reinforced and was reinforced by the political activity.

The tremendous variety of committees, collectives, coalitions, caucuses and other organizations that made the word "Sixties" synonomous with protest rather than serenity came to be known as the New Left. This term was first associated with Students for a Democratic Society, which called its newspaper "New Left Notes," but it applied to much more.

This was a New Left because, for the most part, it was neither begun by nor connected to older organizations on the left in the United States. Not that what it did was entirely new: The Black freedom struggle, for instance, is as old as the first uprising on a slave ship. Even in our own century, there are plenty of precedents. The tactic of filling the jails to protest denial of constitutional rights, made famous in the 1960s by the Civil Rights Movement in the South, was pioneered by the Industrial Workers of the World in their "free speech" fight in the West in the 1910s. Among the earlier activists going to prison for opposing foreign wars and the military draft was American Socialist Party leader Eugene Debs; while still in jail, in 1920, he received 900,000 votes as his party's candidate for U.S. President. Five thousand women demanding voting rights were, in 1913, the first demonstrators to stage a counter-inaugural parade in Washington.

But the most recent major organization of the U.S. left had dwindled to near-invisibility by the late 1950s. In the 1930s and '40s, the Communist Party had led the fight for industrial unionism, economic security, and racial justice at home, and support for national liberation abroad. The Party and its activities had drawn significant support from large numbers of citizens. But partly through its own mistakes (especially its unquestioning loyalty to the Soviet Union) and partly through vicious government repression (which jailed all the Party's leaders and made membership a legitimate reason for losing your job and being excluded from any other organization), by 1960 the "Old Left" was small and unpopular. Most of the activists who made up the New Left considered the Old Left "irrelevant."

Most New Left groups nonetheless came to see themselves as socialists or communists of one stripe or another. But their paths to this conclusion, like their paths to power and growth, were their own. The emergence of movements for Civil Rights, for Black Power, against the Vietnam War, and for Women's Liberation were new, radical responses to conditions in the U.S. in the 1960s.

To say that the political movements that burst on the scene in the 1960s began with the Woolworth's refusal to serve the four students in Greensboro is not to say that Woolworth's could have served four cups of coffee and avoided all the trouble that followed. All the laws and customs that kept rich white-run corporations and plantations on the top of the economic ladder in the South, and poor Black laborers and sharecroppers on the bottom, made such an act impossible.

Only the growth of a mass movement changed the South enough to make such a simple sounding reform possible.

Likewise, only the growth of mass action in the cities, North and South, made possible a "War on Poverty" or affirmative action in hiring; only the growth of mass protest against the war in Vietnam changed the political climate enough to make possible a U.S. withdrawal; only the growth of mass Women's Liberation consciousness and action has brought the legal and social changes that have put women a step closer to equal rights.

It was mass movements of political protest that brought about both the revolutionary changes in thinking and the reform changes in institutions that characterized the U.S. in the years after Greensboro. Those mass movements are the subject of this book.

This book does not present the picture of "The Sixties" which the mass media are busily trying to sell us: kids rebelling against anything and everything, or a lot of romantic nonsense about radicalism and revolution which really accomplished nothing. It's not a collection of where-are-they-now snapshots of former activists who grow radishes in Vermont or spend their time struggling against "the real enemy inside ourselves." Those images, splashed across the pages of Sunday newspaper supplements, serve primarily to distract us from the actual political movements of that time, why they flourished, and what they did.

Even the idea of "The Sixties" is somewhat of a myth. A number of the essays and interviews in this book deal as much with the 1970s as the 1960s. Describing radical movements as confined to a single decade is a way of containing them, filing them away, hiding their importance for today's problems and today's struggles. The effect of all this media treatment of our past is to make it harder to go on from here—to make us doubt our own memories of the past, and to make each new generation start from scratch.

In the eight chapters that follow, seven participants in these movements, including myself, describe what we participated in and what it meant. This book is a collection of essays and interviews; it is far short of being a complete history.

Many activities and movements are left out, including: the freedom movements of Puerto Ricans, Chicanos, Native Americans, Filipinos, and other nationalities or ethnic groups; the organizations of welfare recipients and of tenants, and a number of other approaches to community and workplace organizing; the religious and pacifist groups that played steadily important roles in the Anti-War Movement; the Gay Liberation Movement, which is introduced but not chronicled in Chapter 8; the later Black on-campus student movement, which resulted in the establishment of Black Studies programs and other changes.

But the activities which are included have been chosen to give a sense of major mass movements and the lessons and questions they raise. The history of the Civil Rights Movement—which was both an inspiration and a training ground for all the others—is described with a narrative overview and several interviews, focusing especially on the Student Non-violent Coordinating Committee; at the center is an interview taking off from the demonstrations in Albany, Georgia, in 1961 where the mass character of the movement first became obvious to the nation.

The Black movement in the Northern cities is represented by chapters on the Black Panther Party and the League of Revolutionary Black Workers. The new movements that arose primarily in response to the war in Indochina are represented by chapters on the nature of the white student movement, the accomplishments of the anti-war activities, and the emergence of a soldier's movement. The Women's Liberation Movement is portrayed in two chapters: one narrates the emergence of Women's Liberation ideology and organization with a special focus on Bread & Roses in Boston, Massachusetts; the other describes, through a personal history, the position of women within the earlier New Left movements and the impact of the new feminist and lesbian politics.

All the organizations described represent the more radical trends within their movements. But the radicals were consistently the inspiration and the pacesetters for these movements; what was an "extreme" position one year was frequently commonplace the next. While most of the chapters focus more on the strengths and the growth of the organizations they describe, the chapter on the League of Revolutionary Black Workers focuses more on the weaknesses and the eventual break-up; this is not intended to suggest that the other organizations didn't have the same or equally damaging weaknesses. To help the reader get a more complete picture of all the organizations represented in this book, I have included an appendix with suggestions for further reading. To explain references to organizations or events which readers may not know about, I've added historical footnotes where necessary.

The final versions of all the essays and interviews have been approved by the contributors.

Dick Cluster
October 1978

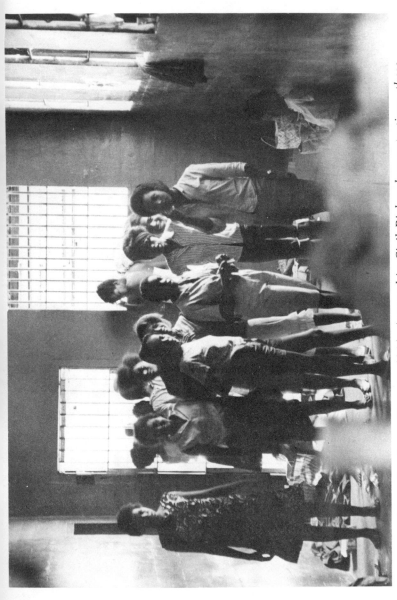

Leesburg, Southeast Georgia, 1964. Arrested in Civil Rights demonstrations, these young women had been in this cell for as long as three weeks. SNCC photographer Danny Lyon reported, "I reached through the glass to the girls. They all reached— 'Freedom.' When I saw them, they were in good spirits." Photo by Danny Lyon/ Magnum.

1

The Borning Struggle:
The Civil Rights Movement

When the Woolworth's in Greensboro, North Carolina closed after the first five days of sit-ins in February 1960, something had suddenly been equalized—if Blacks couldn't eat at the lunch counter, no one could. More important, Woolworth's decision to close while figuring out what to do next testified to the power of the students' actions. Within weeks, other Black students and some white supporters were doing the same thing in cities and towns across the South. They were arrested for trespassing, beaten by angry whites—and sometimes served. And, what was most surprising to observers across the nation, they did not stop.

Picture the Southern states of the United States at this time, the beginning of a decade which was to become synonomous with mass protest. Segregation was complete and nearly unchallenged, both in law and in practice. Blacks were forbidden to eat, ride, play, pray, go to school or go to the bathroom in the same places as whites. They were not allowed to vote (in some counties not a single Black had succeeded in registering in half a century) or to take whites to court. A system of police and Ku Klux Klan terror, erected with a vengeance after the end of Reconstruction in the 1880s, was designed to "keep them in their place."

Yet even before the sit-ins, there were signs that this system was in trouble. Black parents in, of all places, Topeka,

Kansas, went to court to protest against segregated schools, and in 1954 the U.S. Supreme Court struck down its own 1896 decision which had legalized segregation. One important factor influencing this decision was the freedom fight of the African colonies, emerging now as independent nations whose favor had to be courted by the U.S. Another may have been changing corporate needs for a better-trained workforce and a "New South" without the constraints of legal segregation.

But of even greater importance were the signs of rebellion from within. In 1955, Rosa Parks of Montgomery, Alabama, refused to give up her seat in the "white section" of a crowded city bus, sparking a 381-day bus boycott by Blacks which resulted in desegregation of the buses (again by a Supreme Court decision) and the emergence of a young Montgomery minister named Martin Luther King as a leader in the fight for equal rights.

So there was movement by 1960, but there was not yet a Movement. What exploded in that year, beginning with the sit-ins, was a determination by young Black college and high school students to fight for their freedom with a tactic they called "non-violent direct action"—resisting the system of segregation and oppression, not with court action nor even with boycotts alone, but with their bodies.

The sparks that flickered from point to point across the South in 1960 leaped into flames in the spring of the following year. The flames were seen across the nation on Mother's Day of 1961, as a white mob in Anniston, Alabama, burned the bus which was carrying the first of the Freedom Riders. The Freedom Rides, initiated by the Northern-based Congress of Racial Equality, were an effort to test whether integrated groups could travel, as federal law said they should be able to, in the buses and bus stations of the South.

After Anniston and the decision by CORE to call off the rest of the action shortly afterward, members of the new student movement vowed to continue the Rides, and they did.

The organization which the new Freedom Riders joined was SNCC (pronounced "Snick")—the Student Nonviolent Coordinating Committee. First called together in the spring of 1960 as a temporary body to increase communication among local groups conducting sit-ins, SNCC emerged after the Freedom Rides as a permanent political organization seeking to build a mass-based movement among Southern Blacks.

John Lewis

John Lewis, who joined the Nashville student movement while studying for the ministry at the American Baptist Theological Seminary, was SNCC's national chairman from 1963 to 1966. Here he describes the climate of the early sit-ins and the Freedom Rides, and the source of strength which many of the activists found in the spirit—if not the practice— of the Christian Church in which they had grown up.[1]

The Movement during that period, in my estimation, was the finest example of what you could refer to as Christian love. It was highly disciplined. When I look back at that particular period in Nashville, at the discipline, the dedication, and the commitment to nonviolence, it was unbelievable.

Woolworth's was where the first violence occurred. We

1. John Lewis's comments come from the transcript of an interview done for the magazine *Southern Exposure* by Jim Sessions and Sue Thrasher. Their complete published interview may be found in *Southern Exposure* Volume IV, No. 3. Subcriptions to *Southern Exposure,* an excellent magazine about life, power, and struggle in the South, are $10 from P.O. Box 230, Chapel Hill, North Carolina 27514.

had information that the police officials would have us arrested and would let all type of violence occur. We were afraid, but we felt that we had to bear witness. There was a young girl, a young student at Fisk, Maxine Walker. And a white exchange student at Fisk, Paul LePrad. There's a fantastic picture of the two of them around, the two of them sitting at this counter at Woolworth's. And this young white man came up and hit Paul and knocked him down and hit this young lady.

And then just all type of violence started at the counter, pulling people, pushing people over the counter, throwing things like ketchup, grinding out cigarettes on people, pouring ketchup in their hair. Then the cops moved in and started arresting people. That was the first time many of us had been arrested. And I just felt that it was like being involved in a holy crusade. I really felt that what we were doing was in keeping with the Christian faith. It was sort of a moving spirit, something that just came over you and consumed you.

During that night, lawyers and professors and presidents of Fisk and other schools came down to try to get us out of jail. They wanted to put up the bond; altogether it would have been several thousand dollars. We refused to be bailed out. We felt that we hadn't committed any wrong. We wanted to stay.

I did a paper once where I described that early Civil Rights Movement as a religious phenomenon. And I still believe that. You needed something to act on. It was not just the sit-ins and the Freedom Rides, but in order for people to do what they did afterwards, to go into places where it was like going into hellfire—it was like guerrilla warfare in some communities. I'm not just talking about the students, but the community people, indigenous people. It had to be based on some strong conviction, or some strong, I think, religious conviction.

During the Freedom Rides, in May 1961, when we got to Montgomery, personally I thought it was the end. It was like death. Death itself might have been a welcome pleasure.

Before we got there, when we first arrived in Birmingham, Bull Conner took us off the bus and put us in the Birmingham city jail.[2] That was on Wednesday, May 17. Then Friday morning around one o'clock he took seven of us out of the jail, took us to the Alabama-Tennessee state line, and dropped us off. He said, "There's a bus station around here somewhere, you can make it back to Nashville." And I have never been so frightened in all my life. We located a house where an old Black family lived. They must have been in their seventies. We told them who we were, and they'd heard about it and they were frightened. They let us in.

A car was sent from Nashville, and we got back to Birmingham. By this time the total number of us there was about twenty-one. We tried to get a 5:30 A.M. bus to Montgomery. And this bus driver said—I'll never forget it—"I only have one life to give and I'm not going to give it to CORE or the NAACP." Because you see this was after the burning of the bus at Anniston and after the beating of the CORE riders on Mother's Day. We stayed in the bus station all night, with a mob, the Klan, on the outside.

Early that morning a reporter came to us and said he understood that Bobby Kennedy had been talking with the Greyhound people and apparently we would be able to get a bus later that morning, Saturday morning. The arrangement was that every fifteen miles or so there would be a state trooper

2. The CORE Freedom Ride, starting from Washington D.C., had ended in Birmingham, Alabama, when the Riders could not get a bus to take them on to Montgomery, Jackson, and New Orleans. Students from the Nashville sit-in movement then took buses to Birmingham to pick up where the CORE ride had left off. As Lewis describes, Birmingham Police Commissioner Eugene "Bull" Connor, who had allowed the beating of the CORE riders by a white mob, prevented them from getting a bus out of Birmingham for several days.

car on the highway and a plane would fly over the bus, to take us into Montgomery.[3]

So we got on the bus about 8:30. On the very front seat behind the driver I took a seat with Jim Zwerg. We saw no sign of the state trooper cars. We didn't see any plane. It was the eeriest feeling of my life. We got to Montgomery and we didn't see anyone outside of the bus station. We started stepping off the bus and then the media people started gathering around, and just out of the blue, just hundreds of people converged on the bus station. They started beating the camera people, just beat them down. One guy took one of these huge cameras from a guy and knocked him down with it.

People started running in different directions. Two young white ladies that were with us tried to get in a cab, but the Black cab driver said he couldn't take white people. He drove off, and the two young white ladies started running down the street, and John Singer got between them and the mob. Then another part of the mob turned on us, because we were left, just standing, mostly Black fellows. I was hit over the head with a crate, one of those soda crates, wooden crates; and the last thing I remember was the Attorney General of Alabama serving me an injunction, prohibiting interracial groups from using public transportation in the state of Alabama. And I was afraid.

William Barbee was left lying, and he almost died. Jim Zwerg was beaten too.[4] Jim Zwerg was one of the most committed people. And I definitely believe it was not out of

---

3. Robert Kennedy was then U.S. Attorney General and a frequent target for criticism by Civil Rights workers for his refusal to order the Justice Department to protect them or take any action against the Southern police.

4. William Barbee, like Lewis a student at American Baptist Theological Seminary, spent several weeks in the hospital after being beaten into unconsciousness with baseball bats. Jim Zwerg, a white exchange student from the University of Wisconsin studying that

any social, do-good kind of feeling. It was out of deep religious conviction. You know, during Nashville and our nonviolence training workshops, we never thought that much about what would happen to us personally or individually. And we never really directed our feelings of hostility toward the opposition. I think most of the people that came through those early days saw the opposition and saw ourselves really, the participants in the Movement, as being victims of the system of segregation and discrimination. And we wanted to change the system.

We talked in terms of our goal, our dream, being the beloved community, the open society, the society that is at peace with itself. You come to the point where you forget about race and color and you see people as human beings. And we dealt a great deal with questions of means and ends. If you want to create the beloved community, create an open society, then the means, the methods, must be ones of love and peace. And redemptive suffering, if necessary, may in itself help to redeem the larger society.

I think we had grown up with these ideas to a certain degree. Black ministers have a tendency to compare the plight of Black people with the children of Israel. So I think that maybe had something to do with it. And you go to the seminary and you study church history and the battles the church was involved in. And I just had the feeling of a holy crusade—with the music and the mass meetings and without anything else, only with a dream, with a daring faith.

In the Movement, during those early days, maybe 1959 to 1962, I really felt and had almost concluded that the only real integrated society and in a sense the only true church in America was that part that was caught up in this movement. And I think this may have been biased and prejudiced, because

year at Fisk University in Nashville, was forced by police to wait two hours outside the bus station, dazed, before getting any medical attention.

maybe I cut myself off from the larger community at that time, and I'm not prepared to close people out or build a wall. But in the Movement, in that group, you really did have a community, a community of believers.

The Albany Movement

The students carried the Freedom Rides into Mississippi, where with clockwork regularity, throughout that spring and summer, they were arrested for attempting to use "white" waiting rooms and rest rooms. Some of the original CORE riders, plus members of other groups and Northern white supporters, joined them. But once out of jail, the students moved on to even more dangerous ground.

In the fall, SNCC organizers began to fan out to rural communities across the Deep South. Their aim was to help create local mass movements which could mobilize the energies of poor Blacks. It was becoming a question of much more than the right to a cup of coffee at a lunch counter. It was becoming a question of rebuilding the society from the bottom up.

One of the first big local movements was in Albany, Georgia. In 1960, Albany was the booming commercial center of southwest Georgia. This was not its first boom. In the early nineteenth century Albany was the slave trading center for the rich plantation country which stretched for a hundred miles on every side. "Here," according to the great Black historian W.E.B. DuBois, "the cornerstone of the Cotton Kingdom was laid."

A century after the Civil War, Black people made up two-fifths of Albany's population. There was not a single Black elected or appointed official, jury member, or policeman. Blacks were barred from "whites-only" city parks and swimming pools, from the town library, and from all but the lowest-paid jobs. From the "colored waiting room" of the bus station it was eight blocks to a restaurant that served Blacks, and six miles to a "colored motel."

In 1961, the freedom spirit came to Albany. And in Albany what had until then been primarily a student movement in which small groups of protestors defied segregation, became a community movement in which during a single week, more than 800 demonstrators filled the jails of the city and several nearby counties.

During February of that year, local Black leaders had formally requested the city commission to consider desegregating certain municipal facilities; the answer, delivered not by the commission itself but by the *Albany Herald,* was a flat no. In September a few voter registration workers from the Student Nonviolent Coordinating Committee arrived to begin signing up Black voters in Albany and surrounding counties. Under their influence, the Albany Movement was formed—a coalition of SNCC, students from nearby Albany State College, local ministers, and other Black leaders joining together to attack discrimination in bus and train stations, libraries, parks, hospitals, buses, juries, public and private employment, and treatment by police.

As one leader said, "The kids were going to do it anyway. They were holding their own mass meetings and making plans. We didn't want them to have to do it alone." A doctor, W.G. Anderson, and a retired postal supervisor, Marion Page, were elected as president and secretary of the Albany Movement.

In the demonstrations that followed, reaching their heights in December 1961 and July-August 1972, over 2000 local Black residents were arrested—primarily for marching and praying on downtown streets and the steps of City Hall. Police chief Laurie Pritchett defended these arrests by saying, "We can't tolerate the NAACP or the SNCC or any other nigger organization taking over this town with mass demonstrations."

During this time the federal government, though it

claimed to be "watching the situation very, very closely," took no action to protect the civil rights of the demonstrators. Chief Pritchett was praised by news media across the country for limiting himself to wholesale arrests rather than wholesale beatings. When local Black lawyer C.B. King was beaten over the head with a walking stick by county sheriff Cull Campbell ("I wanted to let him know that I'm a white man and he's a damn nigger") and walked across the street to Pritchett's office with blood streaming, neither the police chief nor federal agents took action.

In surrounding counties, voter registration activists were beaten, arrested, and had their homes shot up while they slept. Several churches were burned. Marion King of Albany, five months pregnant, was kicked into unconsciousness while bringing food to a friend's daughter in jail; months later, she miscarried.

As an elderly Black woman, who had begun by relying on the federal government for protection, later told her attorney, "You know what, lawyer? The federal government ain't nothing but a white man." Finally, in the summer of 1963, the Justice Department announced its first criminal prosecution in Albany—of eight Black leaders and a white student sympathizer.

Their crime? "Conspiracy to obstruct justice," in the form of picketing a supermarket to demand jobs for Blacks. The owner, who had been part of an all-white jury which dismissed charges against a county sheriff who had shot a Black handcuffed prisoner four times in the neck, claimed the picketing was retaliation for his role on the jury.

Albany, Georgia, provided a vision of things to come in the United States of the 1960s and '70s. The following interview recounts that struggle and its effects.

Bernice Reagon

Bernice Reagon grew up in Albany and was a member of the executive committee of the Albany Movement. She was suspended from Albany State College for her role in the demonstrations. She has been active in political movements ever since.

(How did you first get involved in the Movement?)

In Albany, Georgia, there's a district called Harlem. It's about three blocks long, and it's a Black district—Harlem's Black wherever it is. There was a drugstore in Harlem. It was owned by whites and they wouldn't hire Blacks. Not anybody—to sweep—nothing. So we had formed, in the summer of 1960, a junior chapter of the NAACP; I was the secretary. We'd go to the drug store in Harlem, to talk to the owners and try to get them to hire a Black person. And they'd run us out, and then we'd go and meet and talk about what to do next.

What I'd known before then about struggle and the Civil Rights Movement would center around Autherine Lucy, who affected me deeply.[5] I think I was in junior high school, so I was 11 or 12, pulling for this woman to get into this university. She had been admitted; she was suspended; she was readmitted; and then they kicked her out again. I thought we were just beginning to fight...and then she got married to this preacher. I was real upset, because for me it felt like when she got married she got tired, like she had been so battered on and this preacher was marrying her and taking her away so she wouldn't fight any more. I did not *want* her to be tired, and I didn't *want* her

---

5. Autherine Lucy, in 1956, became the first Black student to enroll in the University of Alabama but was expelled.

to be taken away, and I didn't *want* her to rest. I wanted her to go back.

Also I remember when the 1954 Supreme Court decision came, my father saying, "Now that's the supreme law of the land!" Like, the Supreme Court, that's it. I remember him reading from it in the house, and it being a really high time.

When I entered Albany State College—the segregated state-run Black school in Albany—we were already watching the other colleges. It was the fall of 1960, and the sit-ins had begun. Students involved in Civil Rights demonstrations were calling all the Black colleges in the South and asking the student governments to protest and give sympathy demonstrations, and to try to get the administrations to come out with a position in support.

We got a call in the spring of 1961. There was a guy named Hogan, a veteran; there was Miss Albany State, Olivia Blalock; there were two or three other people. We wanted to get the Albany State College president, William H. Dennis, to take a stand. We went to the president's house one night; he said he wouldn't see us. So we called an assembly where we wanted him to answer some specific questions, so he would have to commit himself clearly. He said, "You ask all of your questions, and then I will answer." Afterwards we felt like we hadn't really had our confrontation. We had presented some issues, but also we had been outfoxed.

At the same time on the campus there were several things happening. One was that white men would go to the girls' dormitories to solicit women, and a few times women would find these men on the second or third floor. They would call the football team who would run down, catch the men, and hold them until the campus security guards showed up. On two occasions in that particular year, the guard held the gun on the Black male students and let the white ones get away. Also teenage white guys would drive on the campus and throw eggs on you as you walked. At the same time we found rats in the tubs and in the dining hall food. We combined all of these issues and had a rally. The response was that student government activities were suspended. And at the end of the year Irene Asbury, a dean who had supported the students, was fired.

Fall 1961 was when the Albany Movement got underway. There was one particular incident that clarified for me who and where I was in this society.

I was a freshman dorm counselor at the college. I picked up the phone one day and this white guy said, "Do you want twenty dollars?" I said, "Yes"—I thought it was a radio show. So he said, "There's twenty dollars on the seat of my car." And I thought, "Car?...Radio?..." until finally I figured out that he was soliciting and since I was a student dorm counselor, I was supposed to catch him! (Too much TV.)

I made a date with this man, went to my faculty advisor, my music teacher, and he said, "My God, child." He went to the president who was reluctant to deal with it. Then he went to the Albany, Georgia, police. Though I'd made the appointment off campus, the police said they couldn't deal with it because it was a campus issue. The police told the campus security guards not to use weapons in dealing with the case. I was not informed of this. My advisor just said. "It's going to be okay; you go ahead and we're going to have the police there." So I'm on this corner, waiting. I was saving the world, and saving all these freshmen. And here comes this man in this Volkswagen and he says , "Get in the car."

I didn't see the police, and I wouldn't get in. I said, "Where's the twenty dollars?" He said he had to go cash a check. I thought it was really good that I asked for the twenty dollars since he didn't have it. He told me, "I can't give you no money," so I told him, "Well, forget it then." I still didn't see no police, so I decided I'd better start walking back to the campus. He was driving alongside trying to talk me into the car.

Finally, along comes Mr. Chadwell's (my music teacher's) car. That's all. No police, no sirens. I couldn't believe it. I had this crook right here; I thought everybody should come and catch him. I mean, that's the way it happens on TV. That's the way the American system works. I felt like I was plugging right into the American system. The security police jumped out of Mr. Chadwell's car, put his hand on the white man's car, and said, "What the hell do you think you're doing?" The guy drove off.

I went down the next morning to the police station, and the police said, "We're glad you brought this to our attention because we want to stop this, but his wife says he wasn't home. He was out of town."

Two weeks later, I was involved in demonstrations. I was down at the police station, and the major part was getting on your knees and praying. I'm on my knees, picketing the station and praying. There was Chief Pritchett in front of me, asking, "Weren't you in my office, uh, just the other day?" And I said, "Yeah." And he said, "Well didn't we try to help you?" And I said, "No—you didn't catch him!"

That was my awareness, graphic awareness, of what side I was on. I'd always been afraid of police, knew you weren't supposed to run into them, but on some level I must have thought that you really could call on that system and it would respond to you. That experience drew some kind of line. It put me on one side, and a lot of other people, that I really didn't know a lot about, on the other side.

(How did the demonstrations begin?)

The Albany Movement came about as a result of two Student Nonviolent Coordinating Committee field secretaries, Charles Sherrod and Cordell Reagon, who came down to work in the Black belt area. SNCC had decided to do voter registration campaigns and they located the areas of this country that had more Blacks than whites. Theoretically, if those people were voting they could run those areas. With that information Cordell and Charles came down.

I remember when Charles Sherrod came to me and said, "What do you think of Terrell County?" I said, "It's a little bitty town." Another man who was from Terrell said, "That's tombstone territory." After a few excursions into those surrounding communities they knew this—it was too tight, the fear was too great, they would be dead soon. So they thought they'd better center in Albany.

When the SNCC people first came to Albany, they began coming to our NAACP junior council meetings. This caused a clash with the NAACP. Because I was the secretary of the chapter, I went to the NAACP district meetings in Atlanta. They asked me, "What have you been doing in your community?" We had just picketed and done some other things. I thought things were about to happen and I thought I made a good report. They smashed into me and said I better be careful because these people come in and get you stirred up and leave you in jail and the NAACP has to pay the bills and blah blah blah blah.

I was real upset, I didn't know what was happening. At that point I didn't have the ability to deal with "Student Nonviolent Coordinating Committee." Those words had no meaning for me. I couldn't pronounce them; I couldn't even remember to say "Snick." The NAACP might have been a different group but it should have been the same from where I stood.

"I said, "We're working for the same thing, aren't we?" What an answer I got! The Regional NAACP came down to a meeting of our chapter—Vernon Jordon, Ruby Hurley, and the junior district director—and blasted SNCC.[6] These peo-

---

6. Vernon Jordan, then Georgia Field Secretary for the NAACP, is now Executive Director of the National Urban League. Ruby Hurley was Southeastern Regional Director of the NAACP.

ple thought it was important enough to stop SNCC that they came down to Albany to tell us how SNCC would lead us wrong. We had to vote on whether we would go with SNCC or the NAACP. I just couldn't figure out why we were making that decision. I voted to stay with the NAACP because it was familiar, but I never went to another meeting.

In November, we decided to test whether the Interstate Commerce Commission would enforce its new ruling, that had come out of the summer Freedom Rides, that bus and train stations could not have segregated facilities. The NAACP chapter voted that one person would go into the lunchroom, be arrested, and be bailed out; then they would have a court case to test the ruling. SNCC decided that they would test the ruling, but the people would stay in jail.

Bertha Gober and Blanton Hall, students at Albany State, tested the ruling. At this point people were going home for Thanksgiving from the college, and the dean of students was going down to the bus station, making sure that Albany State College students went in the colored side. So what I'm describing is not a Black against white situation *per se.* I'm describing a system that was held intact by almost everybody in it, including major people in the Black community. Bertha was suspended from school right after she got arrested.

Bertha and Blanton were held in jail and when they came to trial we had the first marching and praying at City Hall. We announced the demonstration on campus and then we went through the halls trying to get people out. I remember one teacher we called "Ma Lat," Trois J. Latimer, told her students, "Get out of here and go and march for your rights!" "Ma Lat" was *ancient,* you know, but I remember her yelling at people to go. I remember Bobby Birch taking Mr. Ford and picking him up and moving him out of the way—just so we could get out of his class. We started from the campus and there were like just a few little people, and I said, "My God, I guess we failed." We had to cross a bridge to get to the jail, and by the time we got to the bridge we couldn't see the end of the line. It just kept growing. When we got to the City Hall, we weren't even sure what to do. We were saying, "Circle the block, keep moving..." We couldn't decide whether to sing or be silent. Nothing like this had ever happened before in Albany.

At the end of that march, we needed to meet someplace. The Union Baptist Church on the corner near the college campus allowed us to meet there. Students did not have any place to meet in that city except in the Black churches. NAACP meetings had been held in a church. When SNCC began to do nonviolence workshops, that was in Bethel AME Methodist Church.

Students had to go to other institutions in the community because we did not control the campus or the college buildings and we could not get access to them. I was in the student center when the dean saw Cordell and Charles Sherrod there and said, "Get off this campus!" It was like I was sitting with the bogeyman. They really said, "Get off or I'll call the police!" These men could not walk on campus. So the student movement could not exist except for the larger community.

In December, there was a further testing of the ruling by SNCC. A number of Freedom Riders came down on a train from Atlanta to support us. There was James Forman, Tom Hayden, Sandra Hayden (they had just gotten married).[7] Bertha Gober was arrested a second time. After her first arrest, there had been a meeting. She'd gotten up and talked about spending Thanksgiving in jail. This time, with all the Freedom Riders present, I remember her standing up and saying, "Well...." It was like—here she was again. Julian and Alice

7. James Forman was Executive Secretary of SNCC from 1961 to 1966. Tom Hayden (see p. 111) was participating in and reporting on the Civil Rights Movement as Field Secretary of Students for a Democratic Society. Sandra "Casey" Hayden (p. 188) was a white SNCC staff member from Texas.

Bond were there. Irene Asbury, who later became Irene Wright, was there. The main speaker was Dr. Anderson who was president of the Albany Movement.

After the train riders were arrested, there were more demonstrations, and more arrests. I was arrested in the second group of demonstrations. Each time, as news of the demonstrations and arrests came out—newspapers and TV—Black people came to the mass meetings from just everywhere. It seemed to break loose something basic.

The demonstrations didn't happen in a vacuum. The news, for over a year, had been full of these sit-ins. They had come behind things like Autherine Lucy and the Montgomery Bus Boycott and Little Rock, Arkansas.[8] Everybody was praying for Dr. King when he got stabbed. It was like, "Oh, it's finally gotten here!"

So, Albany was not simply a student movement. There were just swarms of people who came out to demonstrate, from high school students to old people. And there was so much that you got from finding that some older people backed you and were willing to put up bail and things of that sort. That made the Movement much stronger. It was a mass movement.

A lot of the older people in the Albany Movement were entrenched in Black cultural tradition and not as much into the Black culture you'll find in colleges—rhythm and blues and arranged spirituals. A lot of the sit-in songs were out of the rhythm and blues idiom or the arranged spiritual idiom. Those songs, as they went through Albany, Georgia, got brought back to the root level of Black choral traditional music.

8. In 1957, nine Black schoolchildren attempted to attend the all-white Central High School of Little Rock, Arkansas, in accordance with a court-ordered desegregation plan. Blocked by National Guard troops acting under the orders of Arkansas governor Orville Faubus and then by white mobs, they succeeded in entering the school only after federal troops were sent to protect them. The following year, Governor Faubus closed the school entirely in order to delay integration.

Albany, Georgia, in addition to all that it did in terms of a mass movement, also became a place where the music was so powerful that people became conscious of it. People who came to write about the Movement began to write about the singing and not even understand why. They couldn't understand what the singing had to do with all the other, but it was so powerful they knew it must have some connection.

(What did the music have to do with the strength of the demonstrations?)

That was not a question for people who were doing the singing. If you get together in a Black situation, you sing and, during that period, you would pray. If it's Black, that's what you were gonna do.

There is a kind of singing that happens in church that is really fervent, powerful singing. And when people get out they say,"Ooh, wasn't that a *good* meeting!" Ordinarily you go to church and you sing but sometimes the congregation takes the roof off the building. *Every* mass meeting was like that. So the mass meetings had a level of music that we could recognize from other other times in our lives. And that level of expression, that level of cultural power present in an everyday situation, gave a more practical or functional meaning to the music than when it was sung in church on Sunday. The music actually was a group statement. If you look at the music and the words that came out of the Movement, you will find the analysis that the masses had about what they were doing.

One song that started out to be sung in Albany was, "Ain't gonna let nobody turn me 'round."

Ain't gonna let Pritchett turn me round,
I'm on my way to freedom land.
If you don't go, don't hinder me.
Come and go with me to that land where I'm bound.
There ain't nothing but peace in that land,
Nothing but peace.

There was a lady who sang that song who had a voice like thunder. She would *sing* it for about 30 minutes. She would also sing the song in church meetings on Sunday. The song in either place said—where I am is not where I'm staying. "Come and go with me to that land" had a kind of arrogance about being in motion. A lot of Black songs are like that, especially group ones. If you read the lyrics strictly you may miss the centering element, the thing that makes people chime in and really make it a powerful song. Singing voiced the basic position of movement, of taking action on your life.

It was also in the Movement that I heard a woman pray and *heard* the prayer for the first time. It was a standard prayer:

> *Lord, here come me, your meek and undone servant*
> *Knee-bent and body-bowed to the motherdust*
> *of the earth.*
> *You know me and you know my condition.*
> *We're down here begging you to come and help us.*

We had just come back from a demonstration. The lines said, "We're down here—you know our condition. We need you." All those things became *graphic* for me. They were graphic in my everyday life but when I heard those prayers in a mass meeting, it was like a prayer of a whole *people*. Then I understood what in fact we (Black church) had been doing for a long time. The Movement released this material, songs and prayers, created by Black people, that made sense used in an everyday practical way and in a position of struggle.

(How did the singing start?)

I was a singer. We sang all the time. By the time of Albany, there was a tradition of singing in the Movement that came out of the sit-ins and the bus Freedom Riders. "We Shall Overcome" was already considered the theme song. Already there was a musical statement being made that paralleled all the other activities. As that body of music came through Albany, it was changed. You had old ladies leading freedom songs, backed by old ladies and old men who really knew what the songs were like before they'd gotten to the college campus or wherever else. Like the old song "Amen" which turned to "Freedom." That same song has been done for centuries in the Black church. You can put a harmony, 1-3-5, soprano-alto-tenor-bass, to that and get a tight choral sound. A SNCC worker would start to do "Amen" in Georgia and it would be taken over by the congregation who would sing it the way they always sang it. They were singing "Freedom" but they sang it in the same way they sang "Amen." That wouldn't be an arranged hymn. "Amen" is a Black traditional song and it's actually an upbeat song. Lots of songs changed like that.

When SNCC came to Albany, we were singing "We Shall Overcome," because in the church where we sang it on Sundays it was "I'll Overcome." We had seen it on TV and said, "Oh, we sing that song." So at the next meeting they said, "What shall we sing?" "Oh, there's a new song, that we heard on TV, and it goes..." And you do it the way you know it. As far as you're concerned, you are singing the same song they're singing, even though it's different. By the time "We Shall Overcome" got to Albany it had become ritualized as the symbol of the Movement. They were doing it standing, holding hands. "We" was really important as a concern for the group. There were one or two other changes. We were doing it a little faster than they were doing it. We slowed it down a little bit— that's just the students in Albany and the SNCC workers—and by the time it got to a mass meeting, something else happened to it in terms of improvisation and slowing it down more.

In jail, the songs kept us together. I was in jail with about sixty women, and there were teachers in there, and educated people, uneducated people, a few people who had been drunk in Harlem and just ran. (One lady said she was with her husband and the march was going by and she says, "Look there goes my people!" and he says, "You better stay here" and she ran and caught up with us and ended up in jail, and she says, "What did I do that for? I ain't never gonna drink no more."

So there were real class differences between the Black women in jail, and music had a lot to do with breaking down those things because there were several women in there who could lead songs, of different ages, and everybody would back everybody up. It was the first time I led songs and felt totally backed up by a group of Blacks. If you're growing up in a Black church you can background, but I mean the leaders are so powerful, the real songleaders, the old ones, that you think of the day someday when you're gonna do "Let me ride Jesus" or something, but you don't strike out on it. Maybe when you join the church you're so ecstatic, you might lead a song if people will sing with you, but you know you really can't pull the weight.

There was something about the Civil Rights Movement, where leaders were defined by their activism. Not by their age or their class, so within the Black community people began to look up to students, to ask students what should they do about x, y, and z, and follow the leadership of all sorts of different people based on what they perceived to be an integrity and commitment to struggle and stick with that particular struggle.

(What would you say was the feeling of people who became involved in the demonstrations? What were they trying to accomplish? What was this movement that you had joined?)

There was a sense of power, in a place where you didn't feel you had any power. There was a sense of confronting things that terrified you, like jail, police, walking in the street— you know, a whole lot of Black folks couldn't even walk in the street in those places in the South. So you were saying in some basic way, "I will never again stay inside these boundaries." There were things asked for like Black police and firepeople and sitting where you wanted on the bus. There was a bus boycott and we closed the bus company down and brought it back with Black bus drivers. But in terms of what happened to me, and what happened to other people I know about, it was a change in my concept of myself and how I stood.

It was an experience that totally changed the lives of people who participated in it. There were people who did every march, every mass meeting, their whole lives became centered around the Movement. People who lost their jobs, who lost their homes.

A lot of studies of Albany have focused on evaluating the tactics of Pritchett, the police chief. They have called him a "nonviolent police" because he locked people up. He just locked you up and when there was no more room in the city jail he sent us out to counties.

When I read about the Albany Movement, as people have written about it, I don't recognize it. They add up stuff that was not central to what happened. Discussion about Pritchett: discussion about specific achievements; discussion about whether it was a failure or success for King.[9] For me, that was not central. I had grown up in a society where there were very clear lines. The older I got, the more I found what those lines were. The Civil Rights Movement gave me the power to challenge *any* line that limits me.

I got that power during that Albany Movement, and that is what it meant to me, just really to give me a real chance to fight and to struggle and not respect boundaries that put me down. Before then, I struggled within a certain context but recognized lines. Across those lines were powers that could do you in, so you just respect them and don't cross them. The Civil Rights Movement just destroyed that and said that if something puts you down, you have to fight against it. And that's what the Albany Movement did for Albany, Georgia.

9. Martin Luther King, invited to Albany by the executive committee of the Albany Movement, led a large demonstration in December 1961 and was jailed. He also attempted to negotiate with the City Commission on behalf of the Movement.

(There were some established adult professionals in the leadership of the Albany Movement, but other successful Blacks, like the school administration, opposed it. Did this surprise you?)

I've found it real surprising to people outside the South. I'd say I was suspended from school and they'd say, "Oh, it was a white school, a white principal?" If you grow up Black, you know that the manifestations of the system closest to you are Black. We had known Dean Minor (the dean at the bus station and at the jail who made lists of students breaking the segregation barriers) and President Dennis for a while. It was really just behavior that we had always seen.

What we did not know, though, was the numbers of people on that same level who were fighting. I think that's always an unknown until there is a fight. You never know who will stand for you until the issues are really on the line.

You can always figure out the people who are executing the system. It appears that almost everybody's executing it, even you are executing it until you fight against it. The positive thing I experienced was the numbers of people who risked everything they had to work in that Movement. People of all classes. People who absolutely couldn't afford to take those stands, did. The most independent people were the ministers of those Black churches which supported Civil Rights Movement activities. But people who were working and were losing their jobs, that was another thing.

(It's now been 17 years since SNCC went to work in Albany. What is Albany like today? How do you see the difference that the Movement has made?)

There are hundreds of specifics. Albany State College is integrated. Dennis died very shortly after he suspended us; I still think that's connected. You can ride in white taxicabs. There are Black policemen and white policemen (policemen are still policemen), Black firemen and white firemen, Black bus drivers. Schools are integrated. There are Black telephone operators. I wouldn't have to go all the way to Belk's department store to go to the bathroom downtown; there used to be only two stores with restrooms for Blacks—Silver's 10¢ store and Belk's. All those things have happened.

Albany, for Albany, as well as the Civil Rights Movement for whoever was affected by it, raised and answered some questions in ways that changed how people would be dealt with. So that, you know, I could get a job at the Marine base as a secretary. Those are things that you take for granted in Albany now, but I remember when my sister got a job at the Marine base and it was a first. They hired manual laborers at the base, but they didn't hire Black women.

Those are the specifics. Behind those specifics are people who have greater responsibility for who and where they are—and slightly more chance to fight for difference in their lives. In in some way the Civil Rights Movement exposed the basic structure of the country that, as it's set up, cannot sustain itself without oppressing someone. The change in the movement later toward riots, Black Power, Black nationalism, feels to me like it had to do with some learning we did about this country during that first period. It was like learning about the Constitution; quoting the Constitution, saying "All we want is our rights in the Constitution." After Albany, I began to look in the Constitution, and to realize that every time they dealt with property, they were dealing with the slave question. So in the Constitution I am primarily property. And our depending on that Constitution is like me waiting on the corner for the Albany police to save me from that man.

But that was where we were. So one thing the Civil Rights Movement did was give us a lesson in the structure of this country—the most graphic kind of civics lesson you can get— and we began to really see that there were some problems. If you watched TV and watched all them Black people getting beat for all those years, you knew that yours was coming next week. And it became much more difficult to handle that nothing else was coming, and especially that, in some real way, the economic order was not changed by the Civil Rights Movement.

When I say you can work in the Marine base and you can work at the telephone company, the implication is that something basic has changed in the economy. But if you look at where Blacks stand, economically, in the society, it continues to be a society that has maintained itself on the exploitation of groups of people. Though I get the feeling that the groups may be slightly breaking down; maybe now all workers are beginning to find themselves terrified for their jobs, which used to be the way Black people felt all the time—if you had a job you were scared any day something would happen so you wouldn't be working.

(What about the effects of voter registration work on the power relations?)

I think we're still seeing it and I'm not sure what the result will be. There have been some differences in power relations with so many Black elected officials, but the changes are limited. In Charleston, South Carolina, Septima Clark sits on the school board that around 1919 refused to let her work as a teacher in that city. Mayor Daley's little clique was unseated by a Jesse Jackson-led group at a Democratic National Convention. That was 1972, when McGovern was nominated for President, and that was the year of "This is really gonna make a difference; we're gonna turn this party around and make it a people's party." There were all those fights, and then, next time around, 1976, Mayor Daley's back. The Democratic leadership were so glad to have him back, they didn't know what to do.[10]

10. At the 1972 Democratic National Convention which nominated George McGovern for president, the Illinois delegation headed by Chicago Mayor and political boss Richard Daley was disqualified

So you can talk about power changes that occurred—that put Fannie Lou Hamer in the Democratic National Convention—that kicked Mayor Daley out for a little while.[11] It means something; it is more helpful to have more Black people in these positions. But also it means that we're in a system that's very flexible and can absorb some demands based on how much you hammer for them: if you are ever-visible hammering, you will not totally be ignored. You will either be let in or destroyed. And then sometimes the system lets in a certain number and then destroys the radical fringes of it. But the structure has not changed and human beings are still terribly exploited in this country. This is not a country that's focused on human beings.

because it did not give sufficient representation to minorities and women. It was replaced by a delegation headed by Black community activist Rev. Jesse Jackson. Daley and other Party bigwigs and fundraisers refused to work on McGovern's presidential campaign against Richard Nixon, which was one reason for McGovern's devestating defeat in November. Afterwards, all but the most left-leaning of the Democratic liberals quickly made peace with the old-line conservative forces in the Party, and relaxed the rules about minority and female participation.

11. Fannie Lou Hamer of Ruleville, Mississippi, became a leader in SNCC and the Mississippi Freedom Democratic Party after she was evicted from the B.D. Marlowe plantation (where she had lived and worked as a sharecropper for 18 years) for registering to vote.

In 1964, the Democratic National Convention refused to seat her and other members of the MFDP in place of the segregationist Mississippi delegation led by Senator James Eastland. In 1965, the MFDP demanded that Congress seat her in place of Mississippi Representative Jamie Whitten on the grounds that more than half of the residents of his district were Black but less than 3% of these had been allowed to register; this challenge lost by a vote of 276 to 149. Eventually, in 1968 and 1972, mostly Black delegations were seated in the Convention in place of the segregationists; in 1976, the Democratic Party in Mississippi was "reunited" and sent a delegation including both the Eastland forces and Black and white liberals.

The other thing that the Civil Rights Movement has done is make Black people see beyond themselves, to see some parallels in the experiences of other people and other groups. If you're Black and oppressed, you're also isolated. When I joined the Civil Rights Movement everything was Black and white. There were Black people and there were white people and that was it. The Civil Rights Movement has taught at least some activist part of the Black community internationalism, something about the world, and has made the world not so distant and not so irrelevant to our own position. It is like beginning to analyze society and understand where you are in it.

(How have you personally been affected since then by your participation in the Albany Movement?)

Well, the first thing that happened was I lost the job I had at that time. I would get up at five in the morning to clean this beautician's shop. The woman said, "She's a good girl, but..." She thought her windows would get broken because my name was in the paper and I got arrested.

I was expelled from school in December 1961, not to return. It was for something like "behavior unbecoming a student." My parents were pretty worried about me being out of school, and also about not being able to tell me what to do. I was clearly making my own decisions. I was scared but I was really caught up in the activities of the Civil Rights Movement.

The forty-nine students who were suspended got an offer to go to Black schools in Atlanta to complete the year. In February I went back to school in Atlanta, to Spelman College. The most important thing happening was the Movement. I felt like it was my movement as much as it was anybody else's, so being in school during that time was difficult. I tried to get involved in what was happening in Atlanta, but it did not have the community base. The Atlanta movement was student based, and something that I had gotten from the Albany situation was missing. I worked at the SNCC national office; I went to rallies and demonstrations in Atlanta; and I went back to Albany as much as possible. The next year I returned to Spelman but left in November and didn't go back for several years.

I think everything I've done since has to do with the Movement. I'm still an activist, still a singer, a song leader, as I was then. I have moved since that time through being very much in the middle of the pan-Africanist and Black nationalist movement. During the Civil Rights Movement I was in a group called the Freedom Singers. With Black nationalism, I sang with a group of women called the Harambee Singers; we almost only sang to Black people. Now I'm with a group called Sweet Honey in the Rock. We are Black women singing about our lives and our commitment to our community and our commitment to struggle for change.

What I've had since the Civil Rights Movement is a better knowledge of who I am in this society, an understanding of my power as a person to stand and speak and act on any issue that I feel applies to me in some way and therefore to other people. That has included the war in Vietnam, Black nationalism, liberation movements around the world, and other movements I've come to with some support because of what I learned in the Civil Rights Movement. And music is just the way I talk about that commitment and understanding.

I learned that I did have a life to give for what I believed. Lots of people don't know that; they feel they don't have anything. When you understand that you do have a life, you do have a body, and you can put that on the line, it gives you a sense of power. So I was empowered by the Civil Rights Movement.

There have been many times since then that I've felt other levels of oppression, for instance, doors that open for me as a Black person but have another slant on them for me as a woman. I now move through a different level of the society than I did then. I'm seeing what happens when you're Black, when you're a woman, when you are outside of categories that are comfortable. Like I have a doctorate in history, but doctorates are not supposed to sing, and if they sing they're not supposed to sound the way I do, using Black traditional vocal techniques. There are just a hundred different ways of clashing. Yet I somehow know that I have a right, almost a responsibility, to struggle to be all of those things. If I don't work out in my lifetime who I am, and fight for that space, then I will never *be*. I will be somebody else's representation or the society's representation of what it will tolerate me to be.

Mississippi

The movement that Bernice Reagon describes in Albany spread throughout the South. The Civil Rights Movement of those years is always described as "nonviolent," but the nonviolence was all on one side. The entrenched white power holders, represented by the local businessmen's White Citizens Councils, the southern Democratic Party, and the Klan, responded to the organizers and local activists of SNCC and other groups with the weapon they had been using since Reconstruction—terror.

The symbol of this terror was the state of Mississippi. No written list of the murders, the bombings, the beatings can convey the atmosphere in which the fight for freedom took place. Few people outside the state heard about Herbert Lee, a Black farmer of Liberty, Mississippi, shot dead by a state legislator in 1961 for encouraging other farmers to register to vote. Many were shocked three years later by the murders in Philadelphia, Mississippi of three Civil Rights workers—local Black activist James Chaney and northern whites Michael Schwerner and Andrew Goodman.

But the important story of the Civil Rights Movement in the South is not one of terror but one of slow, drawn-out struggle. "We all recognize the fact that if any radical social, political and economic changes are to take place in our society, the people, the masses must bring them about," said John Lewis, speaking for SNCC at the national March on Washington in 1963. Despite the terror, the people continued to join the Movement.

Jean Smith

Jean Smith was a SNCC voter registration worker in Mississippi. In this interview she describes the growing popular participation—and the changes that were won.

I'm reminded when I talk about this of an expression from the Bible which is, "He loved me before he knew me." In Georgia and in Mississippi where I worked, the local people were like that. They loved us before they ever saw us. When you showed up, they didn't even ask if you were hungry. They would just do for you like you were their own children.

I remember that one family I stayed with, I was there about two weeks before I realized that the father was sleeping on the floor so that I could have a place to sleep. They didn't have any reason to trust us, to trust that our judgment was particularly great, but they had good instincts about our good instincts. Having those people love me before they knew me reinforced for me the idea that people have in them the potential for just—goodness.

It wasn't so much a question of heroic acts in the literary sense. I mean, there were some. There was Mrs. Hamer getting beat up in the jail.[12] There were people who really got beat on

12. In June 1963, Fannie Lou Hamer was taken off a bus in Winona, Mississippi, while returning from a conference. She was jailed and, on the orders of a state trooper, two Black prisoners were made to beat her all over her body with a blackjack.

and who said "I'm not gonna stop because of this," there were people who got killed. But mostly it was all one by one. It was one person who's been scared forever deciding to go to the courthouse that day, to try and register. It was the ability to recognize that you might be utterly devastated by an act, even if you only recognized it without talking about it, and still to go ahead and do it.

I remember after the guys got killed in Philadelphia, I went there to work. I stayed in the house of a lady who wasn't political at all, and for whom it was very dangerous for me to be there. And she just never, never double checked herself.

What we had then in SNCC was people who believed in themselves and in the people in the South, and who mostly wanted to maximize the potential of those local people, to help them be the best they could be. Voter registration in particular was a good way to get to that.

In Mississippi now you can see the difference that it brought. The people now have almost no fear of contact with whites. They don't walk on the other side of the street. They don't put their eyes down. You can sue a doctor for malpractice now, whereas fifteen years ago you had to be grateful for anything a doctor did for you. People think they have the right to be in a hospital, whereas I remember one man's daughter died because they wouldn't let you into a hospital nearby; you had to drive 200 miles to a charity hospital.

Economically, Blacks are not that much better off relative to whites. There's almost no more money in hand farmwork for cotton. But for people that have jobs, now, in health services, in manufacturing, the hours are certain, the pay is certain, you have recourse.

Before, everything you had was at the pleasure of the white people. Now Black people have rights. That's the biggest thing that's changed.

...And Beyond

By the middle of the 1960s, the nature and the outlook of the Black movement were changing. These changes were as complex as the task of liberation, but four main trends stand out:

• It was no longer just a Southern struggle. With the passage of the Civil Rights Act of 1964 and the Voting Rights Act of 1965, both in response to the direct action movement, the federal government had finally taken some significant action to extend to Southern Black people the right of equal access to public facilities and to the voting booth. At the same time, the uprisings of Black people in the ghettoes of New York and Los Angeles had shown that in the North, too, a struggle for equality needed to be waged.

• It was a struggle against a larger system. In 1964, Blacks excluded from official Democratic Party proceedings in Mississippi formed the Mississippi Freedom Democratic Party. In local, district, and statewide elections they balloted for a slate of officers to challenge the segregationist Mississippi delegation to the Democratic National Convention in Atlantic City. Many people in the Civil Rights Movement expected the MFDP challenge to win and, by removing the entrenched conservative Southern Democrats from the Party, to open the way for tremendous changes in many areas of national policy.

The convention rejected the challenge, signaling to many activists that revolutionary change toward a free and equal society meant battling a national structure of economic and political power, not just a regional one.

• It was no longer an entirely non-violent struggle. Faced with constant threats and the unwillingness of the federal government to protect participants in the Movement from local police or the Klan, most activists stopped believing in nonviolence as a philosophy, and many began to reject it as a tactic as well. The Deacons for Defense and Justice, of

Bogalusa, Louisiana, were one of the first groups to carry out armed defense of Civil Rights workers.

• It was no longer a struggle for "integration." Under the influence of their own experiences in trying to help poor Blacks gain power in the South, and learning from the speeches and writings of former Muslim leader Malcolm X, SNCC and other groups moved toward a polictics of "Black Power." If Black people were going to improve their lives and the society, they reasoned, they were not going to do it by becoming more like their white oppressors. They had to do it by developing their own self-respect, educating themselves for their own needs, and building their own organizations.

They had to fight not just for a cup of coffee, but for a share of the U.S. wealth that they had created as slaves, sharecroppers, and low-wage laborers; not just a vote, but a way to use it. Also, increasingly, Black movements saw themselves not as a minority among whites in the U.S., but as part of a world majority of colored peoples.

All of these developments brought the period of the Civil Rights Movement to an end. Also at this time, the leaders who seemed most likely to unify a new movement to deal with the changed conditions came under fierce attack. Malcolm X was assassinated in 1965 as he was moving to create a new strategy and program based on international solidarity and challenging not just racism but capitalism as well. Martin Luther King was assassinated in 1968, while leading a sanitation workers' strike in Memphis, speaking out against the Vietnam War, and preparing for a "Poor People's March" on Washington. SNCC leader Stokely Carmichael, who had come to symbolize the concept of "Black Power," was driven into exile in Guinea.

It was no surprise, therefore, that the late '60s and the '70s saw the emergence of a variety of new Black revolutionary organizations seeking ways to confront the new realities. Two of them, the Black Panther Party and the League of Revolutionary Black Workers, are represented in this book.

What surprised almost everyone, though, was the number of *other* movements, among whites and among Third World groups other than Blacks, that grew out of the Civil Rights Movement. The Civil Rights Movement created new room for politics in the United States; it inspired other movements by example, and it served as a training ground for many of the future activists in other movements.

Bernice Reagon

Bernice Reagon talks about the role of the Civil Rights Movement as the "borning struggle" of all the struggles that emerged in the 1960s.

When I look at the Civil Rights Movement, I see an activism that has parallels in periods past. Masses of people are re-evaluating who they are, where they are in society, and what society owes them—and challenging the structures that exist. One of the things that I feel is different about this particular period is that it did not seem to be controlled by the borning struggle, the Civil Rights Movement. Few movements have created as many ripples, and certainly not ripples that crossed racial and class and social lines as happened in the 1960s.

The Civil Rights Movement, being Black at the bottom, offered up the possibility of a thorough analysis of society. People who cared could help Black people challenge the structures of society. They could come to the South and march. When they left, not only was the South changed, but they, the people who came to give their support, were changed.

The exciting thing about the Civil Rights Movement is the extent to which it gave participants a glaring analysis of who and where they were in society. You began to see all sorts of things from that. People who were Spanish-speaking in the Civil Rights Movement, who had been white, when they got back, turned Brown. A few of those people who had worked with SNNC began to do political organizing around issues concerning the Spanish-speaking community. Some of the leaders of the anti-war movement were politicized by their work in the Civil Rights Movement; with the question of U.S. involvement in Vietnam, they found themselves in a movement that affected all sorts of citizens. Here was a mass struggle that took another cut across the society, across class and race. The movement for students' rights, the women's movement, the gay movement, all offer the same possibility. Nobody will rest because everybody will check out what their position is.

For many Civil Rights Movement organizers and supporters, leaving a specific project or struggle didn't mean the end of political activity. These people came away from their Civil Rights Movement experience with a greater facility for seeing a wide range of questions. For many, there was no end nor rest. The Civil Rights Movement was only a beginning. Its dispersion continues to be manifested in ever-widening circles of evaluation of civil and human rights afforded by this society.

The Movement continues. In fact, it is intensifying. People are being threatened in almost every way. If it runs its course, no institutions or values will be left unexamined or untested. I feel like the response to this is society trying to say, "Enough is enough. We cannot have all of this." In Wichita, Kansas, more people came out to vote against gay rights than had voted in any previous election. You really have to be coming from someplace, it's so clearly a civil rights issue, to vote against gay rights. What brand of McCarthyism will there be this time to cut across gay rights, Indian rights, Chicano rights, Black rights?

I don't know about the reactionary presence in this country, how strong it will be, but I feel like the work of the past period of struggle has strengthened the basic feeling that people *do* have the right to be. So we have a chance of not getting knocked down this time.

I also want to say that you cannot present an accurate picture of the movements of the 1960s and 1970s unless you show them resting on the foundation of the Civil Rights Movement. A study that's done from some other point of view will be a myopic report on those other movements. I find, generally, that people who participated in any of the other movements, especially if those other movements were predominantly white, see whatever they participated in as central. It is too easy to make the one movement you worked in the center; from wherever position you stand; that's the beginning. The Civil Rights Movement gets equalized. There might be a sentence that says the Civil Rights Movement is the base but in space and analysis the other movements that are predominantly white rise in stature. I feel it is, again, a distortion of what Black people do to stimulate the salvation of this country.

Most people's images of the New Left are white. Black people who have participated in struggle are presented almost as an adjunct. I have problems with that perspective. My point is the Civil Rights Movement borned not just the Black Power and Black revolutionary movements but every progressive struggle that has occurred in this country since that time. In all organized struggles coming after the Civil Rights Movement, you will find among the leaders those who experienced, on more than a cursory level, the energy and transforming dynamics of the Civil Rights Movement. To that extent, they are children of the Civil Rights Movement.

I want to know whether or not your book is going to look that way, is going to give that analysis of the relationship between the movements. I bring it up because it's important to me and because all the studies that I've read about the New Left or the '60s do this disservice to Black people's struggle which affected everyone in the country. I'm asking that the center of the piece not be anyplace but the Civil Rights Movement. The centering, borning essence of the '60s, of the New Left, is the Civil Rights Movement. That should not be avoided. The Civil Rights Movement should not be segmented out but in fact made an integral part of everything that happened.

Black Panther Party rally, New York City, 1970.   Photo by Howie Epstein.

2
A Way To Fight Back:
The Black Panther Party

In October of 1966, two young Black men sat in the back room of an anti-poverty office in Oakland, California, and drafted a 10-point platform and program for a new political party. Its name: the Black Panther Party for Self-Defense.

The panther came to California from Lowndes County, Alabama, where it had become the symbol of the Lowndes County Freedom Organization. Earlier that year the Freedom Organization had launched one of the first attempts to put into practice SNCC's new doctrine of Black Power by running independent Black candidates for county offices to unseat the white Democratic Party power structure.

Lowndes County was Ku Klux Klan territory. Not only were Blacks routinely attacked and intimidated by gun-wielding Klansmen, but even a Northern white supporter, Viola Gregg Liuzzo, was killed as she drove through the county during the Selma-to-Montgomery voting rights march. The Freedom Organization decided that to organize freely they would have to abandon the position of one-sided non-violence, and that they would have to do what was necessary to defend themselves if they were attacked.

Alabama law required that all political parties on the ballot have an animal as their symbol. Freedom Organization chairman John Hulett explained his party's choice this way: "This black panther is a vicious animal as you know. He never bothers anything, but when you start pushing him, he moves backwards, backwards, and backwards into his corner, and then he comes out to destroy everything that's before him."

The new Black Panther Party formed in Oakland represented one of the most striking and most popular attempts to transfer the inspiration and the new lessons of the Southern movement to the cities of the North.

Huey P. Newton and Bobby Seale, the party's founders, were born in the South but grew up in the Oakland ghetto, where they learned that legal equality was a long way from freedom. They met at Merritt College, a two-year school on the edge of the ghetto with a large proportion of Black students. Tired of academic discussions of Black nationalism and revolution, they set out to form a revolutionary organization of "brothers off the block."

Their program, written primarily by Huey Newton, was and still is as follows:

WHAT WE WANT

1.   We want freedom. We want power to determine the destiny of our Black Community.

2.   We want full employment for our people.

3.   We want an end to the robbery by the CAPITALIST of our Black Community.

4.   We want decent housing fit for shelter of human beings.

5.   We want education for our people that exposes the true nature of this decadent American society. We want education that teaches us our true history and our role in the present-day society.

6.   We want all Black men to be exempt from military service.

7.   We want an immediate end to POLICE BRUTALITY and MURDER of Black people.

8.   We want freedom for all Black men held in federal, state, county and city prisons and jails.

9.   We want all Black people when brought to trial to be tried in court by a jury of their peer group or people from their Black communities, as defined by the Constitution of the United States.

10. We want land, bread, housing, education, clothing, justice and peace.

Each point was accompanied by a corresponding point of "What We Believe," explaining the necessity and justification for the demand.

The Party's first activity consisted of patrolling the streets of Oakland with guns and lawbooks to protect Black citizens from illegal abuse by police—and to back up their knowledge of legal rights with weapons equal to those of the police. Stories of Panther patrols facing down the astounded cops began to circulate around the ghetto.

"It was an educational point we wanted to get over," Bobby Seale explained years later in an interview. "We wanted to get the idea over of self-defense, and then educate the people, not only for self-defense against racist police attacks and bullets, but to defend themselves against hunger, famine, rats and roaches, dilapidated housing, unemployment, etc."

The Panther Party burst into the glare of national publicity in May 1967 when they appeared in the California state legislature in Sacramento with their guns—to read a statement opposing a bill, aimed at them, which would outlaw the carrying of loaded weapons on the street. Misdirected by reporters, they actually marched onto the floor of the legislature rather than to the spectators' gallery as they had intended.

Bobby Seale and five other Panthers were sentenced to six months in prison for disturbing the peace of the legislature. For the next four years, one or both of the Party's founders was in prison at all times, charged with a variety of crimes including first-degree murder. The charges on which they were arrested, except for the original Sacramento misdemeanor charge against Bobby Seale, were all eventually dismissed. Yet both men suffered solitary confinement and threats of death penalties in the meantime, and they were freed only after years of massive outside protests against their actual status as political prisoners.

These charges were part of a national campaign by the FBI and local police forces to disrupt the Panther Party's political activities through arrests, shootings, infiltration, and the portrayal of the Party as mindless, bloodthirsty hoodlums. The purpose of this campaign, as the Senate Select Committee on Intelligence learned in 1976 from an FBI memo, was to "prevent the rise of a 'black messiah' who would unify and electrify the militant black nationalist movement."

The FBI sought to prevent the Panthers and other militant Black groups from achieving "respectability" and "long-run growth." FBI chief J. Edgar Hoover reported to President Nixon that he was particularly concerned about the Panthers because "a recent poll indicates that approximately 25% of the black population has great respect for the Black Panther Party, including 43% of blacks under twenty-one years of age." One memo directed each FBI field office to submit, every two weeks, a report on actions against the Party.

More than twenty Panthers died as a result of this campaign. The most blatant murder—but not the only one— was that of Illinois Black Panther Party chairman Fred Hampton, who died along with another Panther, Mark Clark, when Chicago police raided an apartment where they were staying on December 4, 1969.

The supposed purpose of the raid was to search for illegal weapons which an informer had claimed were in the apartment. Yet the police passed up an opportunity to search the office when it was empty the evening before. Instead they staged a surprise attack at 4:45 a.m., guided by a map of the apartment supplied by an FBI infiltrator; they fired more than seventy-five shots to the Panthers' one. Hampton, who had fallen asleep in the middle of a phone conversation the night before, never woke up or moved during the entire raid; yet he was shot four times, twice in the head. A private autopsy performed for his family found that he had been heavily drugged.

Other Panthers were killed by members of rival groups. In December 1968 the FBI informed its field offices of a growing conflict between the Panthers and a Los Angeles-based group called US. It instructed its agents to "fully capitalize upon Black Panther Party and US differences" with "imaginative and hard-hitting measures aimed at crippling the Black Panther Party." While Black leaders attempted to mediate the dispute, the FBI planted phony letters and cartoons to increase hostility and suspicion; it also used undercover agents to inform US of the times and places of planned Panther events. In the course of 1969, four Panthers were killed by US members.

Despite this disruption, Panther chapters sprang up in cities across the country. Modeled on and directed by the Oakland headquarters, they carried out campaigns against police brutality, conducted political education classes, and encouraged Black people to see that "political power grows out of the barrel of a gun." They also provided community services including free breakfasts for school children, free clothing and medical care, and free alternative schools for Black children. The Party acquired several thousand members, about equally composed of women and men. *The Black Panther*, the Party's newspaper, reached a circulation of 30,000 in Chicago and 35,000 in New York.

The Panthers encouraged Blacks in the U.S. to identify with the socialist countries and revolutionary movements of Asia, Africa, and Latin America. They taught that the enemy is not white people in general but the capitalist system. They insisted on the necessity for a Black-led revolution to overthrow that system, and they pointed to the success of the Vietnamese revolutionaries in resisting the armed might of the U.S. government. "The power of the people, " said Huey Newton, "is greater than the Man's technology."

On the Labor Day weekend of 1970, the Party held a "plenary" (open) session of a Revolutionary People's Constitutional Convention in Philadelphia. More than 6000 people participated, about half Black Philadelphians and the rest representatives of other Panther branches, other Black groups, Puerto Rican organizations, anti-war groups, Women's Liberation groups, poor whites, Indians, and other ethnic and political groups from across the country.

In an atmosphere of tremendous determination and emotion, the convention adopted scores of resolutions explaining the principles of the new society for which participants were struggling. The convention did not, however, formulate any common political strategy or tactics for carrying on the struggle. Huey P. Newton, just out of prison after nearly three years (most of it spent in solitary confinement), delivered a keynote speech about the political and economic origins of the existing Constitution and why the necessary changes would not come from working within it.

The intense government repression and internal problems began to take their toll on the Party. In March 1971, a faction led by exiled Minister of Information Eldridge Cleaver left the Panthers because of the Party's refusal to begin an immediate underground armed struggle. In April, Huey Newton issued a criticism of the Party's past actions from the opposite direction, stating that it had "defected from the community" by overemphasizing the gun and the slogans of revolution while isolating itself from potential supporters in the Black community. He called for renewed emphasis on the service programs, programs of "survival pending revolution," to rebuild the Party's base.

Though many branches eventually closed, the Party succeeded in regaining its strength in Oakland. In 1973, Party officers ran in the city's municipal elections on a platform of establishing community-controlled cooperatives to meet basic needs. Minister of Information Elaine Brown received more than 30,000 votes for city council; Bobby Seale placed second in the primary vote for mayor and got 36% of the vote in the runoff election.

Since that time, Seale and Brown have both left the Party, and Panther support has fallen off somewhat amid charges of corruption and violence within the Party leadership. But, longer-lived than most organizations of the 1960's, the Black Panther Party continues to operate its survival programs and do political organizing and education in Oakland.

Reggie Schell

Reggie Schell was Defense Captain (the highest local post) of the Philadelphia branch of the Black Panther Party in 1969 and 1970. He was interviewed where he still lives in the North Philadelphia Black community, across the street from the first Party office.

(Can you tell a little bit about your life before you joined the Black Panther Party?)

There isn't nothing to tell. I mean, I could say that in three sentences. I was just an average, what I call, a street nigger. We weren't what you call poor—well, I guess we were poor, because there were days we didn't eat, days we went without coal, times that I went without stuff that I figured I needed.

I messed around with street gangs, and then I went out and joined the service. That's when I got my first lesson in racism—in the service. Because you know up until the time I joined, when I was 17, fighting white people was just like fighting with another gang. I was going to South Philly High, which was at that time about 75% white, mostly Italian. We used to have to fight our way in sometimes, or fight our way out. But some Italians we found were just as nice to us as we'd be with each other; if something's jumping and they know you, they'd tell you to watch yourself, and try to take some of the weight off you.

That just wasn't the same degree as what I found out by racism when I joined the service: this deep intent to control and to dominate you because you happen to be something else. It was in the service in Germany where I really got exposed to it. Most of the company commanders were from the South, and they were just openly racist. It really, really brought me down.

I remember listening to Malcolm X somewhere in there. Malcolm was on TV a couple of times, and I was really impressed by him. He was on a show called *The Dissenters*. He used to call white people "devils" at that time, and him and this white guy were arguing, almost fighting on the show. And I was impressed because I thought, "Well, shit, at least he's not just gonna sit there and act like he has to apologize for what he believes."

Then I came home and went to work in a sheetmetal plant. They made porch lights, ventilation screens, everything. And I saw then how the bosses can divide people. Upstairs in the shop it was all white, they ran machines. Downstairs in the foundry, sheetmetal department, punchpresses, it was all Black. The people upstairs got paid more. When I got there we were talking about putting a union in. People were afraid, I guess I was afraid too, but I knew we needed more money, or *something*, you know. So I worked with the union, helped fight to get it in, and that's when I first started seeing how things go.

I worked on that job about four years. I used to argue with the superintendent because I saw shit being done to Black people, and I know he used to tell me, "One day it's gonna get you in trouble, because you try to take up too many people's fights." Well, one day it did.

How I got in the Movement, I guess, is I began to develop

political consciousness around the time of Selma, Alabama.[1] I used to come home from work and just watch how the police beat the women and the children. You know, just about every day I used to think forward to watching that, because it did something to me inside. Like I say, I had started to pick up some kind of militancy on the job. Then I met with some people and started talking about trying to do something or join something that we thought would help change the situation for Black people in this country. After a couple of months of just kicking around, reading, and studying together, we decided that it would be this new group, the Black Panther Party.

I think the first time we heard about them was when the Panthers stormed Sacramento with guns. We heard about it on TV and in the papers. We knew then that after looking at Selma and Birmingham, and continually just watching people being beaten and there was no struggle back—I think that was really the thing that excited me about it: that at least we'd have a chance to fight back now.[2]

1. Selma, Alabama, the county seat of Dallas County, had been a focus of SNCC voter registration work since 1963. On Freedom Day—October 7, 1963—more than 350 local Blacks lined up at the courthouse to register; their applications were taken at the rate of only four an hour, and they were denied food and water the entire time they stood in line. The work continued, as did arrests and beatings of activists by county sheriff Jim Clark and his deputies.

Selma achieved national prominence in February and March of 1965, when Martin Luther King began leading mass demonstrations there demanding the right to vote. Day after day, demonstrators were beaten with clubs and electric cattle prods by the sheriff's posse and Alabama state troopers. John Lewis of SNCC suffered a broken skull. Three people—a local Black man and two northern white supporters—were killed by police and local whites in the course of the demonstrations.

2. In May 1963, mass demonstrations in Birmingham, Alabama, for equal employment and desegregation of restaurants were met with

Of course when we first opened we were just ad hoc, really, we weren't Panthers, we weren't anything. But one of the things that impressed me early on in the Party was when we decided we wanted to be Panthers we called out to California and June Hilliard told us, "Look, you don't got to be no goddamn Panther to struggle."[3] So we went out (this was in 1968) and we were just basically doing our thing because we didn't have any idea what Panther work was. But we set up our first office, right down here on Columbia Avenue. We were doing work around police brutality and situations like that. Police were shooting fifteen-year-old kids, mentally retarded children, and we started calling press conferences and trying to organize the people to do something to fight back.

After a period of time we started sending to California for papers; we were selling the Panther Party paper, though we still weren't recognized as a chapter. Then Field Marshal Don Cox came and inspected the branch, put us through a rigid kind of inspection to see if we were qualified to become a branch of the Party. This was early 1969, and it was also when the cadre selected me to become Defense Captain.

(How did the Party start out its work?)

The politics that we were trying to develop was to inform Black people about things that happened. I mean, we knew they knew, but we also knew that they didn't have any idea what they could do about it and we wanted to try to break them

clubs and high-pressure water hoses. On Sunday, September 13, after the demonstrations had ended and some demands had been won, the Ku Klux Klan bombed a Black church which had been a staging area for mass marches. Four Black girls were killed. No one was arrested for the crime until fourteen years later. Recent evidence suggests, however, that an FBI undercover agent inside the Klan knew about the planned bombing before it happened, and he may even have participated.

3. June Hilliard, brother of Panther leader David Hilliard, was the Party's Assistant Chief of Staff.

from this stranglehold that bootlicking politicians had on them and the white power structure had on them. Our strategy was to win their confidence first, to gain people's confidence in our desire, at least, to make some fundamental changes.

Besides what had been and still is a continuing problem of police brutality, there was a problem right at that time with sewers backing up. These were the kinds of things that we initially started, to get roots into the community. We had blocked off Columbia Avenue in protest at one point and had people come out with us, and after that we were on our way politically, as far as having some validity in the eyes of the people.

We started our free breakfast for children program some-where around September of that year. I think the breakfast program really shot us into the community. It was held across the street in that little blue building right there. We'd cook on hot plates 'cause there wasn't any gas or anything in there. It was hard but everybody enjoyed it because it was our first real program and our first attempt at trying to do something fundamental for people in the community.

We got the bulk of the food from merchants in the area. At first we had problems. They said we were communists, Black radical militants, and they tried to urge people to get us out. Some of the merchants (it was kind of funny because they were white merchants that had spearheaded this) were starting to circulate a petition to try to get us removed off Columbia Avenue. But it really didn't go over anyway, you know. We didn't bother with it, we just felt that if that's what they wanted to do, fine—we had a program we wanted to institute and try to get this community stabilized. So we kept on doing that and after a while that whole petition thing just fell through.

Right after that, though, we had our first confrontation with the police. They busted me because they said there was an M-14 found at my sister's house. I had some papers there at her house that had my name on them. So along with the M-14 they found these papers and right away, bam, they raided the office.

I remember it well. We used to have community classes, community meetings. They were well attended, we always had thirty or forty people, sometimes more, because I think during that period everybody wanted to be identified with at least fighting back. We used to go into this bar over here afterwards, and I'd be sitting, talking to some people about some of the discussions in the classes. The FBI came in there and came up to me, and they had this police inspector with them, George Fencl, the head of the "civil disobedience squad." They asked, "Are you Reggie Schell?" I turned around and said "No." So Fencl said, "Don't play with me. That's the motherfucker right there." And they read the warrant and I was arrested. They arrested all the other Panthers that were on the street, they broke in the office and ransacked every damn thing, all our files and everything. At that point we weren't organized well enough to have our security intact. We were just really getting the feel of the community when we got hit with this raid.

Even though we knew that the system and the police, especially, didn't want us to set up shop, we didn't have any idea about how fast something would come our way. But it didn't stop us from dealing with the police. We did extensive work around police brutality, organizing different communities, getting down with lawyers, helping set up different agencies that we could funnel these problems through.

Probably the most classic example of the way the police acted here was their murder of a young guy, Harold Brown. He was shot and killed in West Philadelphia. He was killed by four highway patrolmen; and the highway patrol in Philadelphia has always had the reputation for being the most vicious and most murderous of all the police. They had stopped this young brother and killed him, shot him. People heard him begging on his knees. Witnesses heard him begging the cops not to kill him, but they just shot him.

We talked to his mother. His father was a postal

employee, his mother was a school teacher. He was a good student at Cardinal Daugherty, which was a predominantly white school. By now the Party had gotten itself organized to the point where we could wage a hell of a campaign. We started circulating leaflets, we went up into the area where he was killed and talked with people, with witnesses. We had tape recordings of conversations with witnesses who saw certain things, who had heard the police tell them to "Get the fuck back in the window before we blow your heads off," and stuff like that. We had taped conversations with his mother and his father and we'd done a 16-page booklet on police brutality; and we spearheaded this by putting out wanted posters on the four police.

That set the city administration off. Rizzo was police commissioner and he was calling for something to be done, because we'd put a price on these policemen's heads by putting out a wanted poster on them.[4] You know, what was actually happening, what was transpiring at that point, was that sides were being taken. I think that people who once feared the Black Panther Party because of the shootouts across the country, began to see it as a legitimate organization that wanted to try to make some fundamental changes. The campaign that we raised with the police killing of Harold Brown was probably one of the most significant to get us involved with people and to get more people involved in the Black Panther Party. It caused a tremendous amount of anti-police support, because even the major papers had to pick it up. The *Inquirer* did a full expose on the whole thing and finally the cops were sent to a mock trial; you know, they walked in with their guns and their uniforms on, and finally they were exonerated completely. But by that time the political atmosphere in terms of the street, the people on the street, was beginning to change.

4. Former police chief Frank Rizzo became mayor of Philadelphia in 1971.

Those who had controlled it before had absolutely no control, or very limited control, over what was happening, and I think that's when the Party started really taking off. Around racial problems, you know, people would call the Black Panther Party with almost any problem that had any significance. The people would call the Black Panther Party first before they would call the old established Black leadership, and I think that the campaign itself—the Harold Brown campaign— probably was the catalyst for that.

(How much did the Party grow?)

I guess, even though I'm no longer in the Black Panther Party, I still have some of the indoctrination about numbers. We never liked to give out specific figures that could be used by the police. We had tremendous numbers up until 1970. After the police raided our office a second time in August, 1970, and shot it up, within a week or two weeks hundreds of people had joined the Party. When we had drill we had to use a schoolyard because there were that many people there. I imagine some of them were just fools or curious people, but we used to have to use a schoolyard because there were that many people; we couldn't fit on a city block or a lot anywhere.

(What was the role of guns in the Party? Was the idea, as the media often put it across, that picking up the gun meant that right then and there the Panthers would conduct a revolution, or was it more of a symbol?)

You know, I think that whole idea was manifested by the police, because I know that the police believed it. The times I was arrested they seemed to put emphasis on the fact that, "We know you all got guns, motherfucker, but we got the firepower, and we'll kill you." Just like the FBI told us, "We got the superior firepower, you can't win." We talked about guns because it was a constitutional right, you know. We also had other ideas about making revolution, but the police and the media had taken this, as you say, symbol and projected it as if we were trying to organize 500 Blacks to get guns and then just commit revolution.

We weren't talking about that, we were talking about people exercising their right to bear arms and to fight in defense of their homes if police come at them, kicking in their door without any valid reason or search warrant. And I think after a period of time Black people understood that.

We did have weapons classes. They were restricted to Panther members, not community workers. If community workers wanted Panthers to come and talk to them about weapon treatment, they would have to set up a meeting at a site of their own choosing and have their own weapons; and then somebody would come in. We did stress that people have a right to own a shotgun or rifle or pistol and that they had best do that; and again, I think that people liked that. Even though they were silent all the years of the peaceful nonviolent demonstrations, they couldn't take it any more than I could take it when I saw what was happening in Selma, Alabama, every day.

It was clear that of course we would take guns and we would defend ourselves and there were times we took guns to situations, like racial confrontations. There was a situation where four Black women had moved into a previously all-white neighborhood through a redevelopment kind of thing and used to get their windows broke out; their children used to be chased home. The women had called us about it. Well, they only called us after somebody fired a shotgun. We went down, we looked at the situation; by that time Fencl and the police were there, but the police offered absolutely no protection. We stayed maybe a week with them, protecting their home.

(Can you say more about the Party's idea, the idea of people who came into the Party at this time, about what kinds of changes were needed?)

In the early stages of the Party when people first joined, the only fundamental change that they thought had to be made was to at least let the world know, and let the system know, that they would fight. Before the Party came into existence, Black people just were looked on as people who will take a nice little ass-whipping, for a job or something.

I know that we had a lot of men coming in that were leaving their families. They'd come in and work part-time, working on the job and then coming in to the Party on the weekend or evenings. They'd go out and sell papers at night; they'd sell 'em through the bars up until the bars closed. And after they'd do that for a while they'd get, you know, that spirit. I don't know what infected them, but we'd find that a lot of them just left their jobs and lived like we lived, from hand to mouth, out on a limb. When we saw them every day, we were seeing that they were fundamentally satisfied with themselves maybe for the first time in their life.

These were people that were frustrated about the entire situation of Black people, and more or less frustrated about themselves, about their own inability to let the system know that "Goddammit, I *will* fight, and I don't like it but I will get down and you just can't keep on messing over me like that." When I joined the Party I was married and I left my wife for fundamentally the same reason: the question was, as we'd talked about it, either go back to work and get out of this crazy shit, or leave.

I'm talking about a man who's been on the job for eight years. He's not satisfied with the wage scale. He's not satisfied with the relationship that the boss has with him and other people around him. But he just takes it and takes it and takes it, because it is essential that he bring home the bread and butter. Now these men, or these individuals, these human beings, are in a constant state of turmoil with themselves; and the Black Panther Party, when it came out, existed as something that was totally opposed to that—kind of "You won't take advantage of us any more." And when they marched into Sacramento with guns they were telling America, "This is it, I mean Selma's gone, all that other, you forget that; this is the new human being, this is the new man and the new woman that's emerging."

When people saw that, you know, they'd take that and say, "Well, let me go into the Party and see how Bobby or Eldridge developed this, what they'd think, tremendous courage to stand up before thousands of people and call Richard Nixon a pig, stand up before corporation heads and call them enemies and just deal with them. That was the thing that people came in for—to find out what was this secret formula that the Party had. And they found out later that it wasn't a secret formula; it was just a question of them understanding the forces around them and understanding themselves, knowing what they had to do and what they could and couldn't say.

I don't know if that explains it, but I think that what I'm saying in a nutshell is that people live in a dual world until they find something that they can really believe in. You know, you believe here when your here and you believe there when you're there. But when something exists that has some principled foundations, something that you can believe in and that you know how to relate to and still be free, you know you won't be like a plastic human being.

I found a lot of people, young people, just breaking with their parents for the same thing, for the same reasons. Some were seventeen, coming in and just wanting to be part of what they figured was a tremendous force that was gonna change American society, which I think that the Party did to some extent. People just seemed to be people who wanted a fundamental change. I don't know if it was so much at that point to change or revolutionize the whole society or just to begin to revolutionize their own self over, to make them free mentally.

Based on what I saw as the Defense Captain of the Party, I

felt that at first most people wanted to revolutionize themselves. They saw the Party as the vehicle that perhaps was supposed to revolutionize the whole society, but they came in to deal with themselves first, because only through the Party could they gain a better understanding of what the hell we were talking about. Then, as they began to change, they began to see that it gave them more confidence to go out and change others. But they initially needed that themselves.

(What were the ways that the Black Panther Party changed the society?)

Initially, society looked at Black people as people who, probably legitimately, had some claim for some equality; but at the same time, will these people fight for their equality? Really, what will they do for it? March and pray and get their legs broken with high-pressure water hoses?

The Party said that was the end of that. We're human beings—we recognize we have certain rights, we have a right to fight for those rights, and we have a right to organize for those rights. We'll do what is necessary; confrontations over the years between the police and the Black Panther Party had let the U.S. know that we will. This is not a fad that you're dealing with now, this is a real emergence of a new human being. And you would find that people would readily identify with Panthers: "They're damn right when they see the police brutalizing somebody." "The Panthers are right, they ought to kill you all." Before that they'd just watch the brutality and go on about their way. So it changed society in that respect.

It also had its effect on the people at the controls of society. I believe that the Black Panther Party—and it's still my belief—was close to flipping this society over. We had established international relationships with other countries; this probably was the first time that it was done on this scale by any Black revolutionary movement since this country existed. In the Party we had made contact with people in Hanoi and we were supposed to begin making deals with the U.S. government to exchange pilots for political prisoners here. We were in Algiers, we were in Cuba, and we had better relations with those people than the head of IBM. So the rulers in this country—not the president, but the rulers, the corporate capitalists—understood that they had to do something.

They understood that the more they attacked the Party, the more Black people came into the Party, and that the more Black people came into the Party, then around the world the more Third World people became conscious of the tremendous surge, the tremendous will that was developing in this Black ethnic group or race here in the U.S.

They knew that they couldn't eliminate us, because by the time they really started escalating the killings of Panthers across the country, the seeds of revolution were already sown in the people. When they raided our office a second time, Rizzo really tried to degrade us by stripping us naked and lining us up against the wall and shooting over our heads. I imagine it was to get the people to believe that this is finally what happens to you. The police took everything out of the office, tinned up the front, and put up a sign: "Unfit for human habitation." What happened the next day was that people on the block stripped the tin off and replaced the furniture. When the police told them they couldn't, they said, "Don't tell us we can't!" The very next day the people just went back up there and ripped it all down, put a refrigerator in, chairs and tables, and began to set the office back up—and the police couldn't do a damn thing about it.

This was happening across the country. It happened in Chicago when they killed Fred Hampton and Mark Clark—this tremendous surge on the part of the people. So the ones at the controls had to do something.

So they took the breakfast program from the Party and coopted it into a national organization. They set up the Urban Coalition, they funded neighborhood health clinics, they had this outshoot of food stamps.[5] They came forth with these different reforms—fundamentally the same programs the Black Panther Party had initiated.

All these things came about not so much because it was the Black Panther Party, but through revolutionary action and consciousness on the part of the people. And the government had to do something to stop Black people from going too far to the left, because if they continued to repress and oppress us— as important as it was that they try to break us—they would have lost millions of Black people and they would have been in big trouble around the world.

People can say Rap Brown inspired the riots, or the Black Panther Party inspired the riots, but it wasn't.[6] You know, I believe it was just the development of a consciousness of revolutionary action, of Black revolutionary action, of Black men, Black women saying, "No more; we took this shit, and whatever we have to do we will do." And this became instilled in the people and what they saw in '64 and '65 were like tea parties compared to what they saw in '67 and '68 throughout the cities in this country.[7] I wouldn't say that it was just the Black revolutionary action and the development of these things that called for the corporate capitalist class to do something. I really think it was the Black revolutionary action going from about '66 up until around '71, when things started to just collapse.

5. Formed in response to militant Black organization and urban riots, the Urban Coalition was a federation of business, government, labor, and religious officials created to funnel money and jobs into poor neighborhoods.

6. H. Rap Brown, chairman of SNCC in 1967-68, urged Blacks to arm themselves for revolution.

7. Rioting by angry Blacks in Harlem (1964) and the Watts section of Los Angeles (1965), was followed by even more serious uprisings in Detroit and Newark in 1967 and in Washington D.C. and many other cities in response to the assassination of Martin Luther King in 1968.

(How did that collapse, or that decline in the Party, happen?)

Really, from my point of view, it was right after that plenary session of the Revolutionary People's Constitutional Convention that was held here in September 1970. The government tried to stop it, with the raid on us and other things, but they couldn't. There was a tremendous amount of people here then, and if some kind of clearcut program could have emerged from that, I think that the corporate capitalists would have had a hell of a war on their hands.

There were Indians, Asians, Puerto Ricans, White people, Black people, everybody. Every ethnic group in this country was represented at that plenary session and any kind of clearcut, basic, fundamental plan to go back into communities—if it was nothing else but to make sure that the government couldn't coopt what was existing at that point—could have helped us funnel more and more people into our struggle.

This rag-tag outfit of Black people, with these other little rag-tag outfits of poor whites and Indians and Chicanos couldn't by themselves pull together nothing of that magnitude; but the support we were getting was tremendous all over the country. Masses of people in this country were beginning to side with the left wing, both white and Black.

But I think the U.S. has got a system that people have got to be very, very conscious of. That is, it projects leaders, and then it breaks leaders. I was out in California that summer when Huey P. Newton got out of jail, and I watched it when people from the community came up and talked with him, congratulated him for coming home and told him how much they missed him and supported him. And I saw that he couldn't talk to them. His conversation was gone, he was a million miles away from them.

At the plenary session what he said just lost people. When he spoke to the people at that session, he spoke to ordinary people in the street way over their head, while they were talking about committing themselves to going back to their areas and making some very fundamental changes in people. I'm not sure if it wasn't a pre-arranged plot to allow Huey to come out at that time.

Because, you know, everyone was talking about turning the Party around. Internally there were certain things happening that left a lot of people across the country dissatisfied. There was drug use, there were problems at the top; and Bobby Seale was in jail in New Haven, Connecticut, and Eldridge Cleaver was outside the country and couldn't return. We were hoping that Huey could turn it around, but when he came home we found out that he wouldn't or couldn't do it. and the Party just started falling, people just started leaving it. The desire was gone.

It's not a question of individuals, really. But the people at the top, the central committee of the Party, they were the ones that we looked up to, the ones that inspired us to do more, and when we couldn't get that inspiration any more, then chapters and branches across the country just started to fall apart.

I know one thing that happened to me when I came out of jail after the raid. Money was needed for bail and to replace the things the police had taken from us, even our clothes. I tripped up when I came out to find out about some central committee members talking about buying some damn expensive jump suits so they could look sharp for the plenary session. It took me down to the lowest, just about the lowest point I'd been since I'd been in the Party.

Another problem I would say, based on what I think I saw, is that the Party tried to exert itself too much. It tried to form coalitions with other groups and then it tried to lead the coalition before it had first established what the coalition was supposed to do within the Party's own boundaries—in the Black community, or in their own areas, if there were six or seven Black groups. It seemed like the Party was more interested later in projecting itself rather than dealing with a program.

It's like I said before, what impressed me early on about the Party was when we called California and June Hilliard said, "You don't have to be no goddamn Panther to struggle." You know, that set. Even though I really, I just wanted to be a Panther because it symbolized this new human being ready to fight, when he made this statement we sat around and talked about it and said, "You know what, he's right; it's nothing but a name."

But after a while the Party started to act different—and it wasn't just on the Party's part. I think that just about every group, every ethnic or national group wanted to...seeing what they believed was revolution emerging at a very fast pace, they wanted their politics to dominate, you know, and I think that they just forgot about the fundamental reasons for this developing, that is because people across the country were moving our way, the way of the left or the way of revolution.

In what I'm trying to do today I tell everybody in the Movement I won't be so conscious of being a part of the Movement as much as being a part of the community. Because I think the people carried the Panthers, and they carried the Young Lords, and just about all the other organizations. The people carried them and pushed them forward and they gave them protection when they needed protection.

So to get in a damn meeting without the people in there and try to push your politics forward without talking about the common good, that is what I believe was a tremendous mistake—that the Party and other groups wanted to control and dominate everything. And a lot of people rebelled at that and then when *they* left the coalition, *they* would do the same thing, set up another coalition and the same thing for themselves.

(Another factor was the amount of repression the government brought to bear on the Party. What form did this take in Philadelphia, and did it come from the Philadelphia authorities or the FBI?)

Well I think that the repression, it had come down from both, and I base that on that first arrest about that M-14. I don't even know how to describe the FBI people at that time. They were talking like fools as far as I was concerned. They were asking me questions and answering them for me. "What are you? What's your occupation?" and then they'd say "freedom fighter" and write it down. Just little shit like that, and "You're a fucking freedom fighter, you're gonna end up dead."

Then, well, Fencl and his Philadelphia cops used to get a kick out of fucking with everybody; I guess that was the way he got his. You know, you'd just be walking down the street or driving in a car and he'd pull over, stop, search you, take you down to the station for "investigation." That's the way they used to get all the Panthers, everybody they saw continuing to come to our office; one day they'd just get stopped, pulled over, taken down, and they'd ask for what—"investigation."

I know that people in my family, cousins, old friends, told me that the FBI stopped down and asked them what I was like when I was young. I don't know what the purpose of that was. I know my mother called me; she was worried and said that the FBI came to the house and said that I was gonna be killed by some other Panthers or something, and she had best tell them where I was and what I was doing. You know, that kind of shit, that general harassment. There were infiltrators, too. Even a cop told me about one. I don't like to have any relationships with no kind of police because I don't trust them, but I had one that called and told me about this one fellow that was in the Party for a while; he says he's a cop. Sure enough, he was a Black highway patrolman.

But the August 1970 raid was the big climax between the Panthers and the police here. A police park guard was killed, and Rizzo was making all kind of statements, saying he was gonna round up every revolutionary in the city before sun-up, citing us as being fundamentally responsible. We had an idea they'd be coming. About five o'clock that morning I was asleep, and somebody woke me up (we used to pull guard duty in the Panthers anyway) and said, "They're here."

I looked out the window, and they're lined up across the street with submachine guns, shotguns; they're in the alley. I saw the head man clearly, he had a pistol and a gas mask strapped to his leg; he was bending down, and then all hell broke loose. Finally, we had children in there and the gas got to them too much so we had to come out.

Each cop took an individual Panther and placed their pistol up the back of our neck and told us to walk down the street backward. They told us if we stumble or fall they're gonna kill us. Then they lined us up against the wall and a cop with a .45 sub would fire over our heads so the bricks started falling down. Most of us had been in bed, and they just ripped the goddamn clothes off everybody, women and men. They had the gun, they'd just snatch your pants down and they took pictures of us like that. Then they put us in the wagon and took us down to the police station. We were handcuffed and running down this little driveway; when we got to the other end of it, a cop would come by with a stick and he'd punch us, beat us. Some of us were bleeding; I know I was bleeding, but really I thought it was gonna be a whole lot worse.

We had three offices at that time—West Philly where 14 Panthers had barricaded themselves, the North Philly office up here, and a small office in Germantown. They raided them, and they raided everyplace where we stayed. When they took the office, they took everything, they even took the rugs off. And I couldn't understand the reason, but they took all the clothes, the machines; they took everything. I mean I never seen anything as thorough as that—kitchen tables, kitchen chairs, everything we got, refrigerators; they didn't leave us nothing. When we finally got out we had to pay for suits from the prison.

They arrested everyone from the North Philly and West

Philly offices, and set the bail at $100,000 apiece. But the support out on the street was really picking up. I think something about them stripping all the clothes off and taking pictures was the shit that backfired. Meanwhile Rizzo was talking all this shit about how he wanted to take us all, one Panther and one cop, and we'd do battle on the street. Finally bail was lowered down to $3500 apiece, and we got out after a week or ten days and got together for the plenary session.

(What happened after you left the Party?)

Well, the branch here kept operating until I think 1973 when they took what was left of the cadre and called them out to California to help on Bobby Seale's campaign. But I left a little while after the plenary session, and there were some other people that left then too.

I don't know, if things had been different I might have just said "Fuck revolutionary struggle," and gone back to doing what I was doing before the Party—hustling, working, trying to be slick. But it was really because of the dedication I saw in the Panthers I had known: their loyalty, not to me as an individual, but their loyalty to try to really turn this shit around here in this country. I didn't want to do anything else but to try and do something to carry that forward.

I would say that 98% of the people that joined the Party, of the real cadre of the Panthers, were dedicated, were truly serious. The work load would be so tremendous, like going to sleep at 2:00 and getting back up at 6:00, and people would just do that without crying all the damn time. They never asked for nothing, the women or the men. You know women may like to look sharp from time to time, to dress up from time to time. But we'd be going out selling papers at night and they'd be wearing combat boots just like the men. They stayed in that kind of garb. Some women would be wearing shoes with holes in them. They wouldn't complain. Somebody else would have to come up and say something to the finance officer, say "You know, so-and-so ain't got no damn shoes." And then we'd send somebody to look at them and jump on the person for not saying something sooner, so we could have got them shoes. Some of the people were on DPA, and they would use that money to finance the revolution, to help finance it.

I never saw anything like it before, you know, because people—listen, you're out on the street, you know people are fundamentally selfish because they have to think about themselves as being number one; but when those people came inside the Party, it was something else. They were very good people.

So anyway, in 1970 we set up an organization called the Black United Liberation Front to fundamentally do the same things around police brutality, a free breakfast for children program, a free clothing program, a bus that used to take people to visit relatives and friends in prison. For the first time that I know in my political activity we took a militant stand against drugs and on crime, Black crime, gangs.

We organized all the gangs on this side of Broad Street at one point in 1971-72 and got them, instead of fighting each other, to start turning over abandoned cars, throwing trash and garbage that the city wouldn't collect, and blocking up the street demanding that the city turn over the abandoned houses in the Black community and allot money so that they can hire people to clean them up and to begin to rehabilitate them and make them liveable and sell them to the people at what it cost. That was successful; and we ran a breakfast program and then we became involved in different political activity, like a campaign to stop Rizzo from becoming mayor again. We helped to knock off politically some of the Blacks who supported Rizzo in the past. We'd go into different communities and do extensive work and we'd find that Black people would really get down with that.

Our organization folded about 1975 or maybe early '76; that's when the shit started coming down on us, funds were cut off, we just couldn't get any kind of outside help to do anything so we just had to shut down the office in 1976. In the last two months people have told me a new theory that you're allowed to become a civil rights leader, or a political leader, but you don't do both. And I know when we did the anti-Rizzo campaign we used to get arrested quite frequently, and bail would be high and stuff like that.

Lately I've been trying to fix something up, get something going again, some of the things that we did. And to begin to do some other things. The gang problem doesn't hardly exist here anymore. Most of the young guys now are hustling dope or something, just trying to live and be sharp, so they don't have time just to kill for nothing. They kill you for your money. The city, they're statistical, they like to say there's only one gang death now, or gang-related death. But murders still are being committed because of drugs—for $45 a man get his head blowed off. In the course of a year there might be fifty dope killings and they never include that. So I'd like us to do something around that situation.

Really, you know, I guess I still got too much of that what you call street niggerism in me, because I know people over the last couple of years, they're telling me I don't have no upward mobility, I don't want to change. Probably one of the reasons I've been catching so much hell for the last two years is that some people are afraid of me. It's not so much that I'm a violent person, because I haven't been violent with anybody, but I think this is a question of me not being ready to adapt to reevaluating my entire political perspective. I've made some adjustments, but some things you know I'm gonna stand firm on. What the Party gave me, fundamentally, principally what I joined the Party for was because it did not limit my right to fight for what I believed I should be fighting for. I still believe that.

It would be a relief to me to know that at least people have an idea of what the hell happened then, because the dedication that I saw from people across the country—it shouldn't go unnoticed and like it was just a faddish kind of period that they were entering in and nothing more than that. I know now I see a lot of people that for some reason or another left the Movement, and they see the necessity of something happening again because they see this tremendous economic crisis. And I'm almost confident...well, one thing that I am sure of is that revolution will come about; you know, I believe what Mao Tse-tung said, that it's inevitable, it's independent of people's will and people can't stop it.

I would like to see more and more people who had some faith in the Movement become reinvolved in it so that the mistakes that were made, we won't allow them to happen again, so we don't keep setting our own self back. Outside of that there's nothing you can say, really, to prove that it wasn't a passing fancy, a fad, some kind of fetish that people were supporting. There's only what you can do.

Photo by Bill Fibbens/Liberation News Service.

3
Dying From the Inside:
The Decline of the League of Revolutionary Black Workers

In July of 1967, years of pent-up frustration and rage exploded in the city of Detroit. Crowds of angry Black people filled the streets, looting the stores that siphoned their money out of the community, burning the slums to which economic exploitation and housing discrimination confined them, and fighting the police force which harassed and often brutalized them. Lyndon Johnson insisted this "lawlessness" had "nothing to do with civil rights" and fanned the flames by sending in the army. By the time the rebellion was over, at least forty-one people had been killed and 3800 arrested; 1300 buildings had been burned, and 2700 businesses looted.

Widespread unemployment among Blacks in the Motor City was certainly a major cause of the rebellion. When, afterward, companies announced small increased in hiring as a token gesture, thousands lined up at the personnel offices. But it wasn't only the unemployed members of the working class who had spilled into the streets in July. Blacks and even whites who put in their days and nights on the automobile assembly lines of Chrysler, Ford, and GM were seen taking part in the "shopping for free," getting back some of what was theirs.

The following May, their anger took a new form. Four thousand workers shut down the Dodge Main assembly plant in the first wildcat strike to hit that factory in fourteen years. The issue was the incessant, nerve-destroying, and accident-causing speed-up of the line. A key element in making the strike happen was a group of radical Black workers who called themselves DRUM—the Dodge Revolutionary Union Movement.

Black workers had been kept out of many auto plants entirely until the Second World War; now they were the holders of the lowest-paying, most dangerous jobs, and they had the least seniority and job security. In the old, unsafe, and overheated Detroit plants, the auto companies kept up the pressure to produce more cars with fewer people. Black workers, especially, paid the price; they called this process "niggermation." The United Auto Workers, dominated by an overwhelmingly white officialdom interested in negotiating primarily for pay increases, not better conditions, offered little help.

DRUM set out to attack all these issues—discrimination in the plant, discrimination in the union, and the power of the auto companies to dictate working conditions. Within a few months DRUM had dramatized its seriousness to both the company and the union by publicly calling another illegal strike which was honored by 3000 Black workers and some whites; demonstrating at union and company headquarters; and putting forward a DRUM candidate, Ron March, who pulled out the largest number of votes in the first round of the union election.

Company and union officials responded with injunctions, arrests, firings, and vote-tampering. Still, the model was imitated in other plants. The most successful new attempt was ELRUM, in Chrysler's Eldon Avenue gear and axle plant; others included FRUM (in Ford's River Rouge plant), CADRUM (at Cadillac), and UPRUM and HRUM (among United Parcel workers and health workers). In an effort to keep up the momentum and marshall a strong enough force in the plants and the community to defend the RUMs against growing repression, the League of Revolutionary Black Workers was formed.

The League was initiated by a seven-member Executive Board of local Black revolutionaries from working class backgrounds. This group, associated with a newspaper formed shortly after the 1967 rebellion called the *Inner City Voice,* had been working and studying together for some years, and had been instrumental in organizing and supporting DRUM. One of its members, General Baker, had been working at Dodge Main at the time of the first wildcat and had been fired by Chrysler as a result.

The history of the RUMs and the League—their successes and failures and the continuing role of the League activists in later political activity in Detroit—has been chronicled in a number of books and articles listed in the Appendix. Unlike the preceding chapters on the Civil Rights Movement and Black Panther Party, the following essay by Ernie Allen is not intended to tell the organization's history, or to capture the flavor of participation in rank-and-file workplace activism. It takes a more limited and negative focus, but an important one. It seeks to isolate the internal structural and political weaknesses that caused the League of Revolutionary Black Workers, like many of the later New Left groups, to come apart two and a half years after its founding.

In general, the effectiveness of New Left groups in attracting support and carrying out action and education was not matched by an ability to create stable organizations. Particularly in the later years, splits and splinters multiplied as rapidly as they ever have on the left. This essay examines a number of dilemmas and failings in the League which were common to many other groups. Among them are:

• A temptation (already noted by Reggie Schell) to seek coalitions and expanded organizations which look impressive in their formal structures—which allow more people to have some kind of contact with the organization and its politics—but which are often much less solid than they appear.

• A related tendency for leaders to lose contact with their

base, and to see what is happening only in terms of their own ideas about what is needed.

- A lack of structures to encourage democracy and full participation by members.
- A lack of clarity or agreement about strategies and goals.

In dealing with these issues, the essay delves into the internal conflicts and factions of the organization, and it embodies the author's personal judgement about the roles played by specific individuals, including himself. The readings which he suggests in the Appendix offer other points of view. In this chapter, the footnotes are the author's.

Ernie Allen

Ernie Allen was active in the Civil Rights and Black Power movements on the West Coast during the 1960s. He joined the League of Revolutionary Black Workers in 1970 and served as its Director of Political Education. He is currently a Corresponding Associate of the Journal of Ethnic Studies and teaches history in the W.E.B. DuBois Department of Afro-American Studies at the University of Massachusetts at Amherst.

The founding of the League of Revolutionary Black Workers (LRBW) in the late 1960s proved to be one of the more significant manifestations of Afroamerican political maturity since World War II. Though only a short-lived organization, the League, by virtue of competent leadership and the right conditions, and despite opposition from both company and union, was able to mobilize hundreds of black American workers in the factory—where the material wealth of the country is produced.

The LRBW's approach differed in several ways from those of other black organizations seeking civil and social rights. Rather than place primary emphasis on combating the awesome *effects* of Afroamerican oppression, it directed its efforts toward organizing that specific sector, which as a result of its strategic position within the economy, harbored the greatest potential for effecting ultimate political and social change. Rather than view the local police as the *principle* enemy of the black community, the practical implications of which would lead other, less sophisticated black organizations into fruitless and bloody encounters, the League, while taking concrete steps to combat police oppression, continued to view that phenomenon as only one important aspect of *class rule*. Rather than attempt to resolve the social problems of blacks in piecemeal fashion, as had the majority of Afroamerican reformist organizations, the League envisioned the creation of a socialist society in the United States in which all forms of exploitation of human beings by one another would be eliminated forever.

The LRBW was an organized outgrowth of the 1967 black urban rebellion of Detroit. Beginning in May 1968 with the creation of the Dodge Revolutionary Union Movement (DRUM), by early 1969 the more or less autonomous formation of additional Revolutionary Union Movements underwent partial consolidation as the League. With a central-ized leadership in command and important material resources at its disposal, the LRBW quickly embarked on a program of expansion into community organizing, film production, and legal defense, as well as the establishment of a small printing plant and a bookstore.

Outwardly, the League operation was extremely impres-sive. Even those with prior political experience could not help but be moved by the seriousness, dedication, and camaraderie of League members who followed impossible schedules to get the job done. The print shop was always especially busy: a computerized typesetter was pushed to frequent breakdown (not a particularly difficult task), presses ran at all hours, and the continual going and coming of people to drop off "copy," pick up completed work, or contribute labor was a striking phenomenon.

Striking, too, was the activity around the workers' center in Highland Park, despite some of its internal problems. At all hours of the day and night, black workers facing specific difficulties on the job knew they could stop by to discuss their problems. Organizers on their way to meet the morning shifts would often assemble there before dawn to pick up leaflets and other materials. Regular visits from community people wishing to talk over problems of drug abuse, police harassment, or even personal crises, could always be anticipated.

In short, the League—particularly in its earlier days—was both highly visible and highly respected in the Detroit metropolitan area, in the community as well as at the plant gates. At a time when New Left and Black Power organizations were in the process of decline, League membership gave one the distinct feeling of being part of a "winning" organization. But by mid-1970, when the League began to attract considerable attention nationally as well as internationally, cracks had already appeared in its organizational foundation. The following year witnessed the ultimate crumbling of the edifice: the League of Revolutionary Black Workers was no more.

Today, in 1978, as we "prepare" for further cutbacks in social services, lower standards of living, and increased political repression which invariably oozes from the seams of a deteriorating social situation, it is essential that we avoid, where possible, the more salient "movement" errors of the late 1960s and early 1970s—not to mention earlier periods.

In examining the development of the League from an "inside" perspective it shall become quite apparent that its demise, like that of too many other progressive organizations of that period, was due more to *internal* than external pressures. With that experience behind us, and with adequate reflection, we *can* do better. At the very least, we must attempt to understand how organizations such as the League, which held so much political promise for so many people, were unable to surmount their internal contradictions. If the following study does no more than aid that process of understanding, it will have accomplished its purpose.

The Problem With Structure

By 1969—the year the League was founded—the spontaneously formed RUM groups were declining in influence in the plants. Whereas the larger RUMs had often been able to attract hundreds of workers to their meetings in 1968, the following year they were fortunate to pull out a handful.

Several factors account for this decline. The wave of popular discontent unleashed in the 1967 rebellion—upon which the Revolutinary Union Movement had built itself—had now subsided. It might be more accurate to say that it had been engulfed by increasingly violent gang activity and street crime—often drug-related—within the black community. Moreover, by 1970 Chrysler Corporation had visibly increased the number of black foremen on some of its assembly lines, thus robbing the RUM groups of one of their most pressing issues.

RUM activists, meanwhile, had been identified and were constantly surveilled. Even those who had been fortunate or skillful enough to survive the purges by plant management felt a sense of isolation and ineffectiveness. And RUM leadership had furthered its isolation from a large strata of potential constituents by launching indiscriminate verbal attacks on older workers for their "conservatism," as well as tasteless commentaries on the personal lives of numerous union "misleaders."

In the face of these problems, one of the intended

functions of the League was to overcome the isolation of the RUM groups by coordinating their activities and linking the plant struggles with wide, community-based support. There were also several other pressing problems which the formation of a consolidated organization was supposed to deal with. Due to the refusal of local printers to handle the *Inner City Voice,* concrete means had to be found to fill the movement's publishing needs. Also facilities had to be secured to provide a permanent home for the organizations, as well as to alleviate problems which had fallen on particular activists' families. General Baker's family, for instance, had to contend with a literal "army of unemployed" organizers and leafleters who, having no other place to go, bivouacked nightly on their living room floor. And, overall, the haunting problem of scarce financial resources had to be resolved if the movement was to survive over the long run.

The formation of the League was a creative response to these difficulties: but it proved to be as ominous as it was creative. The drive by the top leadership to provide a supportive apparatus for black workers' struggles paradoxically ended in its abandoning them. The League did not succeed in confronting the problems of declining mass revolutionary sentiment, tactical maneuvers by management, and tactical errors by RUM leadership which were curtailing the in-plant revolt. But in 1969 and 1970 such *political failures* were masked by a false sense of organizational successes in other areas: the creation of the League film "Finally Got the News," the proliferation of LRBW offices in the Detroit area, participation in a book-discussion project which had enrolled hundreds of liberal whites, as well as the growing media attention which the League was attracting nationwide. How did such a situation come about?

The reorganization of the existing RUMs into the League was accomplished by the Executive Board from the top down. This was made possible by money which the EB succeeded in raising from outside sources—the Black Economic Development Conference in particular.[1] As a direct consequence, decisions concerning specific allocations of funds (and, more importantly, decisions about what activities the League would become involved in) could and did occur without the participation, or even the knowledge at times, of the rank-and-file.[2]

Due to a lack of participatory democracy or even of adequate communication in the new organization, many of those who remained active in the RUMs were not even aware that they had "joined" the League.

With reorganization also arrived a qualitative shift from in-plant organizing to activities nominally supporting that goal: the gathering of resources, development of printing, publishing, and film-making operations, participation in struggles around control of the schools, etc. An unintended but direct consequence was an influx of political and technical personnel who staffed these new projects—and whose personal loyalties generally went to individual EB members heading such operations. (The fact that some harbored "middle class" outlooks also had a bearing on the changing character of the organization.)

Two other factors prevented an open recognition of the League's drift away from its original base. First, the money

1. The National Black Economic Development Conference—later shortened to BECD—first convened in April 1969 at Wayne State University in Detroit. Sponsored by the Interreligious Foundation for Community Organization (IFCO), BEDC was not originally intended as an independent organization, which it later became, but as a means of bringing "together a broad spectrum of black leaders to explore strategies for more rapid black-directed community development." However, after adopting a "Black Manifesto" under the leadership of James Forman, BEDC began pressuring religious organizations to provide "reparations" to the black community. At least several hundred thousand dollars were raised in this manner, with a significant portion going to the League. For further information, see Robert S. Lecky and H. Eliot Wright (eds.), *Black*

from BEDC served to lubricate the sharpest edges of personal or political dissatisfaction both among RUM members and inside the EB. Second, eminently aware that it was the talented members of the EB alone who had secured necessary legal and material resources for the organization, until mid-1971 the politically inexperienced rank-and-file tended to follow a strict policy of "deference" in regard to top leadership, despite private criticisms which they occasionally voiced.

On the positive side, then, the formation of the LRBW in early 1969 led to organizational consolidation at several levels: a centralized leadership was constituted—albeit not in the most democratic of terms; material resources were secured, and in turn funneled to the RUM groups as well as other projects; and various offices and facilities were established. On the questionable to negative side, the transition to a more complex structure and its associated activities placed the Executive Board largely out of touch with the rank-and-file— the plant workers in particular. There arose a problem of organizational democracy, by which I mean the absence of any *structural* possibilities for the general membership to impose its collective will on either the overall political direction of the League or its internal affairs. And, finally, League energies

Manifesto: Religion, Racism, and Reparations (New York: Sheed and Ward, 1969).

2. Not withstanding the fact that BEDC funds underwrote a number of League activities which, under other circumstances, might not have been immediately feasible, had *political* emphasis been placed instead on a dues-paying apparatus financed by membership, a more structurally sound organization might have resulted. This approach is to be distinguished from implementation of the League-proposed International Black Appeal through company "checkoff" procedures (by which money for the United Fund or union dues is secured), but rather through a more direct means of collection— certainly not the *most expedient* means at hand, but an important process if *political organizing* in itself.

were poured into a number of diverse activities—some of which proved absolutely necessary—while consolidation and further expansion of the RUM groups was virtually neglected.

To understand this process as it unfolded, concretely, in the League, we must look at its social and political make-up, at its seven-member Executive Board, and at the EB's decisions (or lack of them) about organizational discipline, relations with the membership, and political education. Then we can look at the specific internal conflict around these issues that was the immediate cause of the break-up of the League.

Social Make-Up

Who was the LRBW? Large numbers of people participated at one time or another in the RUMs or in League-sponsored campaigns, demonstrations, or discussions. But active members in the League itself usually totalled about sixty.

In the early stages of the League's formation, the plant workers made up the majority of the membership, but by late 1970 they found themselves outnumbered by other elements. A second important group who joined the ranks of the LRBW were the high school students who had organized themselves as the Black Student Union Front, a league affiliate. The majority of the workers earned their livelihood by toiling in the auto plants, of course, while the high school students still relied on their parents to provide them with the basic necessities.

From time to time, however, the LRBW has to provide shelter and money for both workers and students, who, as a direct result of their participation in LRBW activities, experienced personal crises: job firings, expulsion from home by politically conservative parents, etc. This situation created a third type of League member, whose dependence on LRBW resources could last indefinitely, Also in this third category were "free-floating" elements, or "hangers-on," who might enroll at Wayne State University or a local community college for a semester or two, work at the Eldon Avenue axle plant for a few months, and then quit or be fired. Either way, the members of this third group had the "free time" which allowed them to provide the League with indispensable services: the printing and distribution of plant leaflets and other organizational literature, office and transportation maintenance, security details, etc. At the same time, this sector also provided the League with some of its greatest disciplinary problems.

Finally, a fourth group of people provided the LRBW with services and political leadership. Its members often drew salaries from League components, but unlike the third group they tended to assume *permanent* responsibilities within the LRBW. They usually possessed political-intellectual, administrative, or technical skills as well. Here would be classified people who, for example, managed LRBW operations such as Black Star Printing or the bookstore, who oversaw the technical aspects of the printing operation, who orchestrated legal-defense strategies, who furnished typing or clerical services, or who conducted political education classes. With the expansion of the RUM groups into the League in early 1969, it was this strata which increased in absolute numbers, while the number of workers decreased.

Political Make-Up

The RUM groups attracted primarily people who had never become involved in politics before. Caught up in the militant spirit of the urban rebellions and Black Power demands, the hard-hitting, "tell-it-like-it-is" approach of RUM leaflets captured the imagination of these younger workers. (But as others have stressed, the tone of such leaflets also tended to alienate older workers as well as white workers in general.)

Of the two most important worker components, DRUM and ELRUM, DRUM's leadership was by far the most stable, experienced, and politically sophisticated. Ron March of DRUM, for example, had acumulated considerable prior experience working within the UAW black caucus, including political interaction between white and black workers. Such was not generally typical of ELRUM cadre, who became largely dependent on DRUM leadership for direction.

In this period, national consciousness on the part of younger black industrial workers far outweighed any manifestations of class consciousness, though the latter was by no means completely absent.[3] For the most part this nationalism was expressed as anti-racist sentiment, but the negative experiences of black workers within the plant and union also led to anti-white attitudes in general.

Nationalism was hardly limited to the "non-intellectual" strata, as one writer recently asserted. Whether at a sophisticated or elementary level, it manifested itself in varying degrees among most LRBW members. It was the principal motive force behind the Black Student United Front, and it surfaced in a more sophisticated form among those Executive Board members who advocated a "black-led Marxist vanguard party." By far the least progressive manifestations of national consciousness came from the "free-floating" elements within the LRBW—the least disciplined of all.

---

3. An important issue facing any group like the League of Revolutionary Black Workers is how much to focus on the way black workers are treated because of being *workers* and how much to focus on the way they are treated because of being *black*. Are the members of organizations banding together primarily because of their common class, or their common nationality? In a note at the end of this chapter, the author explains his use of the terms "class consciousness" and "national consciousness," and some of the political and historical issues connected with this question.—ed.

Until mid-1970 the main political divisions inside the League rested mainly within the Executive Board. These divisions were basically two-fold. At the level of direct political ideology, there was a struggle between one section of leadership putting forward a general Marxist orientation who proved to be more amenable to working with white (mostly middle class) allies, and more nationalistically oriented individuals who tended to oppose such alliances. Mike Hamlin, Ken Cockrel, John Watson, Luke Tripp, and John Williams belonged to the first tendency, while the second was characterized by General Baker and Chuck Wooten. At the same time both Wooten and Baker nominally subscribed to Marxist principles as well.[4]

The second division on the EB represented a clash over immediate tactics as well as long-range strategies. Nominally, all EB members agreed that the principle political task of the League was the organizing of black workers; however, a number of the other activities in which the League was engaged from 1969 onward tended to become ends in themselves. A highly pragmatic section of the leadership advocated expanding League activities into many spheres at the same time, both locally and nationally. Another group favored a more coordinated expansion but also concerned themselves with the consolidation of existing organizational ventures. Finally, there were more people who tended to resist involvement in any activities that were not immediately connected with the direct organization of black workers in Detroit. On these sets of issues Hamlin, Cockrel, and Watson were identified with

---

4.   One cannot become a Marxist in the sense that one becomes a Christian. The latter requires that one believe; the former should require some degree of study, and the translation of that study into practice. It is difficult to distinguish, among all the EB members, between those who were *consequent* Marxists—that is, whose

the first tendency; Tripp and Williams with the second; and Wooten and Baker with the third.

The two-fold political division on the EB was to produce curious alignments and realignments among its members, depending on the specific issues involved. In the case of gross violations of organizational discipline by rank-and-file members, the necessity to enter specific support activities, as well as in confronting the issue of narrow nationalism, Williams and Tripp tended to align with the Hamlin/Cockrel/Watson faction. When it came to the question of the League's over-extending its limited financial and human resources, the two generally—but not always—sided with Baker and Wooten.

Practically speaking, then, it became difficult if not impossible for any one of the factions within the top leadership to win a clear-cut victory. This, plus the fact that each group needed, or thought it needed, the particular skills cultivated by the others, stalemated any clear-cut direction of the League from the very beginning. As funds began flowing into the LRBW in early 1969, the shifting alignments within the Executive Board resulted in the establishing of three different "headquarters" for the organization; Baker and Wooten oversaw the Highland Park office, main center for worker organizing; Tripp and Williams were associated with the Linwood office, from which were coordinated the public school decentralization and control struggles of 1969-1970 as well as a fundraising project called the International Black Appeal; Hamlin headed the Black Star Publishing operation. (Cockrel and Watson, due to their involvement in legal and film work, respectively, tended to be the least visible of all.) Political division had become physical division as well.

concrete political practice was logically and cosistently informed by Marxist theory—and more pragmatic, but capable people whose knowledge of Marxism failed to extend beyond the reciting of key phrases or principles.

Rank-and-File Nationalism and the EB

Initially, the EB as a whole tended to recognize the virtues of the mass-based nationalism which had brought the League itself into being. A long-standing history of white, working class racism in Detroit had created a fierce climate of mistrust among black workers regarding "black and white, unite" slogans. Moreover, in an apparent projection of Detroit conditions onto the rest of the country, the majority of the EB subscribed to the dubious proposition that black workers *by themselves* had the power to shut down the strategic centers of U.S. heavy industry. In consequence, even those among the top leadership who were the most adamant concerning the need for black and white labor unity were led to advocate, or at least tolerate, certain tactics. An example is the League's refusal to distribute plant leaflets to white laborers, in order to avoid losing credibility with blacks.

In time, however, due to numerous internal problems which surfaced within the organization, some of the more Marxist-oriented members of the EB developed an extreme aversion to Afroamerican nationalism in general, thereby jettisoning its positive sides along with the negative. Undoubtedly the most delicate and volatile issue concerned "sniping" by rank-and-file (and sometimes EB) members in regard to interracial personal relationships engaged in by a number of these leaders.

This "white woman question" was complicated by male chauvinism at all organizational levels. In particular, a double standard allowed League males to seek relationships outside the organization even where "competing" political groups were concerned; similar action on the part of League females was often viewed as a "security risk." In response, the women would frequently raise hell over the white woman question.[5]

5. Parallels can be found in the experiences of black women within

For some male leaders, anxious to squelch this personal critic-ism, nationalism itself became a major enemy.

The Problem With Leadership

Generally speaking, the individuals comprising the Exec-utive Board—the top leadership strata of the League—were eminently capable and creative. Some were even congenial. Without the presence of those particular individuals in Detroit, it is doubtful that an organization such as the LRBW would have emerged when it did. But a measured, political evaluation of that same strata must draw some harsher conclusions, as well: many of the internal organization problems of which EB members chronically complained were the immediate or delayed result of decisions which they themselves made, or failed to make at the appropriate time

Among the numerous, interrelated difficulties facing the League from the beginning was that of an extremely lax organ-izational discipline. Most of the earlier members of the LRBW had been swept into the organizational fold as a result of their involvement in earlier RUM struggles. By the time of the first general meeting of the LRBW in July 1970, when wholesale recruitment occurred, the EB either was or should have been keenly apprised of the strengths and weaknesses of individual rank-and-file members.

At that point, those who had posed constant disciplinary problems could have been placed on probationary status or eliminated from the ranks altogether. Although the League might have lost some of its best leafleters in the process, instances of equipment abuse and, on a lesser scale, petty theft,

the Communist Party during the 1930s and 1940s. See, for example, Claudia Jones, "An End to the Neglect of the Problems of the Negro Woman!," *Political Affairs* (June 1949).

might also have been curtailed. Instead, nearly everyone who had worked informally for the LRBW in the past was drafted into the organization. And no organizational code of conduct was adopted to be binding on all League members.

Moreover, extremely poor choices were made by the EB in matters of "security" personnel. Rather than security forces being comprised of the most disciplined and emotionally stable members of the LRBW, volunteers were sought; the result was that the members most anxious to carry weapons became the security force—and fights which could have been avoided sometimes occurred between these "revolutionary" versions of Starsky & Hutch and rank-and-file members.

A deeper problem, though, was that in many ways the Executive Board conducted itself almost as an autonomous organization. Its relatively "hermetic" (sealed off) nature, made worse by the proliferation of LRBW activities from early 1969 onward, resulted in a relative *lack of visible or responsive leadership* for the organization as a whole. Perhaps the best illustration of this particular state of affairs can be found in the fact that the LRBW's first general meeting did not take place until almost a year and a half after its founding. A large number of individuals who had more or less informally participated in League activities until then, were not even aware of their own formal membership until receiving letters from the EB requesting their attendance at that first meeting in July 1970. The mail, rather than face-to-face discussion, tended to be a primary form of communication between the EB and general membership from then on—even though the League was comprised of roughly sixty members.

The term "lack of visible leadership" should not be taken in the crude sense that individual EB members were never seen by the membership. Due to the priorities which they assigned to plant organizing, General Baker and Chuck Wooten, for example, were among those most accessible to the rank-and-file on a day-to-day basis; other EB members could usually be located at the various League offices which they supervised. (Though there were some who spent almost as much time in Europe as they did in Detroit, or whose job responsibilities or personal temperaments tended to prohibit regular interaction with general membership.)

But even where leadership was highly visible, it was not always responsive. There was a very acute problem (to be discussed shortly) of members not getting any guidance as to how they should carry out assigned tasks. Even in matters of ideology or information about the League, different EB members had different positions and it was not clear to members what "the League's position" was on a number of important issues: Was the LRBW a mass organization seeking to organize the greatest number of people around general issues, with a hope of eventually becoming a more selective group of "professional revolutionaries?" Or was it already in fact that more selective group with a strategy for taking political power? What would be the League's eventual relationship to white workers or to other people of color within the United States? Would it become an "integrated" revolutionary political party, or was there envisioned some sort of federation which would seek to unite all nationalities around revolutionary issues? Such questions had as many answers as there were EB members.

Finally, the problems of leadership were reflected in the inability of the organization to coherently resolve day-to-day difficulties which regularly surfaced in financial or disciplinary areas: numerous problems either went unresolved or received partial and unsatisfactory solutions because there was no visible chain of command within the leadership structure to which aggrieved parties might appeal.

The closed quality of the EB manifested itself as well in the failure of political education among the membership—here, not so much in the sense of formal classes as in the general lack of internal political discussion: the *collective reflection* of the rank-and-file on their own political activities. For example, the political development of the Executive Board itself had been nurtured by the experiences of its individual members prior to the RUM and LRBW formations, the sharing of these experiences in regular EB sessions, as well as the collective reflection of this body on League tactics and strategies in progress.[6] In contrast, although open, political discussions among the general membership sometimes occurred, such were left to the "laws" of chance: no *structure* existed whereby leadership could communicate its concrete political experiences to the rank-and-file, nor was any formal mechanism developed in order that the organization might collectively and systematically analyze itself.

Formal political education fared little better. The fundamental problem here, I believe, was a failure on the part of instructors to relate the subject matter to the existing political level and needs of those attending classes. For example, the principle staples of League internal education were the philosophical essays of Mao Tse-Tung ("On Practice" and "On Contradiction," among others). For those living outside China, one difficulty in teaching from these works lies in Mao's exclusive use of Chinese historical references for illustrative purposes. Black workers who possessed meager historical background in regard to their own struggles, whose political sophistication was only beginning to develop, and who had

6. It should be noted, however, that the internal discussions and debates within the EB tended to center around *pragmatic* questions bearing on strategies and tactics rather than the more basic political-ideological underpinnings of the former. Given the fragile unity of the EB from the very beginning, such political discussions might very well have resulted in a miscarriage of the LRBW at its moment of conception. But that remains an academic matter: fundamental political divisions resulted in the eventual fracturing of the EB anyway.

little time to devote to studies in the first place, simply could not maintain an interest in material which seemed so remote from their own needs. Later efforts were made to correct some of the most glaring difficiencies of the internal education program, but basic difficulties remained.

Similar to its allowing internal political education to seek its own level was the general failure of the EB to provide *particular guidance* to members in the carrying out of organizational tasks. An example is the LRBW newspaper, the *Inner City Voice*. The EB had actually come together around the paper, which began publication after the 1967 rebellion. Once the *ICV* became the official voice of the League, it should have been accorded their greatest attention. But the EB concentrated on other projects and essentially abandoned the newspaper by turning it over to a new, committed, but untrained staff.

It is true that formal journalism classes ended in failure partly because of the narrow nationalistic attitudes on the part of the incoming staff. But the fact that they regarded the classes as futile exercises in "white journalism" and that they received little guidance in the actual gathering and writing of news in the field, also suggests that insufficient effors were made to relate such training to League members' actual needs and political outlooks.

Another example occurred after the first general meeting of the LRBW in mid-1970, when several plant workers were assigned the tasks of organizing Detroit's east- and west-side black communities. Though lacking prior experience, the two workers, after having been assigned funds and told to look for office space, were simply instructed by the EB to "organize." With neither guidance nor prior experience to draw upon, projects such as these were destined to fail. (Fewer difficulties existed with training of a purely technical nature, such as the development of printing and typesetting skills among the membership.

The "hermetic" nature of the EB was manifested in its

relative self-dependency and its monopoly of organizational skills, information, and political expertise. All this, contrasted to the behavior of a number of undisciplined, politically unsophisticated personnel whom EB itself recruited into the LRBW, eventually tended to create in the minds of many upper-ranking leaders the idea that the EB alone constituted the League. This apparent self-deception contributed to attitudes of arrogance and contempt which some EB members exhibited at times in regard to the rank-and-file.

The flow of discussion from the floor during organizational meetings, for example, was effectively curtailed not only because of a basic lack of political self-confidence among the general membership, but also by a justifiable fear on their part of being subjected to ideological terrorism. They risked stepping into scenes like courtroom proceedings, with the EB "prosecution" fervidly attempting to unnerve a "hostile witness." Given the shortcomings of political education and the very real lack of coordinated political discussion within the organization as a whole, the fact that political sophistication remained the "property" of the EB while the general membership remained in relative political ignorance, should come as no surprise.

The result was that at the very top level, the League was nominally a "Marxist-Leninist" organization; middle to lower echelons assumed the character of mass organization which generally deferred to the EB in matters of Left politics, but whose cohesiveness for the most part derived from a shared nationalist sentiment and within that context, a specific commitment to the struggles of black workers.

Evolution and Decline of the Central Staff

An attempt to rectify some of the organizational problems and create a "second-line" leadership beneath that of the EB was the "expanded Central Staff." First discussed in

November 1969, the Central Staff idea was written into the 1970 League program. In contrast with the Executive Board, which had the responsibility of formulating policy, the Central Staff (CS) was to function mainly as the "implementation arm" of the LRBW. It was to consist of the "heads of committees and representatives of lower organizations."

The CS first convened on August 22, 1970. Save for the EB, not one of the thirty or so persons present at this meeting had asked to be there: they had simply received letters stating that their attendance was required. Further, though the CS was to represent the "implementation arm" of the League, and though some did play leading roles in the plant, community, and publishing components, its members apparently had not been chosen with any political criterion in mind. CS members were no more politically experienced or aware than most League rank-and-file. Consequently, this first CS gathering was a poor one indeed. If the CS was to be the place where "second-line" leadership was to emerge, it was clear at that point that the League was in trouble.

A second meeting was called some three months later, and then only after one of the more politically conscious CS members began pressuring for it. Because there were so many issues to be discussed, it was decided that a CS "retreat" should be held December 19-20, with reports to be submitted by various persons. (The sole EB member to volunteer for the "retreat" planning committee attended not a single one of its meetings.)

The December "retreat" opened with a report by EB member Mike Hamlin, who attempted to place the principle contradiction within the LRBW on a *quantitative* footing. There existed two trends within the League, according to Hamlin. Certain people, who wanted to proceed at a rapid pace, advocated continual expansion and involvement in more activities and struggles; others desired to proceed more slowly, concentrating on one aspect of the struggle at a time.

Hamlin affirmed that he was one of those who represented the first tendency; espousing the need for 24-hour-a-day struggles, he felt that individual black revolutionaries should, for example, be completely "interchangeable" with their Vietnamese counterparts then battling against U.S. imperialism. Hamlin, moreover, was pained to think that the LRBW had to take time away from life-and-death struggles in order to discuss organizational problems. He indicated that if the League were involved in continuous struggle against the enemy, organizational difficulties would cease to exist.

Shola Akintolaya and myself, on the other hand, viewed the LRBW's main contradiction as that existing between the *concrete political tasks* which the League had mandated itself to carry out, and the *actual organizational structure* which in our estimation, stifled the effective completion of such tasks.[7] We viewed the *central political task* of the LRBW as the organizing of black workers in general, and the developing of working-class political cadre in particular; second, we saw the *central organizational task* as the reconstruction of the Central Staff in order to lay the basis for working-class leadership and control of the League. The numerous organizational problems, we reasoned, either resulted from or were reinforced by the existing structure.

Even the unimplemented paper structure in the program was rooted in an anti-Marxist division of tasks which would effectively relegate the practice of mental labor to the EB,

7. Akintolaya and I had first met one another, as well as General Baker and Luke Tripp, on a student trip to Cuba in 1964. We renewed our friendship in 1969 when both of us were living in New York City. En route to a UAW convention in Atlantic City in early 1970, General Baker recruited us into the LRBW. Initially we were unaware of the existence of factions among League leadership; as the drama of League internal politics unfolded in our minds, we lent our political support to the Baker-Wooten forces, whom we believed to be correct in their stressing of plant organizing activities. By late fall

manual labor to the CS. In other words, the proposed structure called for a division between those who would conceptualize League policy, and those who would carry it out. Second, there were members of the EB itself who possessed no concrete, spelled-out responsibilities; their activities, rather, were more or less spontaneously determined according to circumstances. (Which is not to say that many EB members were "non-functional," but that their activities were neither integrated, cooordinated, nor channeled *structurally* in accordance with the role that a leading body of this sort must play within a revolutionary organization.) Third, the unimplemented structure contained no effective guarantee for workers' control of a workers' organization. Most importantly, we argued, the League, in its own pragmatic way, was attempting to appropriate the structure of both a vanguard party and a mass organization *at the same time.*[8]

On the one hand, the LRBW had failed to show itself to be a true "cadre" organization (seen as a formative stage of a Leninist vanguard party). Without an effective political education program, there was no way in which the League could ever become a formation of "professional revolutionaries." Moreover, "democratic centralism," the organizing principle behind the Leninist concept of revolutionary party, was haphazardly imposed by the EB—and then only from the "centralist" side.

On the other hand, the hierarchical structure of the League had actually robbed the organization of some of the

---

of 1970, when it had become clear that the EB was hopelessly deadlocked, we suggested to Baker and Wooten that they continue to struggle for this policy within the EB, while we would mount pressure from without. But we had no agreement or discussion with them about the form that our pressure would take.

8. See note at end of chapter for a discussion of the dilemma that these forms—mass organization and vanguard party—are attempts to deal with, and of their meaning in the Leninist tradition.—ed.

most positive attributes of a mass organization: internal democracy, spontaneity, and the consequent ability to efficiently resolve organizational problems. Finally, workers and students, according to the League program, were not able to join the LRBW merely on the basis of their demonstrated willingness to struggle around concrete social issues, but were first required to commit themselves ideologically to Marxism. Such a measure could only hinder future mass organizing efforts by the League.

Thus within the revolutionary political forest of 1970, the LRBW could be counted as neither flora nor fauna, although it had begun to exhibit remarkable vegetative characteristics!

In concluding, we called for: the reconstitution of the LRBW into two structures—a cadre (pre-party) formation on the one hand, mass organizations (RUM groups, Black Student United Front, Parents and Students for Community Control, the community organization UNICOM, etc.) on the other hand; dissolution of the Executive Board; and reconstitution of the Central Staff on the basis of concrete participation of its members in LRBW mass organizations. Admittance to the League's mass organizations would require only demonstrated willingness to struggle against prevailing social and political conditions; such mass organizations would project no strict doctrinal line. On the other hand, admission to the League's inner cadre would be much more stringent, based upon one's practice as well as effective mastery of Marxist theory. The highest body of the League, according to this plan, was to be a conference of the entire membership of the cadre organization; it was to meet every six months with the power to review decisions made by the CS during each interim period.

Not unexpectedly, the CS "retreat" was thereby plunged into a rather sharp ideological battle which lasted some twelve hours the first day, and four hours the next.

Despite the inordinate amount of time consumed in the wake of this presentation, the response of the EB proved to be quite limited. The *real* problem, reiterated the more vocal members of this body, Ken Cockrel and John Watson, time and time again, was that "people weren't doing what they were supposed to be doing," and that whatever internal difficulties the League harbored could be resolved if such people would only "implement the program." (No matter that even the best political program cannot tell one how to function on a day-to-day basis: it cannot tell one what to do when faced with a specific problem, nor how to react in a specific situation.)[9]

The overt response of the main body of the Central Staff to the proposed restructuring of the League, as well as the criticisms of the EB, was one of silence. Privately, many expressed solidarity with the critique; in open discussion, the same persons became tongue-tied. Ultimately, however, after the proposal had been "much cussed and much discussed," the CS as a whole voted to make itself "functional" within the existing League structure.

Things Fall Apart

A follow-up meeting to the December "retreat" was scheduled to take place January 16, 1971. CS members were to have reported the proceedings of the December gathering to

9. This lack of response to the specific criticisms and suggestions caused an impasse, in which further discussion was impossible. Cockrel responded to the expressed need for particular guidance in daily work only by saying he "didn't have time to be holding motherfuckers' (people's) hands." Watson explained that the League had to call itself "Marxist-Leninist" to distinguish itself from existing black reformist organizations. In regard to restructuring, he said the EB "was not about to turn over resources which it had spent years collecting."

their respective components, engaged all members of these components in collective discussions, and then reported their conclusions back to the CS. But on the eve of January 16 the EB cancelled the scheduled meeting. Believing that the EB's decision to stay the Central Staff gathering was based on a fear of criticism by the membership, several CS members decided to act by holding the scheduled meeting anyway.[10]

The meeting was held, but under confusing circumstances: some CS members, hearing only of the cancellation, did not attend; others participated only because they were unaware of the EB's decision; and still others attended in open defiance of what they considered to be an arbitrary and damaging decision on the part of the leading body. Chuck Wooten, the only EB member to participate, excused himself halfway through the proceedings with the remark that he would "fight out any differences he had with the EB, within the EB itself."

The week which followed was one of uncertainty. A "reprimand" meeting of the CS was held January 23, where the communications secretary was castigated by the EB for refusing to notify CS members of the cancellation, and CS members in general were put on alert that further actions of this sort "would not be tolerated."[11] The once-lively internal political discussions which had been sparked by the December

10. Chuck Wooten initially agreed with this assessment of the reason for the cancellation. Both he and Baker were absent from the EB meeting which had made the decision—Baker was out of town, and Wooten could not be contacted in time. The EB's stated reasons for cancellation were not all convincing to some CS members who viewed its failure to set a new convening date as an ominous sign.

11. Apparently as a balance to the harsh tone of the meeting, John Williams announced an "incentives" plan which would single out for recognition members who had accomplished exemplary work. But his comparison of this program to the toilet training of infants, where

CS meeting now came to an end, replaced by less stimulating rumors of possible splits as well as membership decisions to side with whatever faction controlled the most League real estate.

Splitting the League was the very thing that its small handful of "reformers" wanted to avoid at all costs. We pushed for radical structural changes within the organization in order to establish some degree of workers' political control internally and thereby return the League to its stated interim task of plant organizing. But we did so on the assumption that the organization would be able to tolerate principled political dissent within its ranks. We did not agitate among the membership for support for our action, sensing that any attempt along these lines would result in the fracturing of the League.

Meanwhile, the EB had decided on its own plan for restructuring the LRBW. Rather than convene a general meeting to openly thrash out the issues point by point, the leading body sought instead to gauge membership loyalty by means of what one irreverent soul termed a "revolutionary Gallup poll." On February 11 a mimeographed questionnaire was sent by the EB to all League members requesting "confidential" information: "state your commitment to the League from the standpoint of priority, i.e., does it rank first or fifth, in relation to other priorities, i.e., job, family, school, or other aspirations and commitments." And so on ... only a few members chose to respond to this "dialogue."

In March, a general meeting was held in which some EB members spoke of the "disrespect for leadership and authority" in the CS, and others directed their remarks mainly to upcoming organizational activities; none addressed the role of the Central Staff or organizational structure in general. Shortly thereafter, and despite the fact that there had been no

rewards are given by parents for appropriate "potty behavior" provoked further anger.

political "unrest" within the LRBW for several months, the EB unanimously voted to expel seven members from its ranks, of whom only four had really been active in attempting to change the organization's structure: several, Akintolaya and myself included, were specifically charged with "insubordination;" spouses were purged because they constituted "security risks."

The "Easter purges" and the events leading to them produced an effect on the LRBW which no one could have anticipated. Principled criticisms of the organization, as well as measures designed to address its fundamental problems, had been offered; the only "counter" which the EB could find in its political repertoire was that of "hard-line" policy. The effects of that policy on the rank-and-file as well as on the EB itself constituted the *immediate* causes leading to the break-up of the LRBW.

We Will Take the Hard Line

While the majority of the League rank-and-file loyally supported the EB in all organizational matters—including the expulsions—within a period of only two months following the latter event, that support had fully evaporated. From April through mid-June, 1971, the League met in a full body at least every two weeks, and sometimes weekly—an unprecedented event. Prior to this time, the leadership was not always accessible to the general membership; now the strengths and weaknesses of the EB could be regularly viewed by all. And with the EB's "hard line" in effect, the rank-and-file began to sense more and more that they had little control indeed over the affairs of the organization. Moreover, they were forced to see the extreme arrogance and verbal pomposity of several EB members, which only heaped insult upon injury. The result was that workers and students within the organization met during the second week in June to formulate demands for greater worker representation on the Executive Board—one of the very proposals which had surfaced in the December CS meeting.

On yet another front, the "hard line" was having its effect on relations within the EB as well, with Wooten and Baker—the EB members closest to the in-plant organizing—singled out for attack. Their base, the Cortland Street Office in Highland Park, was indeed often in filthy condition and the scene of abusive treatment of women and generally uncomradely behavior. But to place matters in a slightly different perspective, it should be noted that those who had been previously expelled from the League for their internal political activities had also been Baker supporters. (Baker backed these expulsions out of a desire to "preserve the unity" of the EB.) Outvoted on the issue of new expulsions for disciplinary reasons (which were necessay, but which would have cut even more into their constituency) as well as a decision to close down the Cortland Street office, Baker and Wooten resigned from the League on June 11, the day before the next scheduled general meeting. In order not to undermine rank-and-file political momentum, Baker and Wooten did not broadcast the fact of their resignation.

Meanwhile, anticipating strong opposition from the EB, the workers and students who were preparing to make demands for greater representation practiced their debating skills, one by one, far into the next morning; onlookers, intending that such skills be properly tempered, hooted them down with derisive shouts. Ultimately, the charges of the rank-and-file against the EB were registered on a tape recorder.

But at the general meeting of LRBW on June 12 (which must have appeared rather surreal to participants) League protagonists unfortunately lost the will to speak and instead confronted the remaining EB members with the *previously taped* demands for three workers' "slots" on the leading body. Following a brief intermission, John Watson returned from his caucusing with Hamlin and Cockrel to inform the organization that workers could have not only three seats, but *all* of them—Hamlin, Cockrel, and Watson were leaving the LRBW. To the tune of a few tears and numerous jeers, thus effectively ended the League of Revolutionary Black Workers.

That August the Black Workers' Congress—originally conceived as a national body in which the League would play a leading role—became an independent organization with Cockrel, Watson, Hamlin, and James Forman at the helm. The BWC replicated many of the errors of the League. The initial unity of its leadership was forged in the final battles with League members; as such, it proved to be a very fragile one. Moreover, without the mass upsurge which had initially brought the League into being, it was but a matter of time before the BWC itself would experience a number of purges, resignations, and ultimate collapse.

The remaining and greatest portion of the League at first toyed with the idea of reconstituting itself along more nationalistic lines as a mass organization.[12] But in September it decided instead to fuse with a pre-party organization called the Communist League, whose initial base was in southern California. That organization is now the Communist Labor Party.

The collapse of the League of Revolutionary Black Workers was more than just another knot in a long string of political disappointments over the past decade; happily, it has

---

12. Meanwhile, Baker and Wooten rejoined the League, and the victims of the "Easter purge" were invited back—by mail, of course—into the organizational fold. At a meeting held partly for this latter purpose, the "purgees" expressed a desire to return, but only on condition that the body entertain a full discussion of the events which led to the ousters. Although some LRBW members— Luke Tripp, John Williams, and General Baker among them— strongly supported that provision, the measure was voted down in a heated debate.

left a certain positive legacy for the present. Most importantly, small groups of black workers throughout the country, impressed by the League's example of organization and political direction (though largely unmindful of details), persist in seeking solutions to the problems of economic exploitation in general as well as domination by existing union leadership.

In Detroit itself, "wildcat" strikes led by black workers have continued. And in Michigan's electoral arena where, as elsewhere, personalities tend to predominate over concrete issues, two former LRBW leaders have attempted to inject more profound debates into the formal political process. Recently, General Baker ran for the office of state representative from a district including Highland Park, which he lost. Somewhat more successful in his own political career, Ken Cockrel is presently a Detroit City Councilman. It is perhaps too soon to tell what kinds of differences—if any—successful candidacies will make in regard to the overall process of political change.

What Can Be Done

In the latter 1960s activist-oriented New Left and Black Power organizations worshipped at the twin shrines of anti-intellectual tradition in the United States: *historical amnesia* and *pragmatism*. Pragmatism, of course, has had a long-standing past in this country; on the other hand, the present historical rupture in both black and white progressive tradition is rooted mainly in the abrupt decline of the left in the World War II and immediate post-war eras. Now, as a recipient of the radical, working-class milieu which began in Detroit during the 1930s, the League of Revolutionary Black Workers—its leadership, at least—had a much better sense of its historical antecedents and of its role in history than many. By way of contrast, it was the consummate pragmatism of the

League which I consider to have been the greatest short-coming in its practice.

In 1967 the people who were to eventually comprise the dominant leadership of the LRBW came together for the practical purpose of organizing the popular, insurrectionary sentiment of Detroit's black working-class. Some of these people had, from time to time, worked together politically since the early 1960s; sharp ideological disputes had split them before. But in 1967 such divisions *seemed* tiny compared to the vast wave of popular upheaval which had to be given coherent form. By 1969 some of these same disputes would surface again, to the detriment of the LRBW in particular, and the movement in general: score "one" for pragmatism.

With the formation of the League in early 1969 came the arrival of funds from the Black Economic Development Conference, and the resulting proliferation of LRBW offices and activities. BEDC (along with funding from private sources) proved to be the "windfall" which made expansion of the League possible. The immediate availability of monies, however, tended to stifle plans for securing long-range financial backing from the constituency the League purported to represent; the only plan to surface in this regard—the International Black Appeal—was based on the expediency of company "checkoff" procedures rather than direct solicitation. Similarly, financial arrangements between various LRBW enterprises operated on the principle of "robbing Peter to pay Paul," with predictably chaotic consequences. Expansion of League activities and facilities followed no coherent, overall plan, but tended to mirror the ideological divisions on the Executive Board as well as the purely personal inclinations of leading individuals. Pragmatism triumphant! And, finally, the selection of "bodies" by leadership for the purpose of their carrying out specific assignments was also of a highly pragmatic nature.

To be sure, League leadership can hardly be held responsible for every political misstep within the organization. Nor can the source of the LRBW's internal difficulties always be traced to the altar of pragmatic spontaneity. Problems of structure became so thoroughly intertwined with those of negative personal behavior on the part of leaders and followers alike, as to make it quite difficult to determine which was the greater culprit. But with a structure properly attuned to the tasks at hand, at least some of the more glaring deficiencies of behavior could have been checked. Had that been accomplished, the League would have been in much better shape to deal with larger political questions. Since that was not done, the organization was ultimately faced with the spectacle of workers attempting to gain control over their very own organization—a situation which had to appear all the more ironic, since it was that very same situation in the established unions which had initially led them to join in the founding of the Revolutionary Union Movement.

The collapse of the Black Power and New Left movements in the late 1960s and early 1970s left a number of bitter recollections in the minds of many participants. Those who were psychologically geared to resist anticipated government repression were far less prepared to accept the human failings of the organizations to which they belonged: the innumerable splits, petty maneuvers, and poor judgments which, in retrospect, might have been avoided. Rather than reflect more deeply on these failings in order to avoid their repetition in future upheavals, far too many political "refugees" of the period, it seems, either cast their lot with self-assuring, sectarian political organizations, or withdrew altogether into personal cocoons—not to mention "born-again" Christendom. But escape in whatever form is a diversion most of us can ill afford today. With little but long-term social stagnation in sight among the advanced capitalist nations, our situation appears ominous indeed. The preceding account of the decline of the League of Revolutionary Black Workers, though highly critical and fraught with negative examples, may nonetheless end on a optimistic chord: with adequate reflection and study in the process of improving the quality of our lives, we *can* and must do better.

Notes

1. Class and National Consciousness

Without dwelling on all the essential nuances at this point, let me define *class consciousness* as the *collective* consciousness of a given social class in regard to its objective interests, as well as an understanding of the historical role which that class must exercise in order that its interests might properly safeguarded. In a parallel manner, *national consciousness* is here defined as in the above, with the substitution of "nation" or "national minority" for "social class." The ensemble of human relations which defines the social structure of the United States, gives rise *simultaneously* to elements of both national consciousness and proletarian class consciousness among black laborers. The two tendencies are far form being mutually exclusive in all aspects—e.g., black workers in differing locales and at different periods have certainly been conscious not only of their interests as workers, but as *black* workers. Nevertheless, one or the other tendency appears to predominate at any given time depending on regional or national conditions.

Historically conditioned by racist oppression—the most visible aspect of a social formation, as Frantz Fanon once noted—and cutting across class lines within the national black community, Afroamerican nationalism in the United States has come to acquire a distinctly "racial" character. The phenomenon may be contrasted to the predominance of language and cultural questions within French-Canadian nationalism, for example, or to religious forms of nationalist expression among Irish Catholics in their divided homeland. The positive aspects of Afroamerican nationalism—as that of the nationalism of any oppressed people—resides in its celebration of national pride (not to be confused with chauvinism) in its motion towards political self-determination. Generally speaking, such nationalism remains a formidable weapon in the struggle against exploitation and domination.

But not *all* expressions of nationalism on the part of the oppressed are necessarily helpful. Under the leadership of the black "middle class," for example, popular manifestations of nationalism have, on numerous occasion, been diverted into escapist channels or utilized as a mechanism for mass support of private black business enterprise. But an even more critical tendency—since its manifestation undercuts the possibility for uniting the U.S. working class as a whole—is that of nationalist distrust of all whites: a situation difficult for even black workers to avoid when faced with trenchant, racist attitudes and practices on the part of white laborers themselves. Here the *main* (but not the sole) burden for eradicating such divisions necessarily lies with the whites.

Historically, then, from at least the late 19th Century until today, there has existed a recurring tension between national consciousness and a more fleeting working-class consciousness on the part of black laborers. In part, the degree to which white workers have been willing to demonstrate, in concrete ways, their support for the demands of black labor—demands, incidently, which represent the cutting edge of U.S. working-class interests as a whole—appears to be an important factor in the predominance of either nationalist or class consciousness among black workers at any given time. (Though far from constituting the only factors involved, might there be some correlation between the following historical phenomena?: the exclusion of black labor from craft unions, eruption of race riots, and the rise of mass-based nationalist organizations such as Marcus Garvey's UNIA during the World War I era; the efforts expended to organize blacks into the CIO during the latter 1930s, on the one hand, and the rise of working-class consciousness and parallel decline of nationalism among that same strata, on the other; the collapse of white working-class support in regard to the struggles of black labor during World War II, and the re-emergence of mass-based, Afroamerican natinalism epitomized by the growth of A. Philip Randolph's March on Washington Movement; and, finally, the hostility or relative indifference of most white laborers to the Civil Rights demands of blacks in the Fifties and Sixties, and the unprecedented burgeoning of popular expressions of black nationalism in that latter decade.)

2. Mass Organization and Vanguard Party

In order to effect fundamental social change, one must be able to draw upon the broadest possible range of mass political experiences. A revolutionary organization must therefore be able to provide room for spontaneous and creative political experimentation on the part of its mass following. Aimless and non-reflective experimentation leads nowhere, however, and for that reason, as well as for its own sake, the greatest expression of participatory democracy on the part of the basic masses must be encouraged. On the other hand, faced with the immense resources and power of organization which an oppressive ruling strata has in its control over the state apparatus, a tightly structured and centralized organization is also indispensable to the revolutionary political tasks at hand. Thus, in the present epoch, one of the most critical organizational problems for revolutionaries lies in fusing the practical necessities of internal democracy with the equally necessary qualities of centralism.

In attempting to tackle this complex problem, New Left groups in the U.S. have, for the most part, blindly followed the dictates of V.I. Lenin's celebrated 1902 essay, "What Is To Be Done." Basing his concept of the "vanguard party" on the highly questionable assumption that revolutionary class consciousness on the part of workers could not derive from the trade-union struggles in which they themselves engaged, Lenin thereby assumed that such consciousness had to be "imported" from the outside by professional revolutionaries. Briefly put, the party, to be comprised of a tightly knit group of revolutionary intellectuals, is to embody the principle of "democratic centralism." Political decisions are to be exercised democratically, but once made are to be absolutely binding on all party members.

Within the Leninist framework the contradiction between centralism and democracy is to be resolved thusly: mass organizations (trade unions and the like) are to be organized around the principle of democracy; in order to assure maximum political effectiveness, the vanguard party is to be organized around that of democratic centralism. In "normal" times, the principle of democracy would override that of centralism; in times of crisis, the roles would reverse themselves, with centralist tendencies held at a premium.

In the absence of a strong and independent workers' movement, however—as our own New Left experience clearly demonstrated—

self-anointed "vanguards" have a tendency to degenerate into highly centralized, bureaucratic, sectarian organizations. (Moreover, New Leftists exhibit a tendency to incorrectly apply the principle of democratic centralism—with centralism generally administered in heavy doses—to *all* types of organizational structures, not just the party.) In light of the continuing failure of the Leninist party to effectively function in advanced capitalist societies, the concept itself has recently come under considerable attack. See, for example, Antonio Carlo, "Lenin on the Party," Telos, 17 (Fall 1973), 2-40; and Lucio Magri, "Problems of the Marxist Theory of the Revolutionary Party," *New Left Review,* 60 (March-April 1970), 97-128.

Columbia University students occupy campus building, 1968, to protest military research and the destruction of a Black community park to build a student gym. Occupiers are singing moments before police raid the building. Photo by Miriam Bokser/Liberation News Service.

4

Rebellions Outside Ourselves: The Emergence of White Student Protest

Among the Freedom Riders arrested at the Albany, Georgia, train station in December 1961 was a recent University of Michigan graduate student named Tom Hayden—the lone field secretary of a tiny organization of campus radicals called the Students for a Democratic Society. Within five years SDS was to become a household word, cheered or feared around the country as the leading organization of a new radical movement that touched the lives of a generation of white students and youth who, as Bernice Reagon says about the children of the Civil Rights Movement, found it was time to "check out where their position was."

In the early 1960s members of SDS's five to twenty campus chapters engaged in Civil Rights work, did research and agitation around the issues of disarmament, poverty, and university reform, and began to develop a deep-seated critique of basic U.S. institutions and values which they felt underlay many of the nation's visible social problems. In 1964, several hundred SDS members embarked on a program of community organizing in poor white, Black, and racially-mixed city neighborhoods, to find out, as Hayden asked, "Can the methods of SNCC be applied to the North?" SDS's goal was "participatory democracy;" its motto: "Let the people decide."

Nonviolent direct action, meanwhile, was finding its way to new locales. In the fall of 1964, the Berkeley Free Speech

Movement erupted, initially over attempts by the University of California administration to suppress student support for local Civil Rights work. Demonstrators surrounded a police car for thirty-two hours to prevent one student's arrest, and eventually 814 people were arrested while sitting-in at the administration building. In March 1965, forty-three out of several hundred SDS demonstrators were arrested outside Chase Manhattan Bank headquarters in New York in a protest over bank loans to South Africa; that same month, students in many cities occupied U.S. government buildings to demand protection for the voter registration campaign in Selma, Alabama.

But what turned a relatively small network of activists into a nationwide mass movement was the U.S. government's escalation of the Vietnam War. The beginning of systematic bombing of North Vietnam in February 1965 had been met with a wave of hastily organized demonstrations. As U.S. troop strength in Vietnam grew from 23,000 to 170,000 in the course of 1965, it became clear that the U.S. was truly at war, and that much more than occasional picket lines would be required to get us out.

In the years that followed, the unprecedented movement of college and eventually high school youth took literally hundreds of forms. Campuses were closed down by student strikes, made uptight by building occupations, and severely shaken by police busts. Teach-ins and teach-outs, draft card burnings and draft counseling, community organizing and communal living were all part of the same revolt.

There was a leading organization (SDS) and a leading issue (the war). But there was a tremendous amount of work done by other organizations and outside of any organizations. There were tremendous bursts of anger, insight, and action around many issues besides the war—and the essence of the movement's developing worldview was that separate issues were not really separate, but reflections of a single "system."

In this chapter and the next, I want to look at two questions about this web of consciousness and activity. First, why was there a white student movement—what forces and what personal needs prompted us to think and act in this political fashion that none of the country's rulers expected and that all of them today would like to make us forget? Next, in Chapter 5, what was accomplished by the movement against the Vietnam War—and why have many of us failed to see this accomplishment?

In both essays, I'm drawing on my experience in the New Left from the Cuban Missile Crisis of 1962 through the signing of the Paris Peace Agreements ending the active U.S. presence in Vietnam a decade later. The major forms of that partici-pation were civil rights work with the Congress of Racial Equality (CORE) and the Northern Student Movement as a teenager in Baltimore, Maryland; active membership in the Harvard-Radcliffe chapter of SDS as a college student; work as a staff member of the SDS-affiliated Boston underground newspaper The Old Mole *from 1968 to 1970; and anti-war education and action in a variety of local groups and coalitions thereafter.*

The Cards

With hindsight, it's tempting to say that it was all in the cards. For university presidents in their concrete-and-steel towers, generals in the Pentagon, and even Lyndon Johnson in the White House, it was a question of read-em-and-weep. If they had taken a close look at the people and the circumstances that were to give rise to a radical student movement, what would they have seen?

We were mostly the daughters and sons of professionals, managers and small businessmen. There was a smattering of children of actual capitalists, and a steadily growing number of children of workers, salespeople, and clerks; but the white New

Left was dominated by "middle class" students at private colleges and state universities.

We had grown up in America's most seductive image of itself—the suburban, consuming world you see on TV. Many of us could not expect to rise too much higher in income or independence than our parents had. If we were fed up with what we had, we weren't likely to think we could individually rise to something better.

As to our immediate surroundings, we found ourselves in colleges that had just been transformed into modern, competitive, computerized knowledge factories, dependent on Pentagon research money. If we thought the university would be a privileged community of intellectual stimulation where we could find refuge from our fate in the rat race, we found it to be a rat race as well. And the future looked like endless decades of conforming to what was expected of us, competing for what was supposed to be safe, and taking the world of Ed Sullivan and atom bombs as it was dished out to us.

In another period, our dissatisfaction might have turned to self-hatred, cynicism, and escape. We could have felt like freaks, with none of the pride some of us came to take in calling ourselves "freaks" in the late Sixties. But history provided us with rebellions outside ourselves. We found a social reality to back up our dissatisfaction. We saw we were not alone in finding something rotten, something to want to fight against in 1960s America.

The United States was losing a major imperial war in Vietnam, losing to a "hopelessly" outgunned national liberation movement. Similar movements threatened U.S.-installed dictatorships elsewhere in Asia, Africa, and Latin America. The U.S. had failed to defeat new types of socialist revolutionary regimes in China and Cuba, and was now trying to pretend that they didn't exist.

At home, our country was revealed as a land of conflict and oppression by the massive protest, repression, and rebellion of its Black citizens. The Civil Rights and Black Power movements were the biggest social movements in the U.S. since the 1930s. We found that the struggle (and the culture) of the Black people in our country challenged us to stand up in rebellion ourselves.

We were not satisfied with the prospects for leading privately fulfilling lives. The emptiness of our middle-class futures made us willing to risk them—to a degree—in actions against racism, against repression, against the war.[1]

The identity we found in supporting other people's struggles and discovering other people's cultures made it possible to begin some of our own. First came a movement for freer, less competitive, and more socially useful university. Though campus struggles were generally aimed at ending university involvement with the war or racism, underneath they were always fueled by desires for fewer requirements, more flexibility, more student control, sexual freedom, and more socially relevant curriculum.

Later came struggles for new and collective ways of living and working, both inside and outside of political organizations. Latest but in many ways most originally came the battle for Women's Liberation, and for the liberation of everyone from stereotyped and limiting sex roles.

1. Conflicting arguments have been made about the effect of changes in the class structure of the society on the consciousness of "middle class" young people at this time. One argument holds that as small business people and independent professionals were replaced by larger corporations and service bureaucracies, the children of that class faced a future of declining independence, which fed the feeling of having nothing to look forward to. Another view is that the same growth in monopoly business and government bureaucracy was creating a new middle class of technicians, managers, planners, educators, and the like; students, as members-in-training of this class, had a heightened sense of their qualifications (though not power) to run the society.

As the movement for all these goals grew—and as it met increasing resistance from police, from university and public officials, from corporations—we began to put two and two together. Students also went outside the university to poor neighborhoods, to factories and hospitals, to strikers' picket lines, to socialist countries.

Our identities as radicals solidified, and we asked ourselves why we were on one side, and the holders of economic and political power were on the other. Our enemy, which we had thought of as a disembodied culture or a very clearly embodied set of evil men, began to look somewhat different. We concluded that both the values and the policies we opposed had their roots in an economic and political system whose motivating force was private profit.

We did not make this connection lightly. It took a lot of evidence to overcome the Cold War propaganda which made "the problem is capitalism" seem as silly and outdated a statement as "the earth is flat." But there was no other way to explain the society we saw: Where corporations had a right to produce napalm, but poor people had no right to decent housing. Where dictators friendly to U.S. business were given American troops to put down popular revolutions, but Civil Rights workers seeking to increase the power of poor Black people were left unprotected against the attacks of county sheriffs and the Ku Klux Klan. Where students sat-in to keep radical teachers and ban corporate recruiters, but university authorities fired the radicals while protecting the "free speech" of the corporations.

Through our involvement in specific struggles, then, we came to understand that what we were opposed to was a system, and that our enemy was the class that ran that system. Some form of capitalism was what we had to destroy, and some form of socialism was what we wanted to create. None of our goals were entirely new in the history of the U.S. left—and certainly our conclusion was not new. But all our goals were

articulated in new ways—and in ways that emphasized how we
wanted our own lives transformed.

What Made It Run?

The major internal dynamic that enabled the new white
student movement to become as strong as it did was the change
it worked in the way its members looked at their lives. In most
basic terms, what the Movement provided for me was a sense
of purpose and a feeling of community which had been missing
from my life before then.

My earliest sense about "Movement people" was that they
had something *different* going for them. They were often self-
righteous and insensitive, but they thought there was some way
out of here. They had a purpose.

One day in 1965 or '66 some stranger who got my name
from an SDS list called to say she was collecting old clothes to
sell at a thrift shop in Georgia. Could I please set up a table in
my dorm? This group in Georgia really needed the clothes to
keep their project going, she said.

What a drag—I had to go through three layers of
bureaucracy to get "permission" to sit in the dining room en-
trance and collect *old clothes* for a thrift shop I didn't know
anything about. But if I was part of something that stretched
all the way to Georgia and they thought they needed me to do
this, I figured I ought to do it. So there I was sitting at this table
being that other kind of people and among all the bullshit I had
to go through there was this one guy who shook his head,
honestly impressed, and said, "SDS? A thrift shop in Georgia?
You people really do everything!"

Now compare that to most of my experience as a student.
College wasn't a step *toward* anything. It was a way to
postpone decisions, and it was an extremely competitive game.
Whatever I thought, argued, or wrote had two criteria of success—did it outdo someone else, and did it get a good grade?

As an alternative to that, I began to see the possibility of acting as part of a movement.

An early memory of that sense is the first national demonstration against the war—the SDS April 17, 1965, March on Washington to End the War in Vietnam. The speakers stormed and droned on for too long, the White House sat behind us apparently deaf. But there below the Washington Monument were more people than I had ever seen together except at baseball games.

Then someone at a microphone repeated a couple of times, "If Judy Collins or Joan Baez is in the crowd, could you please come to the microphone." In 1965, folk music was In, and these were Big Stars; I took the announcement for a joke. But sure enough, Joan Baez came to the microphone and as she sang "We Shall Overcome," 25,000 of us moved down the Mall to the Capitol, through the line of police who ordered us to stop. The only thing I could think was, "This is a Movement!"

The choice which that movement presented was: "Okay, be out there isolated, competing for things you don't want; or be in here, making history, here with us."

We were not afraid to experiment, and we were making something new. For myself, writing leaflets and newspapers, one thing that was particualry important was making a new vocabulary and (though we didn't call it that) a new ideology. But for most of us, I think, this new language was a part of what made us feel powerful and useful, not isolated and worthless.

"Participatory democracy" said what we felt we were lacking—participation in and control over what was happening to us. "The war machine" summed up both our political enemy and our feeling about what was wrong with the culture. "Corporate liberalism"—our attempt to define the outlook of the Johnson administration—spoke to our confusion about both *who* ran the country and to what end. Even a tactical gem like "the streets belong to the people" (chanted when we defied police orders to stick to planned march routes, or to disperse) compressed a lot into itself: a breakthrough into disruptive action as well as a growing awareness that our goal was to put the products the people sweat and pay for into the hands of the people.

All this language grew out of our trying to understand what we had done and what we were up against. That's why it spoke to so many people facing the same dilemmas, the same questions about the possibility of accomplishing any change.

Proof that we were really reaching people, really building something, was the Movement's growth. All around us we saw people joining and changing. Young people looked to us to tell them about themselves and their society. Suddenly we found a demand for radical "products." Radical courses flourished on campuses, radical newspapers off-campus.

So the Movement offered meaning and purpose, in a society that offered very little of either. Just as important, it offered community.

Community is a very popular word right now, both because people want it so much and because it's so easily twisted. "University community," for instance, is a euphemism which really refers to the owners, managers, employees, and customers of a university; it's a way of pretending they all have the same interest.

What the Movement offered, most simply, was groups of friends doing work together. That is something extremely rare in this society dominated by nuclear families, large factories and offices, and competitive schools.

For example, when I worked on the *Old Mole,* a radical newspaper, we had a newspaper "collective"—some members were paid, some were not, but all were committed to the paper as their major work in the Movement. The collective was a means to an end: it was the group which decided what our goals were, what would go in the paper, how work would be shared. But it also turned out to decide, both then and for years afterward, where I would look for people to live with, close friends, people to talk to about my work.

Many small things went into making up the atmosphere of community: discussion groups where the purpose was really to learn rather than to show off, parties where you didn't need a date, small groups that traveled and marched together in demonstrations, processes like editing each other's articles for newspapers, defending each other's speeches at meetings, going out in groups to speak about projects we were in or about the experience of working in Cuba—all these activities in which we had to depend on each other. These created the bonds which bound us into a movement as much as the ideas in our heads.

I'm not saying that getting into a community like the *Old Mole* collective was an easy task. The New Left was often cliquish. "There is no Movement outside our friends' living rooms," was a frequent self-criticism. Joining the Movement often meant feeling pulled away from old friends but unable to break into an inner circle of long-time activists.

But in comparison to mainstream America, the Movement offered a pretty good shot at a meaningful community. If you weren't as in as you wanted to be, still you felt a lot closer to what you were looking for. And the Movement, though cliquish, had a significant ability to inspire by example.

Sit-ins against college recruiters from the Dow Chemical Company (makers of napalm), women's consciousness-raising groups, underground newspapers—at different times all of these were found on almost every college campus or in almost every city. They were not organized by conspiring travelers. Sometimes a veteran of one would move, usually for personal reasons, and start another were s/he ended up. But mostly it was by example.

In addition to offering purpose and community, the Movement projected a style that made people want to be a part of it. What did this style say to people?

The most popular page of the *Old Mole* was a page called Zaps. Here's a whole Zap: "PEACE CORPS EXPELS 13 FOR ANTI-WAR ACTIVITY—A real live headline from the Washington *Star*." Who was crazy, us or them? Another Zap told the story of a court clerk in Kentucky, who was supposed to open each day's session by intoning, "God save the Commonwealth and this honorable court. One day he decided to say what was really going on instead: "God save the people from this honorable court!" The Zaps page was popular because in some way it turned the world on its head—and it made more sense that way.

If I had to pick a single statement that summed up the feelings which our style appealed to, it would be these two stanzas from Bob Dylan's "Maggie's Farm":

I ain't gonna work on Maggie's farm no more.
No I ain't gonna work on Maggie's farm no more.
Well, I wake in the morning,
Fold my hands and pray for rain,
I got a head full of ideas
That are drivin' me insane.
It's a shame the way she makes me scrub the floor.
I ain't gonna work on Maggie's farm no more.

I ain't gonna work for Maggie's brother no more,
No, I ain't gonna work for Maggie's brother no more.
Well, he hands you a nickel,
He hands you a dime,
He asks you with a grin
If you're havin a good time,
Then he fines you every time you slam the door.
I ain't gonna work for Maggie's brother no more.

The central thing which experience was telling many of us who ended up in the New Left was, "This is crazy. This is sick. There has got to be some better way to live. I want out." A big job of the Movement was to validate that feeling. To say, "Yes, you're right to feel outraged and oppressed by it. Your rulers are the ones who are destructive, not you." Not to fine you every time you slam the door.

The New Left was willing to recognize feeling crazy and isolated as a form of oppression. It saw expressing that feeling as a beginning of resistance. So it needed a style that was responsive and gave some room for self-expression, a style that didn't immediately set the Movement up as a new authority to be followed.

In the fall of 1969, most New Left forces in Boston were working on a demonstration at the Massachusetts Institute of Technology which would interfere with weapons and counter-insurgency research, and would openly support the National Liberation Front in Vietnam. The *Old Mole* had run the call to this demonstration on its cover and was clearly identified as a sponsor; a main effort that fall in our articles had been to explain the war as an outgrowth of U.S. imperialism.

Nonetheless, we knew that a number of other local and national actions were planned, with politics ranging from liberal to left. We ran a capsule summary of the various actions and their political goals, with this introduction:

This fall you can have your pick of demonstrations. Gone are the days when only the Mobilization Committee would call a national demonstration and in the end everyone would go. Now everyone calls a demonstration and no one knows who will go. So here's a brief rundown.

Many papers from an Old Left tradition would have written the paragraph: *In past years the Movement suffered from the opportunist policies of the Trotskyist-dominated Student Mobilization Committee, which declared so-called "national demonstrations" to take advantage of lack of clear political leadership from other groups. This year that demon-stration is being challenged by a clear anti-imperialist coalition action in Boston, as well as...*[2]

The first way of writing the paragraph shows a lot more confidence in the reader's ability to think. We had a position about which demonstrations were more important, but we were willing to present the situation as it was: a choice which our readers had to make. We were willing to talk about this choice in English, as opposed to using a jargon in which our position was the only possible one. Since the first problem of our audience was isolation, it was more important to us to be understood than to be absolutely correct.

Also, the first approach shows more confidence in what we were pushing. It was true that no one knew who would show up for what; we preferred to admit that rather than ignore it. We thought we had enough strengths that we could laugh at our weaknesses without driving people away. (In some liberal paper, that thought all demonstrations were silly, that paragraph would just be smug; but in the *Mole* it was not.)

Last but not least, New Left style at its best projected an image not only of power vs. power, winning this demand and that demand, but of liberation. By an image of liberation I

2. After organizing the first large national anti-war demonstration in 1965, SDS emphasized continuous local action and education around the war and related issues. The task of calling periodic national demonstrations was taken up by a series of less radical coalitions, including the Spring, National, Student, and New Mobilization Committees. In general, the Mobilization Committees avoided confrontations with the police, called for de-escalation rather than total U.S. withdrawal, did not talk about the causes of the war, and did not link the war to other issues. Much of this limited approach was characteristic of the Socialist Workers Party and its youth group, the Young Socialist Alliance, Trotskyist organizations which came to control the Student Mobilization Committee and were active in the others. SDS chapters and independent radicals usually ended up supporting these demonstrations in spite of tactical and political criticisms.

mean an image of bursting free from the restraints of capitalist society and taking up the task of building a new world. Like the feeling of community, we built this image in many small ways. We created alternative institutions (free schools, free buses...) to meet some needs of today and give some idea of the possibilities of the future. We renamed the buildings and parks we occupied; I remember a photograph of students in one college administration building re-arranging the letters on the building directory to spell "liberated area."

This vision of liberation was more fragile and less clear among white students and dropouts than it was among Blacks in the South. We had no tradition of a centuries-long struggle for freedom, no heritage of music or any other cultural form except for the spirituals-turned-freedom-songs which we borrowed. Looking for expressions of this feeling, I want to send you back to the record player to listen to Dylan's "When the Ship Comes In." Certainly the music and the outlawed drug experiences of what came to be called the "counter-culture" were an important part of the way we defined ourselves. At their best, they too represented a shared experience of standing the world on its head and having it finally make sense.

(It is, in fact, impossible to convey the spirit of my own experiences or of politics among white youth in the '60s in general without conveying the atmosphere of grass, acid, hitchhiking trips, Janis Joplin, Rolling Stones, and "We Are All Outlaws in the Eyes of Amerika" in which they floated. But that is really the subject for another essay; the connections were not simple or permanent, and—at its worst—the "youth culture" could be merely a parody of the "straight" culture of rushing after the latest product, isolation and private depression, and self-destruction.)

For myself, when I think about these feelings of idealism and of liberation, I'm also reminded of my reaction to the first man on the moon. All the time I was growing up, the first landing on the moon seemed like the most exciting thing I could imagine. It represented something very pure and promising—the opening up of a whole new world by and for the human race. I kept hoping it would happen in my lifetime. But when it did happen in 1969 (I was 22), it turned out to be just another piece of military-industrial hardware allowing two aging white male Korean War fighter pilots to plant the U.S. flag on another piece of real estate that didn't belong to us. I didn't pay much attention anyway, because I and the people I was close to were deeply engaged in an effort to open up a new world down here on the ground. And the question we kept asking each other was, would we see revolution in our lifetime?

Would we see a time when the values that we tried to incorporate into the Movement were the values of the society: When people's daily work was a collective effort toward a common goal. When the institutions of the society pulled people together rather than forcing them apart. When mass media and schools educated rather than confusing and deceiving. When no one was better off because of someone else being worse off—or as Marx put it, "the free development of each is the condition for the free development of all."

Where Did It Go?

You cannot run forever on purpose, community and style. I've stressed these things because they made the Movement possible—and helped it to thrive by making it a more human place to exist than the society it was fighting against. But there were ways in which this movement was not so human, and there were external factors with which it was not so well-equipped to deal.

We often felt that we failed to live up to claims and pressures to live in a new way. Then we blamed ourselves, rather than the society or the pressures of the Movement, for our bad attitudes, our hidden fears, our need for some personal space, our tiredness.

Likewise leadership often took the form of being a star, a "heavy," more-revolutionary-than-thou, rather than the form of being a learner and a teacher. Male-dominated organizations put a premium on acting cool and together even when we had no idea what to do next; manipulation rather than honest decision-making was often the result.

We also suffered some from our need for everything to be new, experimental, an emotional high. If you try too many things that don't work, you get burned out. Without any socialist tradition to rely on, only our newfound language and our own limited experience, we were quick to jump from conclusion to conclusion, from strategy to strategy. We sometimes got so caught up in our vision of liberation that we could not stay sane unless that vision materialized immediately.

All of these weaknesses made it harder for us to stay confident and organized in a period when the Movement— partly because of its own success in pressing for de-escalation of the war—started declining rather than growing.

But in understanding what happened to this movement in the later years, it's equally important to look at the historical forces that muted it, just as it was important to look at the historical forces that created it.

By about 1968, a minority, mostly middle-class movement had concluded that it was a necessity—and our duty—to make a socialist revolution in the United States. For the next few years, in meetings, in newspapers, in the private spaces we carved out for solitary worrying, we beat our heads almost every day against the question, "How?" How could we possibly do this?

Again, with hindsight, it is possible to say that it was not yet time to make a revolution in the U.S. But we were not experienced enough, not enough used to thinking historically, to see that revolution would be a long process.

To begin with, most working people did not share the

unusual source of our particular radicalism—a privileged
rejection of the middle-class life that Americans are supposed
to strive for. Likewise, it was relatively easy for us to identify
with and a little bit understand the struggles of the Blacks and
Vietnamese because our social positions (self-rejected or not)
were not so threatened by the consequences as those of white
workers could be. We had been taught to gain self-esteem by
thinking we were smarter and more important than workers,
so we didn't need to get it by thinking we were smarter or more
important then Blacks or Vietnamese. Yet the active participation of the various parts of the working class was crucial to
overturning capitalism.

Also, there were quite serious limits on how far all but the
most politicized students would go with their newfound,
exciting, but quite fragile radicalism. For instance, we often
argued that, to help end the war, the universities should be
paralyzed simply because they were important capitalist
institutions. Paralyzing any capitalist institution raised the
cost of the war. The argument made sense, but most students
would not go along with it except at times of crisis, even if they
understood how well the schools functioned to train, to track,
to brain trust, and to brainwash. For the long haul, most
students knew which side their bread was buttered on.

There was a lot of talk and a certain amount of organizing
of a cross-class revolutionary youth movement. But the main
stable organizations to emerge among white working class
youth were in the sectors in the most similar positions to
ourselves—college students and GIs. The movement continued to grow in the more working-class colleges, in fact, well
after it was declining in most elite schools. One of the sources
of this growth was the returning Vietnam veterans.

Soldiers ended up in a position a lot like middle-class
students because—much more than us—they were desperate
to reject the way of life and the institution they were stuck in.
The Vietnam-era army was a dead end (sometimes literally)

and was the opposite of what it claimed to be—in a way that a
secure job, a home, and a family which might rise a little higher
were not. (Letters from GIs, more than from any other readers
except prisoners, said that the underground press provided the
only touch of sanity in their lives.)

We learned our historical dilemma slowly and with
difficulty. Our strategies and identities zigzagged all over the
map as we did so. Particularly we got confused about the
question of self-interest. One day we would want to express
our own needs. (I'm through fighting *for* anyone else; that's
liberal" was a common theme.) The next day support for Third
World struggles was key and any hint of a "student power" line
would be liberalism. One day we thought anyone who was
different than us was "Pig Amerika," and the next day we
thought we were totally useless unless we could abandon all
our middle-class pleasures and hang-ups and become "prole-
tarianized."

I'm exaggerating—each individual in the Movement
didn't zigzag so dizzily. But the mental stress was like that. In
the simplest terms, we mistook a historical event (revolution)
for a moral choice. We were right about the need to make
choices and take action. But we interpreted that duty to mean
that if only we could be good enough and smart enough
communists, we could have, right now, a revolutionary
organization, a revolutionary strategy, and pretty soon a
revolution. The shortest cut, usually, was applying this or that
foreign model.

Our organizations couldn't stand the strain. Faced with
the insistence on becoming a revolutionary party without a
revolutionary base, SDS fragmented—first into two groups,
then into many. One direction, taken by a number of groups,
opted for a rather dogmatic Old Left style with China
replacing the Soviet Union as the model to be followed.
Another direction, Weatherman, tried to create an immediate
armed New Left revolution based on transformed lifestyle,

support for Third World struggles, and put-your-body-on-the-line.

Both tendencies called their approach Marxism-Leninism. In or out of these tendencies, almost everyone in the Movement in the years 1969-1970 went a little bit crazy with the expectation of revolution around the corner and guilt for not doing enough to bring it about.

The early Seventies saw the end of this mass radical movement of white students and youth—the end of great numbers of people self-consciously taking action as part of a group of people like themselves taking similar actions across the country. The end of the mass movement, however, did not mean the end of the critique of American society it generated. "You can't argue with any of this now," marvelled a student in a class I spoke to a few years ago as she leafed through some sample *Old Moles* from 1969. "It's all been proved."

The end of the mass movement likewise did not mean the end of the commitment of many of its members to struggle for the fulfillment of the vision which we had gained. Neither did it undo the concrete changes and reforms that the Movement had brought. The largest victory, as I will argue in the following chapter, was the U.S. withdrawal in defeat from Vietnam, and the popular resistance to "any more Vietnams" which has sapped the government's ability to drum up support for foreign intervention in the years since.

Signing the treaty which got the U.S. out of Vietnam, at counter-inauguration demonstration, January 1973. Richard Nixon, who had been balking for months, finally signed a few days later.

It Did Make A Difference:
The Anti-War Movement

Ten years and 12 days after the first busloads of *APR.29 '75* demonstrators rolled into Washington to protest U.S. involvement in Indochina, the last planeloads of Americans left Saigon and the Provisional Revolutionary Government took control. The standard American histories of the Vietnam War, when they are culled from the memoirs of the generals and politicians, clipped from the files of the Pentagon and the State Department, are unlikely to record this coincidence.

But the decisions about the pursuit of those generals' and politicians' objectives in Indochina were not made only in their carpeted offices. They were also made in the barracks, in the schools, in the streets, by the millions of Americans—Blacks and whites, students, workers, nuns and priests, draftees and draft resisters—who made up the Anti-War Movement.

During this war, unlike any other the U.S. government chose to fight, the number of marchers in national demonstrations against the war kept pace with the number of troops sent to fight in it. In the spring of 1965 there were 25,000 G.I.s propping up Saigon, and 25,000 demonstrators at the Washington Monument. Two years later, some 400,000 demonstrated in New York and San Francisco against the presence in Vietnam of 440,000 U.S. troops.

By the fall of 1969, U.S. troop strength had peaked at just over half a million, and over half a million demonstrators converged on Washington. By the spring of 1971, Nixon had been forced to bring home almost half of the G.I.s, but 800,000 protestors gathered at his door and on the West Coast.

These big demonstrations were only one of the Anti-War Movement's many weapons, but they testify to its size and its organization.This movement irreversibly changed the thinking of Americans about their government and its foreign policy. Witness the publicity and public reaction over the CIA role in the 1973 Chilean coup and the 1975 Angola intervention; the made-in-USA coups in Guatamala in 1954 and Brazil in 1964 excited no such attention.[1] But the Anti-War Movement did more than change people's heads: it severely limited the government's ability to carry on the war as it wished.

In 1965, when the Anti-War Movement was just becoming visible, the government's attempt to defeat the National Liberation Front and make Southeast Asia safe for U.S. business was not going well. The planners in Washington saw the following options for trying to turn the tide: sending more U.S. troops to South Vietnam; invading Laos, Cambodia, and North Vietnam; terror bombing North Vietnam; using atomic weapons.[2] These options were listed again and again in the

1. The U.S. government conspired with right-wing military figures to overthrow the democratically elected presidents Jacobo Arbenz of Guatamala and Joao Goulart of Brazil. Neither of these presidents was a socialist, but Arbenz had offended the United Fruit Company by instituting land reform, and Goulart had begun to break from U.S. Cold War foreign policy and to institute some limits on the profits U.S. companies could take out of Brazil.

2. Legally, there have never been any seperate countries of North and South Vietnam. The Geneva Accords which divided the country in 1954 did so only temporarily and only into two "military zones"; the elections which were to lead to reunification were cancelled two years by the U.S. The so-called "South Vietnamese" government was

Pentagon Papers and other studies and memoirs.

Hundreds of thousands of U.S. soldiers were indeed thrown into battle against the Vietnamese revolution. But in March 1968, despite the Pentagon's insistence that it needed 200,000 more men, U.S. troop strength was limited to the existing total of 500,000. President Lyndon Johnson decided for political reasons that no more troop increases were possible. The period of trying to overwhelm the NLF with American cannon fodder had ended. Withdrawals began two years later.

The U.S. did not invade North Vietnam. The U.S. invasion of Cambodia—met with a massive student strike resulting in six deaths—was limited to two months; almost no U.S. troops were used in Laos.

The regular bombing of North Vietnam was suspended from fall 1968 to early 1972. Bombing the North was a favorite weapon of the Pentagon (which persisted in believing that it cut the flow of supplies from North to South) and was considered useful by the CIA (as an attack on the will of the leaders and the people).

Even though the bombing resumed throughout 1972, the major cities were bombed only for short periods in April and December. Total terror bombing of cities by B-52's was used in December only as a face-saving gesture and a vicious parting shot, when a peace treaty was already written.

Clouds were seeded and dikes were bombed in 1972, but as a threat rather than a real attempt to cause flooding.

always a puppet of the U.S. Nevertheless, these terms will be used here and in the following chapter because they are the only ones most Americans were allowed to learn. However, the correct term National Liberation Front (NLF) will be used to refer to the revolutionaries in southern Vietnam; "Viet Cong," the name by which most Americans knew the "enemy," was made up by U.S. and "South Vietnamese" officials as the Vietnamese equivalent to "commie."

Tactical nuclear weapons were not used.

This list of options denied does not mean that the U.S. military did not cause incredible destruction and loss of life in Vietnam. We all know that it did. But the military was not permitted to do what it believed to be "necessary." Nor does this list mean that the U.S. Anti-War Movement imposed these limits and forced a U.S. withdrawal all by itself. As the Vietnamese often told visiting anti-war activists, the war was always fought in three arenas: Vietnam, the world of international relations, and the U.S. But the Vietnamese attached a lot of importance to what happened in the U.S., and so should we.

Look for instance at the spring of 1968. This was the time when Lyndon Johnson summoned his closest advisers and rejected the Joint Chiefs' request for 200,000 more troops. This was the same time that Johnson, an incumbent president, decided it was too risky to run for a second term. What were his advisers telling him?

As early as the previous May, the Pentagon Papers show Assistant Secretary of Defense John McNaughton warning against "the increased polarization that is taking place in the United States with the seeds of the worst split in our people in more than a century." In February 1968, an International Security Agency memo told Johnson, "This growing dissatisfaction accompanied, as it certainly will be, by increased defiance of the draft and growing unrest in the cities because òf the belief that we are neglecting domestic problems, runs great risks of provoking a domestic crisis of unprecedented proportions."

The next presidential administration—Nixon's—was destroyed by the tactics it used to carry out the war despite the ever-growing domestic opposition. That is the real story of Watergate, which got rolling in the summer of 1970, after the Cambodia invasion and student strike. Nixon ordered the formation of an "Interagency Intelligence Evaluation Committee" to use burglaries, wiretapping, and infiltration against radical groups. The man he put in charge, John Dean, had made his name in the Administration as the Justice Department's man in charge of negotiations with the planners of the 500,000-strong 1969 anti-war march.

By 1971, Watergate testimony later revealed, even a lone demonstrator across the street from the White House was enough to throw Nixon into a rage, and the president's appointments secretary decided to call in some "thugs" to clear the street. In June, Daniel Ellsberg released the Pentagon Papers which showed all along the movement had told the truth and the government had lied.[3] E. Howard Hunt, who later led the Watergate burglary team, was sent to discredit Ellsberg by any means necessary.

Several other pre-Watergate "dirty tricks"were responses to the Anti-War Movement, such as hiring counter-demonstrators to disrupt Washington protests and buying phony ads and telegrams supporting the mining of Haiphong harbor in May 1972. The Watergate break-in itself, as originally proposed, was part of a bigger plan which included arrests and kidnapping of anti-war leaders and demonstrators.

The Anti-War Movement was one of many forces that brought about Nixon's downfall. But, as the testimony of Nixon's key aides before the Watergate investigating committee made clear, it was the force that threw him off balance enough to begin his long chain of costly mistakes.

Having power is not the same thing as having enough

---

3. The "Pentagon Papers" were the Defense Department's own internal top-secret study of Vietnam, where analysts discussed the real history and goals of the U.S. presence since 1945 and the true alignment of forces in Vietnam. It was quite a different story from what the government had been telling the press and the public. Xeroxed copies of this study were released to the press in 1971 by Daniel Ellsberg, a former Pentagon and State Department official who had worked on the Pentagon Papers project and then became opposed to the war.

power. If the U.S. had been able to win quickly, if the Russians had been willing to abandon Vietnam ... a number of ifs in the other arenas could have made things a lot worse. As it was, our power fell far short of the power to "end the war now."

But our power was real. The campus movement's actions consistently disrupted the colleges and the draft. The organized movement of anti-war G.I.s disrupted the army on almost every domestic base and in Vietnam; whole U.S. units refused to take part in the South Vietnamese invasion of Laos in 1971. The leading Black organizations—first SNCC and radical groups such as the Black Panther Party, then Martin Luther King and his Southern Christian Leadership Conference— insisted that the war was not in the interest of American Blacks.

All over, the doubts that our demonstrations, strikes, riots, leaflets, teach-ins, and other tactics raised in everyone's mind made the war the most unpopular in American history. It was much too unpopular, for instance, for the government to raise income taxes to pay for it.

All during 1966, Johnson promised he could provide both "guns and butter" without a tax increase. That December, David Rockefeller, the most powerful banker in the world, proposed a special income "surtax" to finance the war; the ten percent surtax was not put into effect until 1968, when it was both unpopular and too late. In the end the economy could not sustain the war.

Most of all, the radical Anti-War Movement threatened to break down the crucial mixture of people's confidence in government and lack of confidence in themselves which allows the government to govern, the ruling class to rule, at all. As the quotes from the Pentagon Papers indicate, what most scared the government was a vision of ever-broadening circles of disaffection and radicalization. What was the sense, for them, of fighting a losing battle to impose Western capitalist order on South Vietnam at the price of sowing doubt, confusion, rebellion, and even the seeds of a movement for socialist revolution at home?

If even a half-decent portion of what I've said so far is true, why do so many people who identified with the Anti-War Movement feel so negative about it today? Why do so many people I meet say, "I don't think those demonstrations of ours really did anything?" Why, for so many people, is cynicism rather than hope the legacy of the '60s?

The Magic Cleanser Vision

One reason is the need we felt for immediate results. Late in 1967, I argued with my college adviser about tactics for ending the war. He was your too-perfect image of an Ivy League instructor—tall, Yankee, conventional, nicknamed "Buzz." He was going to New Hampshire to work for Gene McCarthy.[4] "We've tried the demonstrations," he said. "We've had the violence. They don't work. Maybe this will work."

I felt his logic was wrong. I knew he was lying with his "we've done such-and-such." When Harvard University's job as training ground for the country's rulers had been rudely interrupted by demonstrators who would not let the napalm-manufacturing Dow Chemical company recruit future research vice-presidents on campus, Buzz hadn't been there. When protestors non-violently occupying the Pentagon steps had been systematically clubbed by federal marshalls a few

---

4. Democratic Senator Eugene McCarthy of Minnesota ran as an anti-war candidate in the New Hampshire and other presidential primaries of 1968. Interestingly, one of McCarthy's stated goals was to draw young people back into traditional, legal forms of protest against the war. By 1972, McCarthy must have changed his mind somewhat, because he publicly supported demonstrators at the University of Minnesota who blocked a highway in protest against the mining of Haiphong.

months back, he hadn't been there to see the violence. How should he know whether these tactics worked?

Yet the only answer I could come up with was, "Well, we voted for peace in 1964, and that didn't work either. I did voter registration for Johnson's campaign and it only brought us the war." I left figuring maybe nothing worked, since the war was still going on. It was a very common feeling.

We started off wanting the U.S. government to admit that its Vietnam policy was wrong and to get out. We thought bringing attention to the war and putting forth facts and arguments would bring this admission. No such thing happened, because the govenment wanted something different than we did. The government wanted to show that U.S. military power could stop communist revolutions, and in that way protect U.S. corporations' interests abroad. We wanted peace for ourselves and self-determination for the Vietnamese.

We didn't recognize this clash of interests between ourselves and "our" government. Though our instincts were radical, our analysis was still liberal. All we knew was that teach-ins, picket lines, and telegrams to Congress weren't enough. So learning from experience, we worked our way up to a strategy of mass confrontation, grass-roots education, and disruption anywhere and everywhere we could pull it off. The many local sit-ins against Dow recruiters, the 32-hour occupation of the Pentagon steps, the 1967 national Vietnam Summer program of community education about the war, and door-to-door work on local Vietnam referendums were all parts of this strategy working itself out in practice while I was arguing with my adviser.

And painfully and oh-so-cautiously we asked why our original liberal ideas had not worked. We studied the structure of power in the U.S., and gradually we learned that the governement was not "ours," and that it had quite different interests at heart. Learning from experience was a strength. It was one of the things that allowed the New Left to grow during this period while various Old Left organizations remained mostly rigid, small, and irrelevant.

But sometimes we insisted on testing our experience too soon. We were impatient. Even when something was working, we often didn't recognize success. That's why I wasn't able to argue for our tactics with my adviser. Nothing in our training had prepared us to do things slowly. We saw no protracted political struggles while we were growing up in the 1950s, but every TV commercial we had ever watched had told us that problems have instant solutions. If you get the right product, it works right away. How could we be prepared for the eight years between the first bombing of North Vietnam and the signing of the Paris Peace Aggreements? We were bound to have trouble supporting a long struggle like that of the Vietnamese, who had been fighting first France, then the U.S., since 1946.

Always, really, we expected victory to look something like our first, liberal, TV-commercial vision of the solution: We spray a little magic cleanser on Lyndon Johnson (or successor). The camera cuts from Before to After and a smiling, slightly sheepish man tells us he has decided that because he was wrong the U.S. will dismantle or abandon its military bases, bring home all its troops, and recognize the National Liberation Front as a legitimate political force. One of our best early books, Howard Zinn's *Vietnam: The Logic of Withdrawal*, even contained a suggested speech for Johnson to give!

In real life, it happened somewhat differently. In 1973 Richard Nixon signed the treaty which committed the U.S. to take exactly those steps, but he claimed that the U.S. had been right all along, that this was a U.S. victory, and that he had bombed North Vietnam into submission. By this time, thousands of us had given up on political action and didn't even recognize that Nixon was doing what we had demanded.

I often get the feeling that some people who took part in the Anti-War Movement think of it as a naive phase precisely because that magic cleanser vision of total open rejection of the war never materialized. But that is not at all a proof that our radicalism has been a failure. It means only that the U.S. failed to conform to our early liberal ideal; we already learned that, with difficulty, in the middle '60s.

The Trump Card

If one reason that many people look back on the Anti-War Movement as a failure has to do with our liberal illusions, a second reason has to do with our radical ones. Many of us who were radicalized by the Anti-War Movement couldn't understand why we had less of an organized mass radical movement by the time of the peace treaty than we did in 1968 to 1971. "How can you say we were so powerful? Look at us now."

Our profoundest weapon, our trump card, in our struggle against the war was our ability to go beyond the war: our ability to work thoroughgoing changes in the way people saw themselves and their country. Radicalizing, we called it.

As long as the war was supported by a broad ruling class consensus, there would be an Anti-War Movement of radicals, who more and more learned to see the roots of the war in a system, not a few misguided politicians who could be replaced.

As long as wanting the U.S. to get out of Vietnam was an illegitimate desire, unsupported by commercial newspapers, politicians, university officials, or teachers, then anyone who came to the very human and simple conclusion that the U.S. should get out had to question the legitimacy of all those authorities. People went through incredible changes.

A high school fullback, former Goldwater supporter, college philosophy major, rejected graduate school to work on an underground newspaper. Later, as a radical journalist, he spent all his spare time for more than a year uncovering a CIA hoax on the American people.

A first-year college student got caught up in a two-week building occupation. In a year she had dropped out of school, visited Cuba, and become a tireless organizer. After the peace agreement, she continued to work to cut off aid to the Thieu regime in the South, and to unionize office workers.[5]

A secretary, very quiet, young-married, uninvolved in politics—a few months later, she was involved in the Women's Liberation Movement and writing an article for a radical paper analyzing a secret report by a major planner of the U.S. Vietnam policy. Later, as a nurse, she worked in a free women's health clinic and as part of a radical health care movement.

A high school senior in a small working-class Massachusetts city, who had never had any contact with the wider Anti-War Movement, joined with three friends to organize a strike and rally at his high school in May 1970.[6] Two years later,

5. This essay ends with the end of the official U.S. military role in Vietnam after the signing of the Paris Peace Agreements in January 1973. But the U.S. continued to finance and control the so-called "South Vietnam" government of Nguyen Van Thieu until its fall in 1975. Pressuring Congress to cut off financial and military aid to Thieu was the major (and quite successful) form of anti-war activity after 1972.

6. Over a million students in at least 450 colleges and universities and 150 high schools went on strike after the U.S. invasion of Cambodia. The demands of the national strike were immediate withdrawal from Southeast Asia, the release of Black Panther Party chairman Bobby Seale and other political prisoners, and an end to ROTC, military research, and other forms of university "complicity with the U.S. war machine." Many local issues were also raised: strikers at New York and Syracuse Universities seized buildings, demanding money to free Panthers being held on $100,000 bail in New York City; at the University of South Carolina, strikers sat-in and blocked police vans to protest the forcible closing of an anti-war G.I. coffeehouse and the jailing of its staff.

Police and the National Guard were called out across the

when his draft number came up and the army wouldn't accept a medical exemption he considered valid, he refused induction.

Just four of the changes I happened to see in those years. How many people like that could the rulers of the U.S. afford to create? How long could they let this accelerate?

Even people who did not become a part of any opposition movement were dislocated. A high school classmate of mine, senior class president, born politician, spent some nights in August 1968 watching the TV coverage of the Democratic Convention and the demonstrations outside. He gave up then and there his plans to go into politics.

A friend of a friend was a buyer in a Midwest department store in May 1970. She experienced the Cambodia invasion, the killing at Kent State and Jackson State and the student strike only through the media, but she decided she had to quit her job and move to Boston, which she thought of as closer to the action. Neither of these people became radical, but how many thousands of de-programmings like that could the society take?

Look at April and early May of 1971. SDS had splintered nearly two years before. The Anti-War Movement and the whole radical movement at this time were in organizational disarray, confused about what worked, bitterly divided. The press had already pronounced the death of the student movement. But what happened in Washington as drama, as testimony to the threat to order and consciousness?

Half a million people came to demonstrate peacefully. An endless procession of Vietnam veterans angrily threw away

country to break up forbidden rallies and angry crowds. Four white students at Kent State University in Ohio were killed on May 5 by Guardsmen firing indiscriminately into a rally on the campus. Two Black students were killed ten days later when city and state police unleashed a shotgun barrage into a crowd which had gathered in front of a dormitory at Jackson State College in Mississippi.

their combat medals in front of the Capitol, while Nixon (Watergate testimony has revealed) was literally freaking out in his corner, demanding hour-by-hour reports, plotting revenge. Then 10,000 traffic-blocking demonstrators were arrested in two days. Former high-level Pentagon think-tank operative Dan Ellsberg was among the demonstrators in the streets. Washington was an armed camp, as helicopters unloaded Marines in the shadow of the Washington Monument. Charges, booking, and other democratic police procedures were ignored; demonstrators were simply rounded up and many were held in a makeshift concentration camp—but neighboring residents, mostly Black, threw food over the fences with the tacit permission of sympathetic National Guardsmen.

In the years 1968-71 the trump card was being played. We showed the dislocation that continuing the war could create.[7] In response to this threat and the economic havoc brought by the unpopular war, the ruling class consensus that Johnson had put together in 1965 broke down. A number of formerly enthusiastic warriors began to feel it would be better for the government to cut its losses.

Such blue-chip types as Clark Clifford, Wall Street lawyer and former Johnson Secretary of Defense, began calling for the U.S. to get out. The fact that the *New York Times* published the Pentagon Papers was a symbol of the changing

---

7. Anti-war leaders, incidentally, often undermined the confidence of the movement by making simplistic and exaggerated claims about what specific demonstrations would accomplish. The Mayday traffic-blocking action was a tremendous success in terms of the havoc it created and the isolation of the government which it made clear. But in order to attract as many demonstrators as possible, the organizers of the action had claimed that it could literally stop the government from functioning. When government offices succeeded in opening, many demonstrators thought the action had been a failure.

times—the truths which the Anti-War Movement had consistently put forward now came out of a liberal establishment mouthpiece. That summer—1971—Nixon began to turn some guns from the left to the center. His "Enemies List" of people he wanted harassed by the Internal Revenue Service was a catalogue of establishment financiers, politicians, and journalists who had been forced to break from the ranks of Vietnam victory-seekers.

For radicals in the Anti-War Movement, this meant a peak had been passed. Troops were coming home; there was no new escalation for two years after May, 1970; the establishment liberal press and politicians had begun to harass Nixon. Increasingly, the war was no longer an issue that belonged to radicals. The sense of the Anti-War Movement as the center of a constantly growing mass movement began to fade.

Of course, much of the propaganda about the "quiet campus" and the "death of the Anti-War Movement" was simply media manipulation. The school years 1970-71 and '71-72 saw demonstrations at over 100 campuses each year, and the 1972 Republican convention saw more protesters, more disruption, and more arrests than the Democratic convention in Chicago four years before. Anti-war sentiment and local organization continued to spread, particularly in middle-class and working-class suburbs where it had not existed before. But the feeling of a peak in the radical upsurge was real.

Early spring, 1972, found us veterans of the Anti-War Movement in a kind of limbo, as far as the war was concerned. Most combat troops were home but the air war was still going strong. Our lack of organization was depressing, and we didn't really understand the causes. But this turned out to be the year of decisive battles, and the last year of the U.S. war effort. A close look at 1972 tells a lot about why both the war and the Anti-War Movement ended the way they did.

I was four years out of college, working for a government-funded organization as editor of a press service for community newspapers. I felt good about what I was doing—it was part of a low-key, long-term effort to build radical media.

But when the NLF launched a general offensive and Nixon decided to unleash the most horrible bombing ever in response, the war took me over once again. Eight years were coming to a climax. I remember only three kinds of scenes from that spring: the TV screen, the meeting halls, and the streets. Everything else went on in shadow, as Nixon tried to hold back history with barbarism.

I spent one afternoon with a thousand other people smashing chairs, windows, furniture, and files at a Harvard University research center which had been home base for two of the major architects of the Vietnam bombing, Kissinger and Samual Huntington. But nothing was enough. Another day I was arrested sitting in front of the Federal Building in Boston; a few hours after I got out of jail, Nixon ordered the bombing and mining of Haiphong. The next day some of us at work sat down to make a poster rebutting the tissue of lies which he called a speech.

It was a desperate and weary spring. The same 1500 people showed up on the streets again and again. Onlookers supported us, sometimes even the police supported us, but the bombing continued. But I remember saying, one night during the news, "I'm daring to hope that this is our last 'spring offensive.' " The hope came from the success of the NLF and from heavy voting for Senator George McGovern, running in the Democratic presidential primaries on an anti-war platform. Thieu was isolated and Nixon was isolated. The most liberal Democrats were seizing the Party with the war issue alone. Years of our work were paying off.

Still, the war went on and the mass Anti-War Movement got smaller. Nixon beat McGovern in 49 states, and his Christmas B-52 bombing of Hanoi deepened the gloom. It seemed that the suddenly outraged press and the ever-timid Congressional opposition were all we had. Seeing the once-menacing Anti-War Movement reduced to circulating petitions and postcards to Congress, I wondered, "Is this the end or is this 1965?"

The Paris Agreements fell upon us like a gift, a beautifully wrapped gift we hardly dared open for fear we'd find the bomb inside. 100,000 of us got to Washington for a "Sign the Treaty!" counter-inaugural much bigger than the previous counter-inaugural of 1968. Still we waited for the gift to explode.

Why couldn't we see our victory? Because our victory had been brought about by a rising tide of radicalism, we expected it to look like a rising tide. But having power is not the same thing as having all the power. There was not a straight line from a powerful Anti-War Movement to a powerful continuing radical movement. It was precisely to defuse that threat that many ruling class figures had turned against the war.

The Vietnam war had become the politicians' turf, Congress's turf, because the Vietnamese and ourselves had held out long enough that the U.S. government and corporate leaders could not afford to continue it. Now that decision needed to be processed through the machinery of government.

The point is, the war was no more likely to end with a pack of warmakers groveling before a triumphant radical movement than it was to end with the warmakers turning into peace-lovers and admitting their sins. Some kind of decline in the mass movement was inevitable once the warmakers decided to slacken up on the war in order to ease the situation at home.

Much of the rest was charade. Since part of the reason to get out of Vietnam was to defuse domestic radicalism, domestic radicals had to be kept from getting any of the credit. Even old Senate hand George McGovern looked too much like the Anti-War Movement (particularly when he wanted to slash the military budget) to be the vehicle through which the war was ended. That's why an unprecedented coalition of businessmen, newspapers, political figures, and even labor bureaucrats lined up temporarily behind Nixon in the 1972 election. (Though they dropped him just as quickly when the Watergate scandal surfaced.) Almost without exception the Democratic Party bigwigs and fat cats switched to Nixon or sat out the race. Then McGovern's erratic behaviour finished the job.

But part of the price for this support was that Nixon had to end the war. He rejected the draft of a peace treaty in October, but he must have known he had to sign it eventually. The treaty he finally signed in January was essentially the same one.

In between these treaties, though, Nixon and Kissenger got in one last fling. The B-52 bombing of Hanoi in December was a last punishment for the Vietnamese, and a ritual of using one of the Pentagon's long-denied pet options as a last resort. But it was also a cold-blooded ploy designed to convince the American people that military power, not the strength of the NLF and the threat from the domestic Anti-War Movement, had brought the treaty.

Nixon is still peddling this tale in his recently published memoirs, though the NLF victory and the flight of Thieu and his American advisers in 1975 make it hard to convince anyone that the U.S. won the war. But as we face our own future in the United States, the question of who won is not the most important question to be answered by the millions of us who took part on the Anti-War Movement, and the millions more who watched it. The most important question is, did we learn that a popular movement can successfully oppose the will of the men in Washington, or that it cannot?

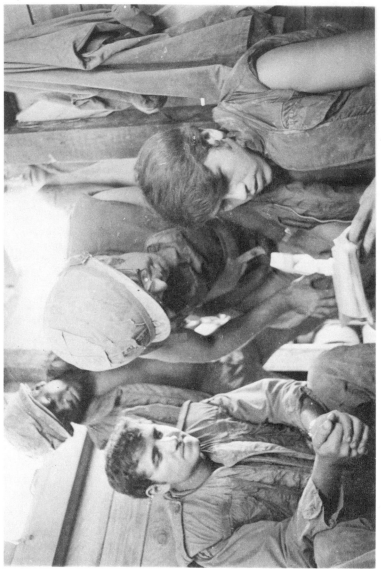

1971: GIs at Firebase Pace, Vietnam, signing a petition to Senator Edward Kennedy calling for an immediate end to the war. Petition was being circulated in the midst of a mutiny, a refusal by these men to leave their bunker to retrieve a jeep abandoned outside the firebase perimeter. Photo by Richard Boyle from Flower of the Dragon, Ramparts Press, 1972.

A Questioning Spirit:
GIs Against the War

"No one had to suggest it," ex-soldier Walter Pawlowski told an underground press reporter from his Canadian exile late in 1968. "That is the classical way you have a demonstration. We had all seen it on television." He was talking about the "Presidio Mutiny," the same incident with which Steve Rees introduces the following essay on the soldiers' anti-war movement. This act of so-called mutiny consisted of twenty-seven men sitting down in a circle and singing "We Shall Overcome." It was another small explosion in the chain reaction set off by the Southern Civil Rights sit-ins eight years before.

The SNCC Freedom Singers, as a matter of fact, had once sung a song about a "Demonstrating GI from Fort Bragg." It concerned a Black soldier who hopped a bus from his base in North Carolina to join his sister marching in the streets of Danville, Virginia; he was criticized by Secretary of Defense Robert McNamara for demonstrating in uniform. But this new movement that sang "We Shall Overcome" wasn't demonstrating against off-base injustices. It was demonstrating against the armed forces themselves.

It shouldn't be surprising that persistent and widespread opposition to the war developed among the Americans who saw it first hand and suffered from it the most. It was surprising only because of the tight lid the military clamps on dissent—and because it had never happened before. From about 1969 until even after the ceasefire in 1973, it happened plenty.[1]

1. Most of the historical facts in this introduction are drawn from David Cortright's *Soldier's in Revolt* (see Appendix).

The biggest organized resistance was stateside, where soldiers had more freedom to maneuver and more opportunities for contact with the civilian movement. In the course of the war, more than 200 underground GI newspapers came into being. Most were local papers at particular bases, but some were national, even international. They had names like *FTA, Fatigue Press, Pawn's Pawn,* and *Your Military Left*, and they served to give a public voice to GIs' growing misgivings about the war and the army. Often they were connected with coffeehouses or counseling centers run by soldiers and civilian activists in the towns near big basic training camps; these centers had a similar aim of giving GIs some space to figure out their reaction to the war, and what to do about it.

Numerous actions grew out of the network of newspapers and local organizing projects. Two nationally coordinated events occurred on May 16 (Armed Forces Day) of 1970 and 1971. The military traditionally used this day to open its bases to the public and bolster its image. In 1970, it closed 28 bases instead—for fear of the resistance the public would see. And in the towns just outside of 17 bases, from Fort McClellan, Alabama, to Fort Lewis, Washington, active duty GIs joined with anti-war civilians for rallies and demonstrations. The next year, GIs staged demonstrations at 19 bases, without outside assistance.

While the newspaper-coffeehouse network primarily involved white GIs, anti-war feeling probably ran even higher among Blacks. They also had to contend with discrimination at on-base clubs, harrassment by white MPs, and a higher casualty rate in battle. In July 1967, during the rebellion in Detroit, Black marines William Harvey and George Daniels called a meeting to question why Black men were fighting "a white man's war." For requesting a chance to discuss this matter with their commander, a court-martial found them guilty of promoting disloyalty and sentenced them to six and ten years, respectively.

Later Black actions understandably took the form of what the press described as race riots. In fact, these actions generally involved Black GIs, joined by some whites, battling MPs and non-commissioned officers. In July 1968, after the beating of a Black inmate in the Fort Bragg, North Carolina, stockade, a group of Black and white GIs seized control of the stockade for over 48 hours, yielding finally to armed troops. Two years later, within a single week, 200 mostly Black soldiers closed off a six-block area of Fort Hood, Texas, and clashed with MPs for several hours, and a similar group took over a section of Fort Carson, Colorado.

But if GI resistance was more visible at home, it was more potent in Vietnam. "You owe it to your body to get out of this alive," as one motto had it, and from about 1969 on platoons and companies would reject orders they considered suicidal and would force officers to change them. When this happened peacefully, it was known as "working it out." When officers insisted on taking a gung-ho attitude no matter what, they were often subject to "fragging"—injury or death from fragmentation grenades which were supposed to be used against the Vietnamese "enemy."

As most GIs learned the war was hopeless and many concluded it was wrong, drug use became chronic as an escape. A random sample study by the Army in 1970 showed 35% of frontline GIs in one infantry division smoking marijuana regularly, and two-thirds having smoked while on field duty. Pentagon studies carried out in 1971 found 10% of servicemen in Vietnam addicted to heroin or opium, and at least 30% having tried heroin at some time. The figures for soldiers toward the end of their hitches are probably significantly higher.

By 1970, combat reporters began to learn of instances of outright refusal to fight. Small groups of infantrymen refused to participate in the invasion of Cambodia. During the U.S.-ordered invasion of Laos by South Vietnamese forces in

March 1971, two U.S. platoons refused orders to advance along Route 9 to retrieve a damaged helicopter as part of support operations; to keep this rebellion from spreading, the entire squadron to which these platoons belonged was pulled out of the operation. At least one other platoon, elsewhere, refused to engage in any combat as part of the invasion.

There were also some public actions, even in Vietnam. Forty members of the Black Liberation Front of the Armed Forces held a demonstration at Long Binh (site of the bloodiest stockade riot of the war) on Martin Luther King's birthday in 1971. That fall, in Saigon, the Vietnam Veterans Against the War began circulating a petition against U.S. military involvement in Southeast Asia. Before the effort was crushed a few weeks later through arrests, discharges, and confiscation of the petitions, some 2000 soldiers had signed.

The plain fact was that the U.S. ground forces became an unreliable instrument for carrying on the war. By 1970, many commanders no longer trusted Blacks or radical whites with weapons except on guard duty or in combat. "Fuck the Green Machine" was a common slogan on jackets and hats. The dissatisfaction and resistance in the Army was a major cause of the U.S. troop withdrawal.

As the change to an air war placed new strains on the Navy's carrier force, resistance mushroomed there as well. In the fall of 1972, one-fourth of the crew members of the U.S.S. *Coral Sea* defied official harassment and signed a petition protesting the carrier's deployment from San Diego to Vietnam. "We the people must guide the government," the petition said, "and not allow the government to guide us." When the ship sailed, thirty-five sailors and three junior officers stayed behind. Another fifty-three sailors left the ship in Honolulu, and others from the "Stop Our Ship" movement continued to circulate an underground newspaper and even meet with civilian journalists as the cruise continued.

That same fall, over 130 sailors of the carrier U.S.S.

Constellation staged a dockside strike, refusing to board ship. The incident occurred after a month of shipboard conflict over punitive action taken against an organization of Black sailors, including a sit-down on the deck by Blacks and white supporters. In order to avoid a possible riot, none of the hundred-and-thirty strikers were arrested, and most were reassigned to shore duty.

All of these reportable incidents took place within a larger context of less-spectacular dissent, desertion, avoidance of duty, and sabotage—and of growing politicization and opposition to the war—in all the armed services. Many Vietnam-era GIs are still paying a price for these activities, by living in exile or suffering the effects of less-than-honorable discharges. That injustice is one of the many wounds of Vietnam that have yet to be healed.

Steve Rees

Steve Rees got involved in the New Left by joining Friends of SNCC in Palo Alto, California, as a high school student. He later worked in SDS and then, in 1970, joined the staff of the underground GI newspaper "Up Against the Bulkhead." His essay describes the soldiers' movement and the soldiers who made it up, through his experiences in one of the many projects that aided and encouraged the revolt in the ranks. It goes on to discuss the continuation of the soldiers' struggle in peacetime.

Steve Rees currently is a member of the founding group of the "Enlisted Times," a new popular-format newsmonthly for disgruntled enlisted men and women.

The last mutiny case I can remember was ten years old this

fall. It happened in October of 1968, which was a bad year for authority all around. This was eight months after the National Liberation Front's Tet Offensive in Vietnam, five months after striking workers and students paralyzed France, and two months after street fighting in Chicago and Prague shook two governments to their roots. Twenty-seven prisoners in the stockade at Sixth Army headquarters at the Presidio of San Francisco sat down together and refused to move—their way of protesting the shotgun killing of a fellow prisoner who was walking away from a work detail. The Army considered this mutinous, convened general courts-martial, and doled out sixteen-year sentences. It fought the resulting public outrage with a determination usually reserved for the enemy.

The Presidio mutiny was not the first skirmish in this battle between the military and the troops they were supposed to be commanding. Nine months earlier, some thirty soldiers at Fort Jackson, South Carolina, went to the post chapel one night to "express misgivings about the war in Vietnam." The previous year, Dennis Mora had refused orders for Vietnam together with two buddies at Foot Hood, David Samas and Jim Johnson.

And only two months before the Presidio sit-down, forty-three Black GIs at Fort Hood refused to board planes for Chicago, where they were to put down the demonstrations provoked by the Democratic Party's presidential nominating convention. Three-fourths of the Fort Hood soldiers had fought in Vietnam. Evidently, none were anxious to fight again, especially if it meant doing riot duty. After all, the winds from Lake Michigan were still carrying wafts of smoke from the Detroit Black rebellion the year before.

1968 was also the year the Army began taking a beating. Put yourself in its shoes. The Army went into the year with the confidence of an undefeated heavyweight champ battling a skinny featherweight whose name no one could even pronounce. Then after getting pummeled with rocket fire, trip mines, sappers, and hit-and-run attacks by an opponent they couldn't even see, the Army dragged ass back to its corner. Instead of consolation, it found its trainer, its sponsor, its promoters, and its water boy all in the other corner, or outside having a smoke.

Experience had been its trainer, experience gained fighting conventional wars against conventional armies, which was none too useful in combatting an indigenous people fighting by the tactics of people's war. Simple Americans had been its sponsor, and now they were having doubts and refusing to pay the costs. The government had been its promoter, and by now even the government was divided: the smart ones said to forget about military victory, the dumb ones wanted to bomb the enemy back to the Stone Age. The government added up the two sides, divided by two, and said "Do what you can."

Soldiers had been its trusty water boy, traditionally faithful, if begrudgingly so. But in this match, the water boy was nowhere to be seen. One report said he was slipping secrets to the other side. Another reported seeing him in back of the arena, watching the events with a special detachment, and smoking up a sweet-smelling storm.

Little wonder the Army came out fighting mad. It swung first on those who had been closest to it: its troops. Grunts. Peons. Or, as the Black soldiers put it, slaves on Uncle Sam's plantation. To the Army's command, the logic was indisputable. If they couldn't whip their own troops into line, how the hell could they take on the rest of the world? So the Army set out to make an example of a rather unlikely bunch of mutineers, these twenty-seven Presidio stockade prisoners who sat down in a circle and sang "We Shall Overcome."

After the courts-martial were over, the military appeal court, no doubt influenced by the breadth and depth of public sympathy for the men, reduced the sentences to two- and three-year terms. Several of the twenty-seven had already escaped and made it across the border into Canada with the help of the new underground railway for deserters. The Army had initiated the courts-martial to make an example of the mutineers. At the end of it all, it was the soldiers who had made an example of the Army.

Once the command recognized the hopelessness of its overall situation, they moved to cut their losses by fighting in the realm of appearances, in the press and public relations world. If the strongest institution of the most powerful nation in the world was going to be knocked down, at least the Army could try to control the way it would be written up in tomorrow's paper. In this, to a degree, they succeeded.

The outright disrespect for the chain of command and the code of conduct which blossomed in the five years following the Presidio sit-down must have caused Army battalion commanders to dream of firing squads, and Navy captains to recall the keelhaulings and whippings before the mast of the good old days. American prisoners of war openly collaborated with their captors. Sailors asked civilians to join them in halting the deployment of their attack carrier to the Gulf of Tonkin. Marines turned over to a socialist member of the Japanese parliament secret maps and photographs of nuclear weapons stored in Japan in violation of the U.S.-Japanese Security Agreement. For every reported event, how many more went unreported outside the barbed wire or ship's hull? For every outright refusal, how many sympathized, shirked, skated, avoided work details, maneuvered around "engaging the enemy?" But much of this treason, sedition, and mutiny was unpunishable. The cost of prosecuting—measured in the internationally recognized currency of bad press—was often prohibitive.

When in 1971 the Navy brought Pat Chenoweth to trial for allegedly tossing a monkey wrench into the vital innards of the aircraft carrier U.S.S. *Ranger*, delaying its departure to Vietnam for three-and-a-half months, Chenoweth's civilian lawyer brought to light over 300 recorded incidents of "willful destruction of government property" in the past twelve months. When the lawyer revealed that dozens of crewmen, including the ship's executive officer, had bragged off-handedly of wrecking the reduction gears which his client was charged with having sabotaged, Chenoweth was quickly found not guilty. The court-martial board backed down, despite their deep-seated desire for a conviction as vengeance on those who'd ruined their once secure and prideful little world.

Who were these pesky "troublemakers" who made the armed forces an unreliable instrument for carrying on the war? Pat Chenoweth was a quiet, unassuming sailor from Puyallup, Washington. And like so many others I came to know in eight years of aiding the Soldiers' Anti-war Movement, he was the most unlikely shit-disturber imaginable. He didn't really want the notoriety that resulted from the Navy's case against him. But he did like the people who stood with him during his court-martial. For those friends he was grateful. If he could wrangle a discharge out of all this (as he did), he would be doubly delighted to turn this misfortune to his advantage. At that point, all Pat wanted to do was get out of the Navy, get himself a Volkswagen bus, and hit the road. It was a common aspiration in those days among GIs I knew who were close to a discharge date, "short" as they used to call it. Pat's time in the Navy had been dead time. He wanted to catch up, and he hoped he'd have the chance to start right now. He knew that the road wasn't really freedom. But it was close to it because there'd be no one who could tell him what to do, when to do it, or where.

This attraction to the romance of the road came from young Americans on their way out of that most American of institutions: the military, the great equalizer. Young guys just off the block, the farm, the baseball diamond were pulled into this thing by their ears and thrown at random into barracks full of a rag-tag, rainbow-colored assortment of young men and old boys. Within thirteen weeks they would emerge from boot camp having endured together the trials, tribulations, and humiliations of their drill instructor. Like watching the same television programs and eating the same fast foods, boot camp was a leveling experience, a democratic experience of the American variety, with everyone treated more or less equally shitty.

The army often did what the melting pot, the Supreme Court, and school busing often failed to do: put all hyphenated Americans together shoulder to shoulder, and forced them to cooperate, or at least get to know each other. It succeeded in giving its recruits common enemies—first the army, and then the "enemy"—and teaching them that their lives depended on their ability to work together. Fitting that such a leveling and democratic experience would be found inside such a top-down institution of state violence engaged in such an unpopular fight against a people's war.

The men I knew who'd been on the ground in Vietnam, or just plain Nam as they called it, rarely considered their time in service dead time as Pat, the sailor, did. Most considered it stolen time, especially after a visit back home with high school friends who'd had two years to try several jobs, take a few courses at the local commuter college, date, get laid, maybe even get married. These 21-year-olds who'd been through Vietnam were not only missing two or three years, but they'd also been fundamentally changed in the process. Having been robbed and then remade so basically that some could no longer talk with family or friends, they wanted their freedom with a vengeance.

We were sometimes the first civilians they saw after that fourteen-hour flight from Tan Son Nhut airfield just outside of Saigon. We were in San Francisco International Airport shoving copies of a rowdy, disrespectful anti-war soldiers newspaper, *Up Against the Bulkhead*, into the hands of any soldier who happened to be in the airport, in uniform or out. In between flights we'd cruise the USO giving copies to anyone the rank of sergeant or under, while one of us would tie up the ladies at the head desk with arguments.

The paper had been coming out since 1970, when it was started by a group of ex-marines and sailors involved in the Movement for a Democratic Military. Our staff of five to ten people was usually evenly divided between women and men, with a third or more veterans and the rest civilians. We were generally something of a surprise to the troops returning from Nam.

After spending maybe eleven or twelve months in the bush humping ammo and hearing on Armed Forces Radio that the folks back home weren't duly appreciative of the job they were doing, many GIs came in from Vietnam thinking mobs of anti-war militants would be waiting to spit on them. Since SF airport was the first civilian ground they'd set foot on back in the States, and since we were the first long-hairs to walk right up and talk with them, many were naturally a bit uneasy. Our opening was disarming. "Hey, soldier, welcome home. Fuck the Army. Read all about it in this paper. No charge. It's on us. *The Bulkhead*."

Four out of five took the paper. The other one would refuse it, telling us he couldn't read and that was why he was in the army, or that he didn't want to read another word about the army, that he was getting out in three months and didn't ever want to think about it again. Others turned it down thinking it was an official Army paper and we were the hip front guard of the USO. We sometimes had a tough time convincing Nam returnees that civilian longhairs like us actually gave a good goddamn about the grunts, enough to spend a Friday night walking the corridors of the airport just to hand them a free newspaper.

No one ever swung on us. Of course, we steered clear of career NCOs and officers. But we learned to rely on rank, not appearances. The toughest looking paratrooper, certified hard-assed and decked out in black beret, combat ribbons, and fatigues tucked into those olive drab and black canvas and leather combat boots, often took our paper and gave us a clenched fist or a peace sign or one of those unbelievably complicated daps that admitted you to a very special brotherhood. We forced ourselves to test our prejudices. Guys with flattops, Green Berets, we tried them all. Some shut us down, especially the loners toting rifle cases. But not one of them ever swung on us, railed at us, called us traitors, or any of it.

Some GIs, when they got over the initial shock of meeting us, pursued us through the maze of concourses at SF International and proceeded to rap our ears off. Why we never carried tape recorders, I'll never know. Their stories were the stuff of which history is made: unrecorded, uncorroborated, almost unverifiable accounts of what they saw, what they did, what they felt. If half their stories were lies, it was amazing enough that they would have imagined them at all. These were the impressions that rarely found their way into letters home. Girlfriends and parents most often didn't want to hear about it, and who would be crazy enough to write home about this?

Wild stories of "six-foot white men" seen fighting with the NLF, allegedly GIs who'd changed sides.[2] Stories of "those fuckin' flyboys" turning half a company of a hundred men into "post-toasties" by mistakenly "naping" their position. Stories of friends—comrades in arms—writhing wounded from incoming rocket rounds, and cursing, not the enemy, but "that fuck Nixon."

AWOL havens in Cholon, the Chinese section of Saigon, where GIs holed up in hash dens with the help of bar maids and

2. The National Liberation Front was the grassroots revolutionary political force which U.S. policy was designed to keep out of power. Its armed forces were officially known as the People's Liberation Armed Forces.

mama-sans, and smoked their brains out, listening to Jimmy Hendrix and the Rolling Stones, waiting out the war. Playing dead in a bunker at an artillery base while NLF sappers made their way over the wire, blew up the ordnance depot, and spiked the barrels of the guns that were the reason for the firebase's existence on that hilltop. Being sent out on night reconnaisance patrols, bedding down not more than 50 yards from the perimeter, and radioing in bullshit reports while lighting up another bowl. Stories of ARVN units trading fire with their U.S. allies.[3] Stories of the brutality of the ROK (Republic of Korea) troops toward the Vietnamese. And yes, the confessional accounts of their own complicity in My Lais.[4]

The spectre of American soldiers turning themselves in for war crimes before an international tribunal must have haunted daydreamers in the Pentagon. We met enough willing candidates at the airport, to be sure. In fact, dozens had come forward already, in 1970, to the Citizens Commission of Inquiry, an American war crimes tribunal sponsored by prominent anti-war activists. Not radicals, these confessors, but troubled and disenchanted soldiers, many of them truly patriotic, and for that reason willing to risk all to unburden themselves to make the people of the U.S. aware of the horrors that were being carried out in their name and at their expense.

3. The Army of the Republic of Vietnam (ARVN) was the armed force of the U.S.-supported regime in Saigon.
4. A State Department strategist once remarked that the NLF was so strongly rooted among its rural peasant constituency that it "cannot be dislodged as long as that constituency continues to exist." Therefore U.S. policy was to remove the peasants by bombing and burning them out of their villages—and by massacring villagers suspected of supporting the NLF. The first of these massacres to come to public notice was the one that took place on March 16, 1968, at a hamlet in the village of Son My in Quang Ngai Province, South Vietnam—a hamlet which the U.S. Army called My Lai. Almost the

Another airport scene, which I'll never forget, is the guys walking off the planes with a friend on each arm and a bad case of the shakes, looking utterly wasted. Drill instructors used to tell their recruits, "When I say 'shit,' you squat." By 1971, the Army had homeward-bound GIs not shitting, but pissing, on command. The catch was that if you wanted to get on that flight back to the States, you had to leave with no opiates in your system. The piss test was their judge. It didn't matter if you left with a heroin habit, going cold turkey long enough to pass the test, and got strung out when you returned. It didn't matter if your skin turned yellow and you threw up your guts on that long flight back. All that mattered was that your piss turned up opiate free, so the Army looked good on paper. If these soldiers had the desire to talk to us in the airport, they lacked the energy.

Others we met were headed back to Nam, some for the dope, some for the money, some because there was little to keep them home. But the most disturbing reason we were given, on more than one occasion, was that Nam was the only place, any more, where life meant anything to these guys. Everything else became trivial.

entire civilian population of the hamlet—perhaps more than five hundred unarmed old men, women, children, and babies—were slaughtered by U.S. troops acting under official orders.

This massacre was reported by Army press officers as a battlefield victory. The truth became known to the public only in November 1969—through the efforts of a verteran who had heard the story from participants and of a journalist who pursued it. In 1971 an Army court-martial convicted Lt. William Calley, who had personally done some of the shooting, of murder. None of the higher-ranking officers who had commanded the operation or covered it up afterward were convicted of anything. After all, if ordering operations that involved killing civilians was a crime, every officer right up to the Commander-in-Chief would have had to go to jail.

Whether they were coming from or going to Vietnam, almost all GIs we met shared a profound self-hatred. Not really a hatred of themselves, but of their role, and of themselves for fulfilling it. "Wow," some would say in an embarrassing moment, "are you sure you want to stand here and talk to us like this, I mean with you having long hair and being civilians and all, and us being short-hairs." It was as if they were some lower life-form.

What we missed by not taping those airport stories, we gained by developing correspondences with the soldiers who wrote us. About every two months—basically whenever we could scrape the money together—we'd put a 12-to-24 page issue of the paper to press. Of the 10,000 to 20,000 we'd run, we'd pass out maybe a third in town at the airport, the bus terminals, the major tourist spots, rock concert lines, and the Navy piers. Another third we'd ship to groups like ours elsewhere in the States, and in Germany, Sweden, the Philippines, Japan, Hawaii, and Okinawa. The last third of the papers found their way to Vietnam through the mail—either as single issues sent to the thousand-plus subscribers we carried, or as bundles sent to our more loyal distributors. With that many papers in circulation, we were a natural attraction for dozens of pen-pal-hungry guys sweating out their time in the jungles and engine rooms of what they liked to call "the suck." These letters, more than anything, show what was happening to Vietnam-era soldiers and to the military machine they were supposed to be a part of. They're the primary documents that should be the raw material of history books, but in our time they remain buried in the basements and attics of three million veterans of Vietnam—the private memories of a war that history would just as soon forget:

August 8, 1970

Dear --------

I joined the Army a year ago in the hope that it could give

me a stability that civilian society could not. A month afterward I began collecting material for a book I was going to write, relating all the experiences that GIs must suffer from the Reception Center to Vietnam and afterwards. My fiancee, who was a model, was to receive my manuscripts and help me edit them. After my leave following AIT, she copped out on me and left for NYC where I hope she makes lotsa money to buy the dexedrine she always liked to take. Anyway, it has taken over 6 months for me to stop feeling sorry for myself.

I was in an Army "instant NCO" school, and graduated as an E-5. So it's easy to say I tried to play it their way as long as I could. I knew then as I know now that the war is a total fuck up. But it was easier to grind my teeth and tell myself I would die a glorious death. I actually believed this.

I came home a buck sergeant over three weeks ago with orders to report to Oakland 3 Aug. Two days after I arrived home I made the decision that I would never go to Vietnam. I decided to try to capitalize on a spinal disk injury that I received last February, and try to get a medical discharge. If not, I planned a big scene where I would publicly announce my refusal to go and be taken away, trial, etc.

Well, due to the graces of a Naval surgeon, I am now a patient in the Portsmouth Naval Hospital. I will not go to 'Nam now, but I may not get out of the Army. That's really irrelevant to me now as what is important to me is helping other GIs from going through the hell I've known, and the worse hell that the guys here that have been to 'Nam and stepped on mines have seen. I don't want to see any more wounded GIs! Not one Marine or soldier I've talked to here has told me the wound he got over there was worth it. Not one.

I can truly say I am scared shitless. Rather than sit back on my ass and shoot up some skag like some of my ex-friends and say "fuck it," I have to do something...

Sgt. J.J.
Norfolk, VA

May 15, 1971

Brothers:

Keep up the work, and maybe we will be able to get the hell out of here and leave these people alone. They (the Vietnamese people) do not want our help anyway, and they have proved that by shooting at us and wrecking our vehicles.

PFC D.S.

A Btry 1/44th Artillery

15 April 1971

Dear -------

I'm at LZ Weight Davis about 30 miles south of Pleiku. Things are going well here. In March a people's hero (still unknown) fragged our orderly room and demolished a lifer's office. Then we got rid of our super pig CO, Capt. "Georgie Boy" Gradner. In addition to spending all his time trying to harass the company and constantly making an ass of himself in front of the EM, he was caught one night, drunk, on his knees, begging a dink whore to screw him for $50. He was for some strange reason "replaced" several weeks later. George was a winner. This is the kind of high quality leadership Sam sends to lead us over here.

The peace demonstrations the beginning of this month were very encouraging to most of us in Viet Nam. It's a relief to at least know that the people cannot be bullshitted by the government. *Please*, keep it up.

Mac

584th Eng Co (LE)

25 November 1971

Dear -------

How is it in the land of the "free and the home of the brave"? I'm sitting with Joe in a corner of his compartment where he sleeps. I won't waste your time by telling you about my hassling experience trying to get that turbine fixed. It's no problem now even though it's still not fixed. We were supposed to get underway Friday the 8th, but someone set fire to two of the firerooms and it did some damage like melting aluminum deck plates and smoking the place up real bad. We didn't leave until Saturday morning. Aw gee. They are real shook up about it, and have about forgotten the booster pump is still out of commission. The lifers are really shook. I was in my bunk the morning of the fires, luckily. That's my alibi. Besides, why would I want to burn a ship? Ha!

B.G.
USS *Coral Sea*

October 2, 1970

Dear T -------
   If your MOS is 0311-Grunt like mine was, it'll be a long tour if you just accept the fact that you're going to serve in the bush for 12 months. I was in the bush for 6 months and then I got out and have a job working with the Koreans. I came over here thinking I was fighting to save my freedom and the people of South Viet Nam. It took me almost a month or two to see that was a lie. By then I had a combat promotion to corporal, and was a squad leader. I felt what we were doing was wrong but I had a squad I really dug. I mean these cats were great. Many times instead of running ambushes we'd "sandbag" a patrol, which means we wouldn't run an ambush where we were supposed to. Most of the time we wouldn't run it at all. We got away with it because the pigs didn't have the balls to go out on ambushes with us.
   Another thing we have over here that really pisses off the troops is when we get a Lt. who thinks he's Chesty Puller. This type of Lt. never listens to his men, always manages to have his nose up the company commander's ass, and writes people up for not shaving. There are exceptions, but not many. Another problem is the pigs are trying to make ambush teams stay 100% awake all night say from 8 o'clock at night till dawn, come back, and go on working parties. It can't be done 7 days a

week. Also, it's not being done. Most lifers are afraid to go on ambushes because they know if the VC doesn't get them, we will.

In our clubs here just like back in the states the pigs try to herd us like cattle. We've got our own status: officers one place, staff one place, and on down the line our place. That pisses off the troops because the officers are eating shrimp and roast beef and drinking mixed drinks while we're eating canned ham and drinking lukewarm beer....

Sgt. P.H.

2nd ROK MC Brgd

5th Bn

July 20, 1970

Dear B --------

I'm a PFC serving in Vietnam. Two days ago my company (D Co., 1/7 Cav) went to the bush. But I didn't go with them.

In our last contact, my company and B company lost 4 men killed and 17 wounded. The lifers kept putting us on line and charging the bunkers. Each time we lost 3 or 4 men. After two days of this they decided to pull back and call in an air strike. What kind of game are these lifers playing? Losing men for no reason at all.

I have been in the bush for 11 months. I don't like anybody playing with my life. And I won't go to the field with someone like that.

There was a man that killed himself yesterday. I myself know guys that have broken their arms and fingers so they wouldn't have to go to the bush with the commanding officer.

We don't need this war. Let's end it.

There are 4 or 5 of us that will be in jail soon. If there is anyone or anything that you can do for us, it would be grateful. Please come and talk to us. I know you are fair persons.

PFC H.P.

3rd Bde., 1st Cav Div

November 7, 1972

Dear B -------

Here we are still out to sea. It's been up to 185° in places in the pump room. The blowers won't work and they claim they are working on them. We are going to have two general inspections today, and more later.

We finally got the exhaust blowers fixed. The difference between the once 170° and now 120° is like coming out of a sauna bath and falling into ice water.

On watch we shut down to checking gear and playing soccer. Just like a puppy finding anything imaginable to amuse himself. It was fun, but it would be a far better life being out, not standing this watch, not having this creeping crawling crazy heat rash, and not knowing that I have helped outfit this tub for another war cruise to Viet Nam.

I want to let you all know how I felt when I was told Jimmy Strick was killed. It was just like I had been informed a real close relative, such as a brother, was killed. It could be nothing but pure misery for all of us involved. We are all getting shorter as every day rolls over to another one. I realize accidents can and very often do happen. Let this that happened to Jimmy live in our minds as a new lesson or thought. Let's all be careful and try and hope the mechanical failures don't outlast us. Losing one good friend and compadre was horrible enough. May there be no more.

B.G.
USS *Coral Sea*

19 April 1971

Dear C -------

So right now my ship is floating towards the great war scene with all its bombs and legal murder weapons. But me, I'm sitting here in the hospital in Oakland waiting to be operated on in the next couple of days. So for the time being I'm away from the war. But I see many war casualties here. For you see, this is a Naval Hospital. There are a lot of Calley's brothers here. But they aren't walking around wondering about 'Nam. They are wondering about what they will do in their new lives ahead of them. See, many of the brothers out here are without arms and legs. It's really a sad sight to see someone my age and younger wheeling himself around in a wheelchair with one leg or arm extending from it. I wonder how many of these people has Nixon seen? I think he must have turned his back on these brothers, the ones who didn't quite give their lives, but parts of it.

As I sit here glad that I'm not on my ship, my mind tends to drift out to sea and feel the sorrow and sad feelings that I'm sure by now are covering the minds of the brothers on my ship. For although I'm away from my ship I can just about hear the conversation of the crew as they laugh a little to try and forget the bad times they are about to engage in. The feeling of that crew right now will never reach the news media because the public would not believe how hard it is to repeat doing something you really don't understand or believe in. I've been to Viet Nam before, and I just about would have gone again. But prior to being hospitalized these feelings of sadness weighed me down heavily.

But there are a few freaks who can't wait to kill as soon as they get over in the land of milk and money. You see, every time we take ammunition into the war zone, that's an additional $65 a month, which is nothing to me, for I value my life and freedom much more than $65. But the lifers get a big charge out of it because they are floating bounty hunters. This military life keeps you down, even when they give you a break, because you still have memories and you still have your uniform.

L.E.
USS *Chara*

The newspapers, coffeehouses, base organizations, and anti-war actions that made up the GI Movement were the political expression of the attitude toward the war revealed in these letters. The reality that brought forth a GI Movement was the reality of Vietnam as those who fought there understood it. But the political climate that made it possible was built by all the social struggles of the decade, begining with the Black Freedom Movement.

Especially, the growth of the civilian Anti-War Movement established the best possible preconditions for the emergence of an anti-military movement inside the armed forces. The war and the military itself increasingly became something to question rather than something to accept unquestioningly. Also, the stronger the Anti-War movement, the easier it was for soldiers to speak out. The whittling down of the sentence of the Presidio 27 is an example of the importance of outside pressure on the Army. The existence of sympathetic communities that would harbor AWOLs and deserters is another. Civilian activists also participated directly in the Soldiers Movement, through base-town organizing projects and information centers, and in some cases by entering the armed forces in order to organize from within.

But the Soldiers' Movement transformed the Anti-War Movement as well. No longer was the Anti-War Movement, as it had been in the early years, a minority movement of leftists on the fringe. It was becoming a majority movement, with a young working class component that was strategically centered within the war machine. With a new ability to affect the day-to-day conduct of military operations, the whole movement had to be taken much more seriously.

One of the activists from the ranks—as representative an example as any individual is likely to be—was Tony. A self-retired Marine who'd left Camp Pendleton when his name came up on a Vietnam manifest. Tony was in San Francisco in

1970 with his wild-eyed Hungarian-born friend to start a chapter of Movement for a Democratic Military. MDM was some GIs' answer to SDS, and like SDS, it represented the more radical trends in the movement. I met both MDM and Tony when I answered an ad in the local underground paper for civilian assistants.

I had just returned rather starry-eyed from Oceanside, where only one month before a thousand anti-war marines had marched through the streets of this city adjacent to Camp Pendleton in the most conservative county in California. Some friends of mine had helped organize that march, and I had stayed with them in a former bungalow redecorated as a large bunker. Sandbags had been carefully piled along the streetside exposure for protection against some local citizens who liked to cruise past the house at night taking pot shots at the shadows. Just before I got there they had finally hit someone, a Black Marine named Jessie, wounding him in the arm. Inside, acid, automatic weapons, and bad nerves combined one time to put some unplanned ventilation in the ceiling.

I'd met Marines hitchhiking up to Los Angeles for a rock concert who bragged of getting Ho Chi Minh discharges. "That's what the suck gives you when you're caught leafleting or rabble-rousing, and you get to be more trouble than you're worth." I'd also met a Marine named Ozzie who gave an hour-long speech to his court-martial board about how the Marine Corps made him a revolutionary. Naturally I was pretty taken with all this, and I came back to San Francisco ready to get cracking. I answered the ad, and I met Tony.

Tony was from Chicago, and he loved to talk about it. A great story teller and a practiced charmer, he liked best spinning yarns about his Golden Glove days. An Italian growing up on the North Side, he knew the youth gang scene as a matter of course. Being short, he had to learn to fight with his hands in order to stay on his feet. He wasn't bad with his mouth, either.

Only later did he trust me with his more recent past. After finding out he'd been sent to Vietnam at a time when Marines were known to be taking more casualties proportionately than any other branch of service, Tony decided that anything was better than shipping out. Even the brig. And the brig at Camp Pendleton was nothing to consider lightly. An expose in *Life* magazine included sketches by inmates of men tied spread-eagled to the wall, while Marine brig guards did to them whatever they pleased. For solitary confinement, they locked you into a sheet-metal hot house on a 100-degree summer day, left you barely enough water to survive, and let you out when they felt like it.

Tony knew of other ways out. He knew of some Marines who, on hearing that their orders had been cut for Nam, went out in the sun, covered one eye, and stared at the glowing orb until the retina of their other eye was good and scarred. Losing an eye was better than losing your life. But Tony somehow got off-base, got a ride to Los Angeles, and in a move very unlike this not-so-religious Italian Catholic, he took sanctuary in a church, aided and abetted by the Los Angeles Anti-War Movement.[5] Then he disappeared before the heat got too close for comfort.

It was not like Tony, I later learned, to take unnecessary risks. That helps to explain why he stayed out of Nam. But it doesn't explain his taking sanctuary—taunting the Marines to come get him by making a public anti-war spectacle of himself. Tony was against the war, sure. He also liked being the star, the hero of the moment, the man everyone wanted to hear from, even the press.

5. "Sanctuaries" were a tactic of the Anti-War Movement which made public political events out of individual acts of conscience. Military resisters and draft resisters would seek "sanctuary" in a church or university, where hundreds of supporters would surround them to delay or prevent their arrest.

Afterward, when he arrived in San Francisco with a new identity, he could have laid low again. But he chose to work on the *Bulkhead* and on a GI coffeehouse project in Oakland. He risked all to stay involved with a group of people he respected and came to like. Friends, ethics, and a strong impulse for survival all shaped Tony's actions and thoughts. In Tony, as in most activists, they combined to make up the motivating force we called politics.

Although he was a great bullshitter, Tony also had a great bullshit detector. Nothing rankled him like false bravado of the New Left armed-struggle variety. He'd been around too much of the real thing to romanticize it. He once told me that he'd sooner join Joan Baez's love-everybody pacifist group than be seen in public with yo-yo's who insisted that the only real changes were made by revolutionaries with guns. And Joan Baez was hardly his style.

The other thing that rankled Tony was a certain kind of textbook revolutionary who came on to him just because he talked like they thought "the workers" talked, or because he was made of genuine GI meat. He was irked by ingratiating gestures of phony friendship. He hated being liked not for who he was, but for what they thought he was. It was a courtship ritual that he saw repeated many times in the course of his three years in the GI Movement. When civilian activists talked differently to him than they talked to others, when they came on too fast or too friendly, he knew someone was putting the make on him, and he usually let them know it.

In 1972, a friend and I went with Tony back to Camp Pendleton. Armed with two lawyers, local contacts, many friends back in the Bay Area, and quite a reserve of self-confidence and courage, he wanted to turn himself in, do his time, get his discharge, and get out. It all went according to plan. Today I'd trust Tony's gut politics, ethics, and intelligence a hundred times sooner than the political sensibilities of "new communist" converts of the late 1970s. I'd like to think that the GI Movement of the last ten years produced more indigenous radicals like Tony than zealots and true believers.

Most of the soldiers I met before 1970 and 1975 were like Tony in that they were reluctant radicals or heroes of circumstance. Too many times people like Tony were recast in a more trendy image by the reporters or "revolutionaries" whose bread and butter depended on such fabrications. Sadly, some soldiers took to the posturing like a 13-year-old trying on his first ducktail and leather jacket in front of the mirror.

GIs as a group had about the lowest self-image going: short hair, bossed around, not smart enough to avoid Nam. So imagine their surprise on discovering that radical civilians liked them for the same reasons they disliked themselves. Those who stuck around soon discovered that if they'd only go one step farther, and assume the model of militance which their new civilian friends valued so highly, they could be the star of the project. Some more cynical ones pumped this infatuation for all it was worth, borrowing money, freeloading, getting laid, in a cycle of use-and-be-used.

What completed the cycle was the reciprocal posturing of civilian activists who affected the language and stance of the soldiers they knew. Feeling like fish out of water, they tried their best to be "fish swimming in the sea of people." They looked more like chameleons changing colors as they crept from one habitat to another. This type of posturing contributed to the break-up of a number of projects in the later years of the war.

There was no mistaking the *breadth* of dissatisfaction in the lower ranks of the armed forces, but there was a generally shared misjudgment of the *depth* of radicalization actually achieved. The radicalization was deep enough to cause many soldiers to question not just this policy or that commanding officer, but the mission itself: the war. Here the questioning, for most, stopped.

This was no shallow achievement; but because so many

radicals staffing civilian projects wanted to carry the questioning deeper, regardless of the costs, questioning the war alone seemed inadequate. As U.S. radicals in the '70s tried to reduce the revolutionary repasts cooked up in other countries at other times into a shake-and-bake communism for the here and now, more and more civilian activists made cadre development, not the quickest possible U.S. exit from Vietnam, their overriding concern. For some, the war and the movement against it in the ranks became simply a means for winning converts to communism, or recruits to one or another of the myriad of Old and New Left sects.

This new agenda required a tightening up of the core groups of counseling centers, coffeehouses, and other projects, and a throttling of the initiatives of new arrivals. Wanting to fuck the army wasn't enough. Now an interested GI had to be able to chant "fuck the army" while doing Chinese calisthenics and reciting appropriate catechism before he'd be accepted. That this was the way to an overturning of authority in the most resilient advanced industrial society was questionable. But as a method of either broadening or strengthening the opposition movement in the enlisted ranks, it was definitely a bust.

By 1975 or so, the not-so-new Left and the anti-militarist movement in the enlisted ranks parted ways. Those civilian activists who had come to lend a hand to a creative movement against the war and military authority were now an obstacle to it. In place of idealism they offered ideology. Tactics such as sabotage, counterfeiting official newsletters, and psychological warfare were discouraged in favor of petitions and picket lines.

Even dope smoking, which most GIs considered an act of elementary personal rebellion, was soon frowned upon by "professional radicals" as "individualistic." Civilians would champion "class war" as they denounced "imperialist war," much to the puzzlement of previously sympathetic soldiers.

And the same civilians upheld a new authority—be it a book, a leader, or a revolutionary party—as they rejected the authority of the brass. In place of military discipline they offered "revolutionary discipline." And so on.

Yet with or without the help of outsiders, and with or without a war, each new wave of recruits came into the allegedly "all-volunteer" military skeptical of authority. After Calley's court-martial, no one wanted to be the fall guy for the military's policies or predictable blunders. The post-Vietnam, post-Watergate, out-for-number-one generation of recruits were doubters, not exactly the stuff commanding officers dream of.

Unlike their conscripted counterparts, recruits for this peacetime all-volunteer force were hard to find. The military had to compete on the labor market with all other employers. Without the assistance of double-digit inflation and unemployment figures, it's unlikely that they would have done as well as they did. The military did not consider themselves to be working in a buyer's market. They had to bend the terms of military service to fit the rising expectations of prospective recruits.

Clearly the old way would no longer do. U.S. Navy Captain Jack Caldwell offered one description of the havoc wrought by the Vietnam-era soldiers movement. Caldwell was chief of the Operations Center at the Supreme Headquarters of the Allied Powers of Europe in 1975 when he wrote that, "In the last twenty years alarming changes have taken place in all of the U.S. armed forces: standards of appearance, courtesy, discipline, performance, combat effectiveness, and loyalty to the nation have suffered a steady decline. Desertion and draft-dodging were excused as evidence of a higher morality. Stong leadership was out. Rap sessions were in."

Faced with so severe a crisis, the Army experimented with an unprecedented grievance system at Fort Carson which depended on democratically elected barracks representatives.

A young enlisted man held the ombudsman post as his sole military responsibility and had the power to by-pass the chain of command and talk directly to the base's commanding officer. Retired Army Colonel Robert Heinl blasted this new turn, calling the experiment a "system of soviets based on the Bolshevik model." His comments were a clue to the intensity of debate that must have characterized policy meetings at the Pentagon. In the Navy, the modernizing Admiral Elmo Zunwalt experimented with a loosening of the regulations governing enlisted people's personal lives: dress codes, haircuts, leave and liberty policies.

With dormitories replacing barracks, women soldiers joining men in all but frontline units, civilians working next to soldiers in all but combat fields, and paychecks replacing patriotism as the key sales pitch, many old guard NCOs tossed it in. Their military's defeat in Vietnam was hard enough. Combine this with the command's kid gloves attitude toward new recruits, and the wave of resignations of crewcut, tattooed, balding, blood-and-guts cold war warriors becomes understandable. Only the Sergeant Bilkos remained, the ones who understood that in wartime maybe they could command, but in peacetime they should manage.

Still, they could manage only up to a point. After the war, soldiers no longer gave much thought to *what* they were doing. But they did continue to question *how* the work got done. Was it necessary to tolerate the many restrictions on personal freedoms—including hair and dress regulations—which remained? Why did ship engineers have to tolerate working in steam generating plants so poorly ventilated that the temperatures reached 150 degrees and sent men to their racks spotted with heat rashes? Challenges to race and sex discrimination, cuts in pay and benefits, and limits on First Amendment rights were continually advanced by young first- and second-term soldiers well after the Vietnam ceasefire.

Even though the network of activist projects and underground soldiers' newspapers had rapidly faded away, impertinent soldier-activists were encouraged by a tradition of opposition that had become legitimate in the course of the war. The military institution was still highly unpopular, and public sympathy for the "little guy" was at times enough to encourage soldier-activists to speak their minds. In many cases, radically inclined civilian lawyers could be retained by disgruntled GIs who wanted to take their fight into the military courts.

These challenges from the lower ranks, coming as they did on the heels of the Vietnam-era GI Movement and the subsequent modernizing reforms of the all-volunteer army, forced a continual redefinition of the terms of service. They posed a possible redefinition of the very meaning of the job of soldiering. How much a citizen and how much a soldier are the non-career members of a massive citizen army to be?

This question was posed implicitly by the initiatives of several major unions toward establishing a trade union for soldiers in 1975-76. And it was posed explicitly by two out of a number of GIs (including Blacks and whites, women and men) who were embroiled in courts-martial over their refusals to cut their hair to army standards. Sgt. Dan Pruitt remarked, "They force us to look different [from civilians] and try to make us different. We're not." PFC Lou Stokes explained, "A citizen does not cease to be a citizen once he becomes a soldier, but becomes a soldier because he is a citizen."

All this becomes thinkable only because of a largely unstated but pervasive indifference to the military mission. As long as the army could depend on its troops to accept whatever war—hot or cold—they were supposed to be waging, it could depend on them not to raise any personal demands which might get in the way. But what the command has faced, since Vietnam, is a vacuum in motivation. It's the military equivalent of the blue-collar blues, and it's not an insignificant factor in determining the combat readiness of the troops. As

James Sterba of the *New York Times* wrote in an article on the New Action Army in the summer of 1975, "It would almost be a shame to ask the Army to put all its progress to a test by ordering it to go out and fight a war."

Such a question could not have been posed without a decade of challenges from the lower ranks to the very purpose of the armed forces during the last war. Despite the fact that soldiers now (unless they have older brothers who've passed the memory on) know very little about Vietnam, the questioning spirit in the ranks has persisted. That spirit is one of the strongest legacies of the GI Movement of the Vietnam era. And its strength will play a large part in determining whether the new generation of soldiers will have to face its own Vietnam.

This critical tradition is a tradition we should feel proud to have contributed to. It's also a tradition that will require rekindling in the future, throughout the society. Among the free-thinkers, anti-militarists, radicals, and revolutionaries who will be stoking up the fires will be the former soldier-activists who are veterans of the Vietnam era.

Singers at a Bread and Roses demonstration, Boston, 1969. Photo by Ann Popkin.

7

The Personal Is Political:
The Women's Liberation Movement

Four years after Mississippi Freedom Democratic Party supporters demonstrated outside the Democratic National Convention in Atlantic City, that resort city's boardwalk was the scene of another protest which marked another political turning point.

This 1968 action was a guerrilla theater satire of the Miss America Pageant going on nearby. Carried out by Women's Liberation groups from several East Coast cities, the action challenged a system of oppression as pervasive and deeply rooted as the one challenged by the Civil Rights Movement. Just as Blacks, in the years after the MFDP was denied official recognition by the Democratic Party, increasingly formed their own organizations to combat the political, economic, and psychological effects of racism, women began to do the same to combat the varied forms of sexism.

The new movement continued the struggle for equal rights under the law and on the job which was begun by the nineteenth century women's rights and suffrage movement. It linked that struggle, often, to the struggles against racism and the war. It also broke new ground, for all movements, by broadening the concept of the "political" to include what had previously been considered solely private, individual dilemmas.

Thousands of women were swept into Women's Liberation activities, from consciousness raising groups to workplace caucuses to newspapers, demonstrations, and organizing projects. Millions more have been touched by the new movement's insights. The issues of women's position in the family and in the paid workforce are at the center of much of today's political conflict and debate.

Women's liberation also posed a challenge for the mixed—and in practice male dominated—groups of the New Left. Would male leftists alter their attitudes toward women and their styles of work to embody the revolutionary principles of equality among human beings which they preached? And would they accept the struggle against sexism as a serious political task? The resistance of men in the movement was an object lesson in the strength of male supremacy in the society.

The following essay by Ann Popkin needs little historical introduction. It begins by tracing the roots of the Women's Liberation Movement in the Civil Rights and Anti-War struggles and in the society at large. It portrays the emergence of the movement as an organized force through the example of the Boston-area socialist Women's Liberation group Bread and Roses.

Ann Popkin says about the essay, "I write this history from my present socialist-feminist perspective and therefore emphasize certain questions, issues, events, and ideas. Another woman might write quite a different history.

"In addition to having been an active member of Bread and Roses in 1969-71, I have done research on the organization more recently. More than seventy-five women who created Bread and Roses or joined during its first year completed a long, open-ended questionnaire about their participation in the organization as well as their own political and social histories. I spent many hours with thirty of these women in individual and group interviews retracing specific moments to better understand what happened and what it means for us now. I want to thank all of the women for their participation in this project of recreating our shared past and for their commitment to translate a vision into reality."

In this chapter the footnotes are the author's.[1]

Ann Popkin

Since Bread and Roses, Ann Popkin has worked in the Women's School, the New England Marxist-Feminist Study Group, the Boston Women's Union, the Socialist Column (a radical faculty group at the University of Massachusetts at Boston), and a local socialist-feminist collective. She had made films about a charm school and about her grandmother, and is currently teaching media & society, women & media, and community studies at the University of California at Santa Cruz.

It is difficult to believe this today, but at the outset of the last decade the idea of "Women's Liberation" literally did not exist. The huge "second wave" of the feminist movement in the U.S., which is all around us today, began to emerge only later out of the protest movements of the 1960s.[2] By '68 or '69, small groups of women were meeting together, excitedly, throughout the country. These groups were to mushroom into larger organizations and a movement with profound effects on the lives of women in the U.S.—a movement into which many of us poured our energy and our hopes.

Bread and Roses, the Boston-based organization which I was involved in building, was one among a number of similar Women's Liberation groups that came into being in the late

---

1. I also want to thank Leslie Cagan, Margaret Cerullo, Vicki Gabriner, and Barrie Thorne for their suggestions after reading an earlier draft of this chapter.

2. This movement was called the "second wave" to distinguish it from the earlier women's rights and women's suffrage movement.

'60s. Because it was one of the first and one of the biggest, we faced certain problems that later organizations would not have to face, and we made certain breakthroughs that others would not get the chance to make. By writing about some of our particular history, while setting it in the context of a growing national movement, I hope to share some of the excitement, challenge, confusion, pain, passion, and sense of accomplishment we felt. This is not merely history. Much of political life for women today is an attempt to work out many of the ideas we first formulated and tried to implement at that time.

Some five hundred women came to a Bread and Roses meeting or passed through our office at one time or another during our organizational life-span of 1969 to 1971. At any one time, about 150 of us formed the activist core. We were mostly white, college-educated women from middle-class backgrounds, in our mid-twenties. Some of us were married, and more of us were single. Most of us saw ourselves as participants in a revolutionary movement, and increasingly as socialists and as feminists. We sought to change our lives—our work, relationships, and forms of politics—as we tried to change the larger society.

The Women's Liberation Movement indeed changed my life. And the change was not something that was true just for me; it was a change experienced by many, many women who went through the same process. Politically, I felt that I had found work that I wanted to do—that I was no longer the "mindless activist" I had imagined myself to be in SDS meetings, or one number (however necessary) out of anonymous thousands in large demonstrations. Rather I was a

This chapter is about the Women's Liberation Movement of the 1960s and 70s which sought, and seeks, radical transformation of the society, believing that the liberation of women requires this larger change. There are other more moderate groups in the contemporary Women's Movement which concern themselves with reforms aimed at equality within this society.

competent political activist, whose political contributions could vary with the activity, the needs of the group, and my skills and interests at the time. (How much this is the story of actual capabilities changing, and how much of consciousness changing, I can't really say.) Socially, I helped to create a close community of comrades present in daily life and able to be mobilized in times of political and individual crisis.

For the last ten years I have been active in a variety of political groups with women whose thinking I trust, whose varied experience I value. A women's community provides support for my and other women's decisions to create new ways of living—choosing what to keep and what to reject of the old ways (usually isolated, competitive, heterosexual, and in traditional nuclear families) that "grownups" were supposed to live. Together, we have had the experience of being part of making a powerful movement, watching it grow and change, and now having to fight to redefine it and reclaim it from both cooptation and repression.

Roots...

It's not that the Women's Movement was my first or even first satisfying political experience. I walked my first picket line with my mother when I was thirteen or fourteen. A Black family had bought a house in our town and some "neighbors" had burned it down; we set about trying to make "fair housing in Freeport." A year or two later I began picketing Woolworth's in support of the sit-ins in the South.

The taunts of the predominantly hostile bystanders, the pleas of the workers who feared they would lose their jobs or their pay if Woolworth's closed down because of our picket line, and the hate letter pieced together from newspaper headlines that the picket organizer received—all showed me early on that the struggle would not always be a popular one. I wouldn't always be able to be "nice" when I was fighting for what I thought was right; and maybe, aside from potential social ostracism, I would get physically hurt. None of this seemed reason enough to stop.

What was true for me was true in a larger sense as well. The other social movements of the decade provided women with examples of people in motion, with models of collective struggle to change oppressive conditions. We had seen—and many of us had joined with—people taking positive action instead of letting things go on as usual.

Those of us who had participated in these movements came away with certain political skills. We were familiar with calling and putting together meetings and demonstrations. We had organized in poor communities and in college dormitories. Many of us, myself included, had gone South (especially to Mississippi in the summer of 1964) in the Civil Rights Movement. We had faced the tasks of registering voters and setting up Freedom Schools and community centers, and faced fear and danger as well.[3] Equally important, we had been intimately and daily involved with the struggle of black people for their freedom.

Our experiences showed us what it meant to "put your body on the line." Shot at, beaten, yelled at, as white Northerners we knew that the dangers were even greater for the black people who lived their lives there. Yet the shared peril, work, and daily life, reinforced by the singing of powerful freedom songs, bound us together. (Still, although many of us did good work, we could not help but notice that many of the "leaders" and public spokespeople were men.)

In the Anti-War Movement, whatever our feelings of disaffection as women who could not directly resist the draft, we shared the fervor and excitement of staging demonstrations

---

3. Freedom Schools were set up to counter the "education"— inferior in quality and racist in content—doled out by segregated school systems.

of hundreds of thousands of people. We watched what had been an unpopular position held by a minority of weird folks change people's minds—the sentiment growing, swelling, and eventually changing both the faces of government personnel and their policies.[4]

Working in these movements we began to identify as members of a growing community of radicals. Being part of "The Movement" was not just a matter of political opposition, but of criticism and withdrawal from the dominant culture as well. Blue jeans, comfortable hair, little or no makeup, and increasingly open attitudes about sex, marriage and "living together" already separated us somewhat from the accepted image of proper young women.

...and Stirrings...

At first we thought all of us—women and men, blacks and whites—were together in the struggle as equals. Our new closeness, vision, and activities provided us with a momentum that pushed us forward, made us hopeful and optimistic. At the same time, we lived and breathed a liberal ideology which said that men and women were treated equally. We were, on the whole, blinded to the realities of our special position as women, both in the society and in the movement. When the fog before our eyes began to lift, the movement for Women's Liberation came of age.

A few women, realizing that the rhetoric of equality was

4. For me, though I was affected in the ways I described by the size of the anti-war actions and the growth of the Movement, the period between my Civil Rights Movement experience and Women's Liberation seems now like a blur of meetings with endless harangues and debates, study groups, picket lines, and occasional huge demonstrations—intermingled with tears of sorrow and horror at

not borne out in movement activity, had begun to forge critiques. In 1964, a group of women in SNCC met to talk about their role in that organization; Ruby Doris Smith Robinson wrote up the results of the analysis of this group in a paper, "The Position of Women in SNCC," presented to a staff meeting that same year.[5] The following year, Casey Hayden and Mary King wrote "A Kind of Memo," describing the secondary role of women in the movement. Like Robinson's paper before, "A Kind of Memo" was ridiculed or ignored by most male activists and did not get much response among movement women until later, when it was circulated in other forms.

In SDS, women made several attempts to raise the issue of Women's Liberation, with little success. In the December 1965 national meeting, some women circulated "A Kind of Memo." Women trying to speak to the issues it raised were met with laughter and derision from male radicals. However, workshops at following SDS regional conferences attracted many women who would later become active in the Women's Liberation Movement. In the summer of 1967, SDS women put

the destruction of human life in Vietnam, a sense of frustration at our seeming lack of power to change this daily fact, and feelings of solidarity with the struggle of the Vietnamese people. The Civil Rights Movement and the Women's Liberation Movement touched something deeper in me: In those two movements I not only believed that the goals and tactics were right and necessary, but I also saw that I could personally and concretely do something that could really change the situation and begin to make our vision a reality.

5. The title of that paper prompted Stokely Carmichael's now quite infamous remark, "The only position for women in SNCC is prone." Ruby Doris Smith Robinson, a major figure in SNCC's history, had been in the organization since the Freedom Rides and was elected its executive secretary in 1966. She died in October 1967, of an internal condition complicated by periodic imprisonment and overwork.

forward a formal resolution calling for full participation of women in the organization, and work in, among other areas, communal child care, equality in household tasks, and abortion rights.

Meanwhile, certain social developments outside of New Left circles created fertile ground for a movement of women.

More and more women were entering the paid economy. Professional women became increasingly dissatisfied with their unequal opportunities. In 1961, in part to quell a rising concern with equal rights, the President's Commission on the Status of Women was created. Many U.S. women were beginning to get restless. In 1963, in *The Feminine Mystique*, Betty Friedan called the malaise of housewives, "the problem that has no name."

The discontent of women in the professional middle class led to their creation in 1966 of the National Organization of Women, NOW. These women wanted economic and legal equality in professional life; however, they accepted traditional sex roles, including women's primary responsibility for the home. They did not, at that time, address the oppression stemming from women's prescribed "private" roles as wives and mothers—or the conflict between women's old role in the home and their growing role as paid workers outside of it. A more basic challenge to the sexual division of labor was needed.

This challenge would come from another, younger group of women. For the most part, we were not yet tied down to marriage, family, or career. We were at a crucial age when, having finished college, we had to face life decisions about these very issues. Our education and training for careers had been (or seemed) nearly the same as men's. But the futures we had to face at home and at work were quite different.

Outside the economic sphere, other developments increased women's self-awareness. To some young women, the advent of the birth control pill and the counter-culture brought expectations of more equality in social relationships. The media heralded "The Pill" as a new foolproof contraceptive and the harbinger of sexual freedom for women—the "sexual revolution." Women's hopes were raised again by the emergence of a "hippie" counter-culture emphasizing gentleness, love, personal relationships, cooperation, and the rejection of the striving competitiveness of U.S. life. But the counter-culture was riddled with sex roles and sexual power trips of its own: Women who did not want sex on (some man's) demand were called "uptight chicks." And who was going to bake all that bread anyway? The raised but unmet expectations made us all the more angry and hurt.

...and a Movement!

The first media-certified Women's Liberation "event" announcing the arrival of a national movement took place at the Miss America Pageant in Atlantic City on September 7, 1968. Women from New York, New Jersey, Washington D.C., and Florida joined together to protest the "boob girlie show" in a highly publicized guerilla theater action outside. They crowned a sheep as their contest winner, and set up a "freedom trash can" to receive (their leaflet explained) "old bras, girdles, high-heeled shoes, women's magazines, curlers, and other instruments of torture to women." Headlines screamed of "bra burners"—a name of ridicule that stuck in the media although, as far as anyone who was there remembers, no bras were burned. Now, however, across the nation, television viewers and newspaper readers realized what smaller groups of women had already known: women were ready to make some changes.

Before this well-publicized action, radical women in many parts of the country had started to meet together in organizations of the mixed (male and female) movement. In Chicago, Seattle, Toronto, San Francisco, New York, Gainesville, and Boston, in all major cities, women began to say "Enough."

In Boston, small groups of women in the New Left had begun meeting informally as early as 1967. Some were groups of friends, others were made up of female members of mixed political groups such as the anti-draft organization The Resistance. Larger weekly meetings of about 50 to 75 women began after the return of five Boston women from the first national Women's Liberation conference in Chicago, Thanksgiving weekend, 1968.

Participants in these small and large groups planned a Female Liberation Conference for the spring of 1969; we expected a few hundred women at most.[6] Instead, over 500 thronged to the conference, attending workshops on such topics as Women in Socialist Countries, Self-Defense for Women, Abortion, Women and Witchcraft, and Working Women.

The five hundred women came away from the conference feeling high. For many it was the first time they had seen so many women gathered together. They joined existing small groups and formed others. Members of several old and new groups spent the summer of 1969 thrashing through the arguments for and against the creation of a new autonomous socialist Women's Liberation organization. In September these seventy women created a formal organization. We called ourselves Bread and Roses, taking the name from the cry of the Lawrence, Massachusetts textile workers, many of whom were women, during their historic strike of 1912.

6. Some of the women in these meetings were from an existing organization known as Female Liberation/Cell 16, which later published the feminist journal *No More Fun and Games*. Both women from Female Liberation and women who would later form Bread and Roses were involved in putting together the 1969 conference.

Small Groups—A New Building Block

The small group was the basic unit of participation in Bread and Roses. These groups were called in many parts of the country "rap groups," "consciousness raising groups," or "bitch sesssions." In Bread and Roses we called them "collectives."

In these collectives of seven-to-fifteen women, we told each other our life stories, poured out our feelings as women in U.S. society and especially as women in a left movement of which we had very high expectations. We shared the hurt, confusion, and anger that each of us had harbored inside, and the excitement and relief that came with the act of sharing. Time and again we said, "You, too? Whew! I thought it was just me!" We also shared the hope that maybe, just maybe, we could, all together, *do* something to change the world around us so that women would no longer be treated as second-class human beings.

First we described our feelings and experiences. We wondered, "How come in my equal relationship with my boyfriend it's always *me* who notices when we've run out of toilet paper?" "Doesn't my boss know how to make a cup of coffee?" And, as recorded in New York Radical Women's *Notes from the First Year*, "I can't stand walking down the street by the construction workers on their lunch hour; they undress me with their eyes and I don't know which way to look." "If you don't want to sleep with him, he assumes you're hung up and then you have to stay up the whole night anyway, convincing him you're not."

Then we tried to analyze the experiences. We looked at the ways we were brought up to be good little girls—at all the agents of our socialization that contributed to our feeling that we could do certain things but we couldn't do others. We took a new look at our families, our schools, our churches, and especially the media. Thus, intuitively, we started a process of analysis that has characterized the Women's Liberation Movement since that time: starting from our own experiences, our own conditions of oppression, and from there generalizing to other women's condition and the larger institutions of U.S. society and from there thinking of strategies for change. In this task we were aided by our experiences in the New Left, by our commitment to a basic change that included all oppressed groups, not just women.

This sharing of painful experiences had models in the Chinese notions of "speaking bitterness" or "speaking pains to recall pains." We began by venting our fury at men, our most immediate oppressors. In particular we talked about how invisible and taken for granted we had felt in the left and in our relationships. And we began to explore our relationships with women—to trust and value women more. A group in Bread and Roses evaluating the first year of the collective wrote, "We've been through a stage of working out our own consciousness, understanding our past. This has taken the form of being angry at men a lot...That's been really crucial for us, a way of beginning to shed self-blame, self-hate for who we are. We're really feeling, instead of intellectualizing, that it's not our fault, as we find other women sharing our experience. And now, as we're ready to reach out, this process has developed our politics."

A theme that ran through many of our discussions was something we began to call psychological oppression. Deeply internalizing the norms of the society, many of us had come to think less of ourselves and other women than we did of men. Each woman reproduced the society's power relationships and the values placed on the different sexes, in her own psyche and in her own relationships.

Our understanding of this phenomenon enabled us to look at the social roots of many of our deep feelings of insecurity and inadequacy. it also led us to the position that damage to the psyche of each individual—to unconscious and conscious values, images, and aspirations—was as important to struggle against as was economic exploitation or physical domination. We were aided in our recognition of this cultural domination by the black movement's pointing to the power of the (white) Man's ideology in forming black self-perceptions. The black movement countered this domination in part with the slogan "Black is Beautiful." Could women, together, make a similar affirmation about ourselves?"[7]

The process of the small group also countered an aspect of women's life that we had come to see as one of the most basic and most heinous—the privatization of personal life." women lived, by and large, alone with their day-to-day problems, separated not only by the walls of their individual kitchens but by an ideology which affirmed that people's problems were, after all, individual problems that required individual solutions.

Redstockings, a New York women's group, wrote in its manifesto about this isolation and the need to counter it: "Because we have lived so intimately with our oppressors, in isolation from each other, we have been kept from seeing our personal suffering as a political condition. This creates the illusion that a woman's relationship with her man is a matter of interplay between two unique personalities, and can be worked out individually, In reality, every such relationship is a *class* relationship, and the conflicts between individual men and women are *political* conflicts that can only be solved collectively."

Not everyone agreed with the description of women and men as "classes," but the political nature of the conflicts between men and women was undeniable. This was one of the many warning of what became a watchword of Women's

7. We looked especially to the women fighters in prominent Third World struggles as examples for ourselves. Posters of Black Panther and Vietnamese women adorned our walls, and we sought ways to

Liberation: "The personal is political, and the political is personal." Our response was to cultivate a sense of sisterhood, of solidarity with women.

From the talks we were having in our collectives, many of us experienced a new kind of life-giving energy, mobilizing both our desire to work for change and our ability to change ourselves. One woman in a Bread and Roses collective remembers, "Even outside the group meetings I think all of us found ourselves acting in a way we called 'living up to the group,' but which often did not arise out of any group discussion. The simple presence of the group in one's imagination—and the public commitment to our sex which joining the group implied—were incentive enough."

Being part of the process of creating the Women's Movement gave many woman a new sense of importance about their lives. Another Bread and Roses woman remembers, "I would not have had the sense of what it felt like to be an active participant in history, in my life, Cambridge, whatever, if I had not been in Bread and Roses. I felt like I took my first real risks in Bread and Roses."

Not that it was easy. After learning each other's histories and making some sense of them, many collectives went on to try to deal with issues confronting members in their present lives: their work, relationships, and politics. Women had to make decisions about what was "right action," and the groups tried to arrive at these decisions collectively. Not all groups were able to provide this support, especially as some members did not meet the expectations of others for commitment and change. The groups that survived this process, though, were stronger for having thrashed it out together.

Examining the lives of the members was only one of the

aid their struggles. Many women from Bread and Roses and other Women's Liberation organizations planned and participated in a large women's Panther Support Demonstration in New Haven and in the Revolutionary People's Constitutional Convention.

tasks of most small groups. Making larger analyses of women in the society, reaching out to bring more women into the movement, carrying out small public actions, such as guerrilla theater and "zap" actions—all were taken on. In addition our collectives socialized together—going on retreats, cooking dinner together, going on day trips.

Consciousness raising in the small group was both a means to mobilize increasing numbers of women and a source for generating ideas and analysis about Women's Liberation. It was both structure and content; it re-introduced to the left the importance of small units which mobilize people for larger movements. The personal, again, is political.

In other cities besides Boston, the creation of these groups went hand in hand with the creation of larger organizations. Examples are New York Radical Women, Redstockings (also New York) Women's Liberation Front in Berkeley, and similar groups in Oakland and Seattle. These organizations identified themselves as part of an automous Women's Liberation Movement.

Autonomy and Analysis

By an "autonomous" movement we mean a movement by, for, and of women—one that would analyze women's position in U.S. society and act to change women's condition in the context of a broader struggle for revolutionary change in the society.

Autonomy differed from separatism in that we saw our struggle as integrally tied to that of blacks, workers, and other oppressed groups fighting for radical change. But as long as a racist, sexist, capitalist society continued to oppress different groups differently, it would be necessary for each group to bring its own experience to bear, in its own way. We had learned from history that unless women are articulating their own demands, these demands are not taken up by progressive movements. The example Bread and Roses women cited most often had occurred one hundred years earlier, when the women abolitionists who had worked hard to free the slaves wanted then to demand universal suffrage for women and men, rather than simply suffrage for black men. Male abolitionists told them, "This is the Negro's hour. Don't ruin it by adding your cause too." The wait turned out to be a long one. We were determined not to be trapped into thinking that the issue of our liberation had to wait until "after the revolution."

The goals of the autonomous women's movement differed, too, from the notions of government commissions on the status of women. We thought of ourselves as revolutionaries; we did not just want equal rights for women in this society—we did not want a bigger piece of the existing pie—we wanted a different, socialist society. From our analysis we thought we could not win either equality or liberation for women without a total social transformation. We anguished over the war in Vietnam and the repression of the Panthers. And, in fact, we felt that the more we acted from our own experience as women, the better revolutionaries we were becoming. Members of a Bread and Roses work group on Strategy and Tactics for the Women's Movement wrote: "Previously we named the enemy as capitalism but didn't really understand its encroachment on our lives; it's been through the understanding of female oppression that we understand how it affects us and challenges us to move."

The idea of an autonomous movement did not come into being instantly. We developed it, in large part, because of the lack of response (or negative response) to Women's Liberation from the male-dominated left, with its supposedly egalitarian and revolutionary vision, in which we had invested our hopes and time and energy.

At first we identified the problem merely as "male chauvinism"—the attitude of condescending to women, and undervaluing women, that men (and women) acquired as part of their upbringing. Two Bread and Roses members wrote, "Chauvinism is when we spoke in meetings only to find the next speaker responding to the speaker before us—as if we did not exist; it is when we found men repeating ideas that *we* had formulated earlier, as if they were original; it is why most of us never spoke at all in meetings."

When "chauvinism" was the enemy, we still thought we could solve the problem by trying to reform individual men; an attitude was, after all, merely an attitude. Reasoned argument would lead the errant men to see the fault of their attitudes and then to change. However, as we attempted to explain our thoughts to comrades, friends, and lovers, we met more resistance than we anticipated.

One famous example that quickly entered early Women's Liberation lore took place early in 1969 in Washington D.C., at a counter-demonstration to Nixon's first inauguration, sponsored by a coalition of anti-war groups. Different groups of women, especially from New York and Washington, planned activities including tearing up their voter registration cards to show that women's suffrage had done little to bring women's equality. Ellen Willis, a Redstockings member from New York, describes what took place: "Our moment comes. M. from Washington group gets up to speak. This isn't the protest against movement men, which is second on the agenda. just fairly innocuous radical rhetoric—except that it's a good looking woman talking about women. The men go crazy. 'Take it off!' 'Take her off the stage and fuck her!' They yell and guffaw at unwitting double entendres like 'We must take to the streets.' "[8]

8. Ellen Willis, "Up From Radicalism: A Feminist Journal," in *US No.2,* Bantam, October 1969, p.114.

There were some men who supported us. Others said it was our problem, not theirs. Others denied that this was an issue on the left, or for the left. Often the response was liberal and paternalistic, patting us on our heads and approving of our "doing our own thing," while the men would go out to make the revolution. There was also a kind of "second-level" chauvinism, which assumed that anytime a Women's Liberation person spoke at a mixed meeting it must be to denounce some example of chauvinism—so they could not hear what we were saying on any other subject.

Repeated instances of ridicule and being ignored led to intense anger and a desire to separate from the mixed movement. A spate of very bitter articles denouncing the male chauvinism and men of the male-dominated movement quickly poured out: Marge Piercy's "Grand Coulee Damn" and Robin Morgan's "Goodbye to All That" reflected and refueled that anger. One verse of a song written by four Boston women ran:

The Women's Liberation Jugband Blues
Papa wants a political woman
Just not very much
Papa wants a political woman
Just not very much
She knows how to type, and she likes to screw
She agrees with all of his theories, too
Papa wants a political woman,
Just not very much.

We had underestimated the power of *male supremacy* on the left and in the society. Convincing men to change, changing attitudes, was not enough. The problem went much deeper. By male supremacy we meant the institutional, all-encompassing power that men as a group have over women, the systematic exclusion of women from power in the society, and the systematic devaluation of all the roles and traits which the society has assigned to women. Slowly we came to realize that we had to confront and attack male supremacy as a whole system.

This understanding required new strategies for change. Argument and moral suasion were inadequate to the task. And arguing with men took our time and energy away from reaching and talking with women.

We had the example of the black movement before us, implying a basic assumption about change—that no white man in a position of power is going to abdicate voluntarily. We drew also the implication that each oppressed group had to analyze its particular oppression. Thus we set about creating our own organizations and our own movement, seeking to build a presence so strong and so visible that other political groups and the society's institutions would have to take heed of our critique and demands.

What We Did

One of the ways we made the new movement visible was through street demonstrations. Most notable among the large demonstrations which Bread and Roses organized were the International Women's Day marches, held on March 8.

First observed in 1908, International Women's Day had been lost (in this country) in the intervening years.[9] In 1970, Bread and Roses and other Women's Liberation groups in

9. The holiday began in the U.S., as Women's Day, in 1908, when a group of socialist women in New York organized a mass demonstration of working women for suffrage. In 1910 it was voted an international holiday by the International Conference of Women Socialists. An International Women's Day march by female textile workers in St. Petersburg, in 1917, was the spark that ignited the February Revolution that overthrew the Tsar. (The "February Revolution" could follow International Women's Day because Russia at the time used a different calendar than Western countries.)—ed.

other cities reclaimed the tradition. We made grand plans. Some of us sewed banners and flags, others crocheted many-hued hats. The flags, modeled on the flag of the National Liberation Front of South Vietnam but with different colors, featured a black band for anarchism, a red band for communism, and a brightly colored star of flowered material—for joyfulness and creativity of women. The day before, Bread and Roses members leafleted (and sang) in downtown streets to publicize the demonstration; one reported that reactions ranged "from curiosity to interest to one elderly woman who said, 'God love you.' "

The march itself, attended by over 500 women, passed the Charles Street Jail so that women prisoners could hear it go by, the downtown office area where thousands of women worked as secretaries, fashionable shops where women's images were sold, and the Massachusetts General Hospital where we chanted for "Free abortions, Free health care." Songs written for the occasion were sung, and copies of a "Women's Declaration of Independence" were distributed to onlookers. All along the way we plastered buildings with stickers bearing slogans: "Not with *my* body you don't!" "This ad insults women!" And just "Women's Liberation!"

But the bulk of our political work went on less visibly—in the collectives, in general meetings, in small actions known as "zaps," and in project groups organized around specific goals.

From the first, structure had been an issue of contention in the new women's organizations. Many of the founding members of Bread and Roses had gone through long debates within the New Left, and especially SDS, about structure; these debates had revolved around criticism of representative democracy and moving toward "participatory democracy," with the slogan "let the people decide." Explicit in this political direction was a distrust of formal structure.

Many Women's Liberation activists equated structure with hierarchy, with emphasizing status differences and stimulating passivity rather than active participation. Most women's groups opted for minimal visible structure. A description of the typical Bread and Roses meeting gives a sense of what this meant. These "mass meetings" (assemblies of the general membership) were held weekly. Often 75 to 100 women attended—most of us rarely if ever having been in a room with so many women.

It is 8:00 pm on a Friday night, and the room is filled. Some women are laughing and joking in small groups. Some are in twos, catching up with each others' lives. Others are hugging or holding hands affectionately. A few people are reading leaflets or notes they're written to themselves. Some are arguing over a recent article or political action.

Between 8:00 and 8:15 several women start suggesting that the meeting begin; it takes a while for this sentiment to waft across the room. After the meeting has come to order, announcements echo from many parts of the room—calls for actions or study groups, a description of a new women's journal, a report on a recent demonstration. Stragglers wander in, many of them quietly, recognizing their disruption; a few playing kazoos, openly challenging the ideas of order and schedule. Most meetings have at least one substantive political topic to discuss. The discussion is carried on haphazardly, with emotional interjections of "This freaks me out!" or "I'm uncomfortable" often superseding substantive debate.

These meetings were important for women in collectives to learn what other collectives were doing and thinking, to coordinate actions, and to hear about the larger Women's Liberation Movement across the country. Examples of discussion topics in the mass meetings in Bread and Roses in the summer of 1970 were, "What does it mean for us as women to be revolutionaries?" "Stop depending on the Man; Learning and Sharing Skills," and "Our Experience in Collectives."

But the women coming to these meetings were concerned about the process of the meeting as well as the content. We wanted as many people as possible to feel comfortable talking, realizing that most women were not confident of their ideas or of their ability to present them. In New York, Redstockings provided each woman with a store of chips. Each time she talked, a woman would give up one of her chips. When all her chips were gone, she could not make any more contributions that evening; those women with chips took over the rest of the meeting.

The interjection of "This freaks me out!" in a Bread and Roses meeting was the near equivalent of a point of order. Whatever was being discussed would be put aside to deal with the particular woman's feelings. In part, this followed from a belief that women have similar feelings and experiences; if one person is uncomfortable with the direction or atmosphere of a meeting, so probably are many others. In part, it was an attempt to remedy the past injustices of women not being heard. The style of emphasizing feelings over structure made strides in the direction of democracy and egalitarianism, but sometimes forfeited progress in planned discussions. In extreme form it tended to install a "tyranny of structurelessness" —without clear procedures or responsibility for conducting meetings, power could drift to those with the clearest preconceived goals, or the most skill in public speaking.

The over-all loose and decentralized structure helped give rise to the popularity of "zap actions." Zaps were often one-shot deals, in which a group of women would go to some public place to expose the sexism of an institution or activity. Often theatrical, zaps usually featured costumes or skits as well as leaflets. The point was to reach new people, women and men, in new ways, and to give a quick jiggle to spectators' normal ways of seeing things.

An example is the Bread and Roses "Ogle-In" of July 1970, where men in a busy shopping area were given women's traditional treatment of stares, whistles, catcalls, and pinches. "Don't hide it all under a suit!" the women urged. "Smile honey. What's the matter, lost your sense of humor?" Female passersby were given leaflets and, according to one participant, "It was beautiful—they understood right away."

Zap actions had been popularized by WITCH, a New York group whose name stood for different words, depending on the situation. (Women's International Terrorist Conspiracy from Hell, or Women Incensed at Telephone Company Harassment). Their first public action was on Halloween 1968, when, dressed as witches, they "hexed" the New York Stock Exchange. One of their leaflets captured what the WITCH women hoped to share: "WITCH is an all-women Everything. It's theater, revolution, magic, terror, joy, garlic, flowers, spells. It's an awareness that witches and gypsies were the original guerrillas and resistance fighters against oppression— particularly the oppression of women—down through the ages. WITCH lives and laughs in every woman."

Women throughout the country delightedly followed their example—to reclaim the power of the broom which had too long been a kitchen implement. Bread and Roses women hexed dating bars. Black-garbed and masked, they leafleted women only, giving them the Women's Liberation poem WITCH:

> *Witch*
> *They told me*
> *I smile prettier with my mouth closed.*
> *They said*
> *better cut your hair—*
> *long it's all frizzy,*
> *looks Jewish.*
> *They hushed me in restaurants*
> *looking around them*
> *while the mirrors above the table*
> *jeered infinite reflections*
> *of a raw square face.*

*They questioned me
when I sang in the street.
They stood taller at tea,
smoothly explaining,
my eyes on the saucers
trying to hide the hand grenade
in my pants pocket
or crouched behind the piano.
They mocked me with magazines
full of breasts and lace,
published their triumph
when the doctor's oldest son
married a sweet girl.
They told me tweed suit stories
of various careers of ladies
I woke up at night
afraid of dying.
They built screens and room dividers
to hide unsightly desire
sixteen years old
raw and hopeless
they buttoned me into dresses
covered with pink flowers.
They waited for me to finish
then continued the conversation.
I have been invisible,
weird and supernatural.
I want my black dress
I want my hair
curling wild around me
I want my broomstick
from the closet where I hid it—
tonight I meet my sisters
in the graveyard.
Around midnight*

if you stop at a red light
in wet city traffic,
watch for us against the moon.
We are screaming
we are flying
laughing and won't stop.

Another zap targeted a Boston counter-cultural radio station whose broadcast of an ad for a local drug program ended with "and if you're a chick, they need typists." In February 1970, thirty angry Bread and Roses women stormed the station protesting its sexism. They presented the station manager with eight baby chicks, pointing out that *"women* are *not* chicks." The statement they presented explained:

"The male supremacist assumption was that 'chicks' by their very nature type; we do fifteen words a minute at birth and work our way up. Many phone calls later, they modified it to, 'If you're a chick and can type, they need typists.' No men need apply—it's beneath male dignity...Could a radio station get away with an ad that ran, 'And if you're black, we need janitors?"

The action was a success: station facilities and time were given to Bread and Roses to prepare a program on Women's Liberation, which focused especially on the sexism of popular music. In addition, the protestors won time for a regular women's program which was one of the first women's radio or TV programs ever aired which did not focus on homemaking, "women's careers," and advice to the lovelorn.

Through zaps we reached people we couldn't reach in other ways. But they were more than outreach. We learned through doing them that politics could be fun. (It could also be risky, as when four Bread and Roses members were arrested for spraypainting buildings.) Zaps also sometimes led to new skills, such as the media skills several women learned as a result of the radio station action.

Some Issues—
Sexuality, Abortions, Chidcare, Work

In the project groups (which were sometimes the same as the collectives, and often not), Bread and Roses members pursued more specific objectives. Work and/or study groups generated ideas and actions around racism, imperialism, and class. But the most concrete issues involved control of our lives, our bodies, our work.

Taking control of our bodies was basic. Redefining our sexuality was a starting point for many women. Anne Koedt's "Myth of the Vaginal Orgasm," was first published in 1968 in the mimeographed New York journal *Notes from the First Year*. The idea that Papa Freud and various boyfriends and husbands had defined a women's orgasm—occurring "from the friction of the penis in the vagina"—was mind-boggling. Acceptance of this myth was internalized oppression at the deepest level. In collectives and among groups of friends, women started saying to each other, "You too?" Reclaiming our sexuality became an important part of consciousness raising. Women realized that "our bodies have been kept from us," and then we set about taking them back.

Seeking more knowledge about our bodies led us to a critique of sex education and the health care system. In Boston, a Bread and Roses project began trying to find non-sexist gynecologists to recommend to women—and compiling a warning list of doctors to avoid because of their demeaning attitudes and practices toward their women patients. This group went on to create a health course for women which was taught at adult education centers, YWCAs, high schools, and colleges, first in Boston and then all over the country. Thousands of copies of a booklet form of this course, "Women and Their Bodies," were distributed by the New England Free Press. Women throughout the nation wrote to the Bread and Roses group asking for advice and information, telling their own particular horror stories about doctors and sex. The group then expanded and revised the book and published it commercially. As *Our Bodies, Our Selves* it has become a classic for women, translated into eleven different languages, in thirteen foreign editions.

Two more specific demands for reclaiming our bodies were for safe birth control and legal abortions. The growing awareness of the dangers of the Pill and the number of unwanted pregnancies pointed to the inadequacy of present forms of birth control. We discovered later that sterilization was being foisted on many poor and Third World women without their choice and sometimes without their knowledge. We came to understand that the basic issue was choice: the right to choose when or whether to become a mother. The right to control our bodies became a basic cry.

Within this campaign perhaps the most sustained effort centered around abortion. Any woman on the street could be raped; any woman who engaged in sexual intercourse could accidently become pregnant. Although many reform groups had sought to liberalise archaic abortion laws in the past, the Women's Liberation Movement sought the *repeal* of all laws limiting abortion, and the provision of free abortions on demand.

In March 1970, Bread and Roses women disrupted the Massachusetts legislature's hearings on abortion. Wearing orange tam o'shanters, several women seized the microphone, made speeches, and performed a skit in which a woman was raped by the legislature. During the same month, a particularly well-known anti-abortion-law action was staged by the Detroit Women's Liberation Coalition. As the Michigan legislature debated a reform bill, fifty women and five men dressed in black, veils over their faces, marched to the city morgue with safety pins, coat hangers, and other means of self-abortion, They then continued to the office of William Calahan, the county prosecutor, to hex him:

Cahalan for you we made this hex
The souls of our sisters called forth the moon
To cover the sun and bring on you doom.

(After many years of struggle around abortion, women's efforts seemed to be successful with the 1973 Supreme Court decision which legalized abortion. Recently, however, forces of reaction have zeroed in on publicly funded abortions and organized to end them. In June 1977, the Supreme Court ruled that each state could decide whether or not to provide funds, and in the course of the following year more than forty states cut them off. At the same time, Congress passed the Hyde Amendment, cutting off federal funds. The 1973 decision showed that laws can be responsive to organized demands made by groups of people; but the 1977 decision underscores the fact that legal changes reflect power and the political climate, and even "rights" can be retracted.)

Another key issue was childcare. We didn't need a political analysis to tell us that primary responsibility for children fell to women. But our analysis did help us to understand the particularly oppressive aspect of that fact: the isolation of adult women separated from their peers, and of young people from other young people; the feelings of frustration arising from an activity that could be, properly organized, very satisfying.

In many cities, Women's Liberation groups addressed the issue of childcare from the start, by creating their own alternatives. In Boston, women organized playgroups which rotated childcare responsibilities among parents and other interested people. Another frequent tactic, there and elsewhere, was to make demands on institutions where women worked or went to school, to set up childcare facilities there.

Work itself was a third important area of concern. Beyond equal pay for equal work, we sought to end sex segregation and sex role stereotyping—to challenge the way work was set up.

Women were tired of getting coffee and soothing the bosses' jangled nerves, of looking busy and looking pretty, of being kept from socializing with other women. One woman, "drowning in the steno pool," wrote of ending the subservience:

"It never occurs to a great many of us—perhaps the majority— that we have a right to challenge being channeled into deadly, subservient, mindless office jobs. Even beginning to think that we have genuine reasons to be encouraged is a major step. How little we expect of our lives! We type, deliver coffee, plug ourselves into dictaphones, smile, take orders— unprotestingly die a little each day.

"But we in offices have our own ways of spittin' in Massuh's soup. We manage to break typewriters, steal supplies, forget to relay messages, use the day's mail to cover our heads on rainy days. These reactions to being dehumanized should be recognized for what they are, sabotage."[10]

Bread and Roses had an office workers' group whose members met and talked together and tried to interest co-workers in Women's Liberation. Secretaries in one downtown accounting firm began dividing up their work themselves, refusing to make their bosses' coffee, and decorating the walls with Women's Liberation posters. Those beginnings were short-lived (the Bread and Roses member in that office was fired), but they were the first steps along a path which has led to a city-wide office workers' rights group and two union locals which are seeking to organize the city's thousands of clericals.

A fourth area of concern was making ourselves strong women. We wanted to stop being targets of men on the street,

10. Madeline Belkin, "Drowning in the Steno Pool," published in 1970 in *Up From Under* magazine. The complete article is reprinted in *Liberation Now,* Dell, 1979.

victims to the whims of passerbys. Many of us studied karate and other forms of self-defense; subway stations were stickered with signs proclaiming "Disarm rapists," with a picture of a woman administering a karate kick to a man. Members of Bread and Roses' "Stick-it-in-the-wall, motherfucker" collective taught women how to street fight, how to stay together when attacked, whether in a political demonstration or merely walking down the street.

A Women's Community

Crucial to working together on all these issues were the new feelings we had about ourselves and each other. Growing up, we had learned that the most important relationship was a relationship with a man, and that the most important source of self-esteem was a man's approval. One Bread and Roses woman commented on the changes we went through:

"What we did focused attention on being a woman and what that means. It's hard to separate Bread and Roses from the Women's Movement as a whole, but in *so* many ways it made me stronger, more determined, conscious, focused, open, and into women. It made me unafraid to be independent and unwilling to settle for less than being as whole as possible."

We became close to other women and expected more from them. We also found that women were fun to be with. We were thinking about the same things. Almost anything one person brought up, someone else would find exciting. We felt, "Ahah, at last, I'm part of a group of people I really belong to— a whole group of people thinking and working together, all addressing the same questions." We began to look to each other for the kinds of support and emotional sustenance that we had been taught to look for in men. The large meetings of Bread and Roses were held on Friday nights—challenging the idea that women were supposed to have dates with *men* on weekends.

Knowing that other women were struggling in their relationships with men gave us the added strength to push through hard times in our own. Or, for many, relationships with men faded into the background. A married woman in Bread and Roses remembers, "I had the typical married woman's set-up, with a husband in the background, a generalized hatred for men, a few other husbands in limited doses, and very little contact with men during Bread and Roses." Other women preferred to remain single, some choosing celibacy over relationships which they found lacking in respect. Still others sought out other women for their couple relationships. Many women experimented with new living situations—living alone, living with other women as roommates or in communes.

As women turned to each other for affection and support that we had previously sought in men, many sensual feelings were liberated. At meetings we gave each other hugs and backrubs; in the streets we began to walk arm in arm. We felt a new freedom to explore our feelings for each other. Some of us made love with women we loved; some of us "came out." For some women lesbianism was an extension of the desire to be completely self-sufficient. Or, many times, the women's movement provided a safe enough place to open up new sexual feelings.

But also, at times, women who were already lesbians found it difficult to be "out" in the Women's Movement. Tensions arose as both heterosexual and lesbian women felt guilty or forced up against the wall about their choice. Was lesbianism *the* logical extension of feminism? (As one woman put it, "Feminism is the theory, lesbianism is the practice.") Or was it just *one* natural outgrowth of our feelings and activities? Both straight and gay women could not help but internalize the heterosexual bias of the dominant culture, and we had to identify it and fight it. However much tension there was, though, an important new option was opening for women, bringing the possibility of being in more egalitarian and respectful relationships.

There were other tensions besides that between gay and straight. Conflicts arose too between married women and single women. The whole process of changing our relationships with women and men was not easy; it was not always a barrel of fun. We spoke of "struggling" toward new types of relationships because it was indeed a draining task, and painful, even as it was energizing. People had such varying expectations, and were never sure how far to push. How much could we moderate jealousy? How much confrontation could we stand? How much should we or could we struggle with this man, or that woman? How could we possibly overcome so many years of socialization? But amidst the anguish we did have a vision of how our lives *could* be which propelled many of us on. And our changing relationships laid the basis for a new and strong community of women.

The theoretical expression of this struggle toward a women's community was the concept of "sisterhood." In part, this was merely a political name for the feelings of closeness, respect, and solidarity. In part it reflected our desire for the intensity, permanence, and reliability of a "family." Also, the family metaphor was borrowed from the black movement, where people called each other, "sister" and "brother" to indicate solidarity and the creation of a community separate from "the Man." We felt, too, the potential power of great numbers of women banding together in "sisterhood." And counting on other women as sisters challenged the idea that individuals had to make it on their own. We quite consciously provoked the surprise and dismay of straight liberal groups who would ask for one speaker on Women's Liberation and get three; they would ask, "Who is *the* speaker?" and the Bread and Roses group would respond, "We are."

Women's Culture

Accompanying the creation of a women's community was the creation of a new women's culture, expressed in poetry, music, dance, song, spraypainting, and a host of other media. One Bread and Roses newsletter encouraged us, "Re media: sayitwriteitsingitplayitliveit." We were actively confronting dominant culture which we labeled as white, male, and middle-class on many levels. Individually and collectively, we rejected the old values and sought to express our new values in many different forms.

Publications mushroomed: in Boston, the newspaper *Hysteria* and the journals *The Second Wave* and *No More Fun and Games,* as well as many stories in the radical newspaper *The Old Mole* which had a strong women's caucus. Nationally, *Off Our Backs, Women: A Journal of Liberation, It Ain't Me Babe,* and numerous others around the country helped us share our ideas and experiences.

Some wrote bitterly of our socialization as women:

It's not that I miss you
But I got into the habit of loving
And I have to be
Retrained
in a usable skill.

Others made angry suggestions:

REVOLUTIONARY
SURVIVAL: LESSON ONE
MORE WOMEN
SHOULD THROW
MORE DISHES
AT MORE WALLS
MORE OFTEN

We sang new songs, often written collectively, at demonstrations and sometimes at meetings. One rousing song by a Bread and Roses member, to the tune of the *Battle Hymn of the Republic* was called "The Battle Hymn of Women:"

Mine eyes have seen the glory of the flame of women's rage,
Kept smoldering for centuries, now burning in this age,
We no longer will be pris'ners in that same old gilded cage
For we are marching on
CHORUS: Move on over or we'll move on over you
Move on over or we'll move on over you
Move on over or we'll move on over you
For women's time has come.

It is we who've done your cooking, done your cleaning, kept your rules,
We've kept this system running but we're laying down our tools,
For we are marching on.
We have broken through our shackles, now we sing a battle song
We march for liberation and we're many thousand strong,
We'll build a new society; we waited much too long,
But we are marching on.

> *(words by Meredith Tax based on a Civil Rights song by Len Chandler.)*

Where before, to dance, you had to go to a mixed party and wait for a man to ask you to dance with him—now you could just dance. Our all-women's dances and parties were memorable. For many it was the first opportunity to dance with other women, in circles and groups rather than couples, and to music that did not denigrate women. Newly formed women's rock bands, singing songs for women, were a far cry from the Rolling Stones' "Stupid Girl."

Some women took up traditional "feminine" crafts—expressions of creativity that had historically been the province of women flourished in new ways in this supportive atmosphere. Women knitted, crocheted, beaded, and embroidered everywhere (in meetings, visiting, on subways, watching television) in bright colors celebrating womanhood.

At the same time, many learned traditionally masculine skills. Sometimes these were called survival skills; they included self-defense, auto mechanics, carpentry, electrical wiring, and plumbing. While some of these women have become full-time carpenters, mechanics, and printers, others were satisfied to develop confidence in being able to fix things when necessary, and still others found the *idea* that such work was within their grasp more important than actually mastering a new skill. One Bread and Roses woman remembers her "few efforts at mechanical self-help (e.g., fixing stereo wires)— mainly what was important was a less helpless *attitude* about such things."

The End and the Beginning

The Women's Liberation Movement's innovative actions, its demonstrations (both angry and festive), and its distinctive culture made us a visible presence throughout the country. We also made serious attempts to reach out to as-yet-uninvolved women personally. We spoke in groups of two's and three's and four's in as many places as we got invitations: churches, colleges, temples, YWCAs, women's organizations—to high school women, older women, housewives, and suburban women. What we said touched women's lives, and they responded. Often there were more requests that we could fulfill.

Bread and Roses also held weekly orientation meetings for new women. So many women came to these weekly meetings, wanting to become part of the Women's Liberation

Movement! Held at Sergeant Brown's Memorial Necktie coffeehouse begun by women and men in the anti-draft movement, these meetings featured introductory raps by members of our orientation committee who would continue to meet regularly with that group of women to help them become a Bread and Roses collective. (Sometimes this worked out better in theory than in practice.) But even some women who never joined a collective found these meetings important. One such woman remembers:

"I was probably never a legitimate member of Bread and Roses, but it was a beacon in a storm for me during the '69-70-71 period. I used to go to meetings in Cambridge where the other women simply would talk and let others know their struggles, pains and frustrations. I was attending a Catholic women's college...and if it hadn't been for women like those I met at Bread and Roses, the literature, the thoughts, the feelings, the very *life,* new life that they let me become part of, they proved did really exist, well, I'd still be hoping to achieve vaginal orgasm, or dressing up for goddamn fashion shows. If it hadn't been for B & R, who knows what..."

Television and newspapers, quick to recognize provocative copy, brought the Movement to far more people than we ever could have. Spreading the word was a help, but the words *they* used weren't always helpful. In diffusing information, they generally defused the message. A sensational image emerged: ugly manhaters, "bra-burners." Or a lifeless one: "Women's Lib," a glib popularization which had none of the emotional meaning of "Liberation," but suggested merely a fad, a craze.

Those media figures who tried to be sympathetic usually weakened the message to the need for women to have equal pay at work, and maybe get some help with childcare. But others pandered to people's fears of change, and some women readers and viewers became afraid that Women's Liberation meant they would be drafted into the army (though mostly, we opposed both the draft and the army), or would have to become competitive career women interested only in money and success.

Still, our ideas about the need for basic change in sex roles, work, and the family touched many women. Those who could find us swelled the ranks of the decentralized Women's Liberation organizations; their newly stimulated feminist rage brought us new insights. Growth brought conflicts as well.

Some new women felt that from reading about the Movement their consciousness was already "raised." They didn't want to sit around and *talk;* they wanted to *do.* Organizations such as Bread and Roses were not equipped with enough projects for them to work on, nor with the structural mechanisms to set up new ones. Nor, really, was there a coherent strategy that could be invoked to help us decide what kind of work should be done. And amidst this confusion, some of us lost sight, too, of the fact that consciousness raising is itself a continual process.

After a time, these first Women's Liberation organizations began to wane. This was in the context of a New Left that was, in the early '70s, seeing most of its organizations factionalize and disintegrate. Our commitment to minimal structure and leaderlessness, while avoiding some of the tendencies toward factional rivalries, infighting, and leadership conflicts that plagued much of the left, beseiged us with problems of keeping an organization running, preserving lines of communication and responsibility, and recognizing and holding accountable the leaders who did emerge. Political disagreements, some which may have been present but tolerable at first, also worsened over time. Among those were polarizations between "feminists" and "politicos," between "gay" and "straight" women, and between those who wanted a clearer structure and those who wanted less formal structure.

In sum, what happened by 1971 was that the original moment of self-definition of a Women's Liberation Movement had passed.[11] The barrage of media interpretations and the decline of organization meant that a coherent program of Women's Liberation, a direction for the Movement, never developed on a national level. We still need to spend consider-tionship, even a one-to-one encounter, between a woman and a Women's Liberation, by feminism, and more precisely by socialist-feminism. We are still working to meet the fundamental challenge that we threw down: how, together as women, to act to change *all* the power relations of our society and its institutions.

Many of our insights, however, have continued to spread. What we called male supremacy—the idea that women are not equal to men in this society—is accepted as fact by many people, and the idea that this inequality should be changed is accepted by a great number. Sexual politics—that any relationship, even a one-to-one encounter, between a woman and a man is mediated and shaped by the fact that men as a group have more power than women as a group—can no longer be denied. We were talking about power, not just discrimination. Recognizing the structured, institutionalized nature of that

---

11. All along some people had criticized others for not being "feminist" enough or not being "political" enough—for being concerned only with "leftist" issues or being concerned only with "woman's" issues. "Feminists" feared that some women were using the Women's Movement to further other goals; "politicos" thought other women weren't making the larger connections.

These tensions often resulted from unclear communication, and usually some kind of uneasy peace could be made. But the identity of personal and political sometimes was questioned when practical programatic choices had to be made. One Bread and Roses member talks about her memories of this issue:

"We went around tripping out on the idea that "the personal is

power pointed, for many women, to the need for collective rather than personal solutions.

The political is no longer conceived to be solely in the realm of government, or even (in the traditional leftist sense) solely in the world of economic forces and economic exploitation. Issues that were once considered private—sexuality, the family, how you look and act—are now seen as political. Personal life does not merely reflect politics; it *is* politics. Even more important was our understanding that the power relations are internalized by both men and women, and that they are continually being reproduced in our daily lives.

Following from this was our insight that we must change ourselves in order to change society—we became the raw material of our own politics. How we live now affects our vision of the future; thus the Women's Movement has continued to emphasize that the process of our lives and politics is as important as our goals. (So too women have continued to form consciousness raising groups, to set up alternative institutions, and to provide support services.)

The need for all people to try out more parts of their personalities and be less stereotyped into rigid sex roles is more and more commmonly recognized. We successfully challenged the idea that men are doers and women are objects; that men are providers and women are nurturers; that men are presidents and women are secretaries.

political" and you could get into orgasms and that was going to revolutionize the state...How to really understand those connections isn't so easy. But that's what Bread and Roses really wanted to do, to say that...it was as legitimate to run the consciousnessness raising group for the eight suburban housewives as to run the anti-war action. The Vietnamese people dying, that's a priority, and on the other hand (it was important) not to get caught up in priorities that you could forget everyone's day-to-day existence. I mean, who can figure that out, of course, (the organization would)fall apart!

The reflections of this changed consciousness—changed by the struggle we began—are all around us. They can be seen in some tiny reforms now taken for granted, such as the right of female teenagers to wear pants to school; in newer reforms such as increasing female participation in athletics; and in larger battles, such as the one over sex segregation in work and affirmative action.

Out of the ashes of the first organizations (and often womaned by the same people) have risen numerous projects such as community health care centers, rape crisis centers, women's schools, and daycare centers. The success of the International Women's Year conference in Houston in 1977 testifies to the spread of the ideas and the continuing recruitment of activists. More than 10,000 women—delegates and observers—passed resolutions in favor of freedom of sexual preference (including non-discrimination against lesbians, and lesbians' rights to child custody) and reproductive freedom (including the right to choose to have an abortion). They supported the Equal Rights Amendment and condemned racism. Women who had previously disagreed on many of these controversial issues now united, showing that these concerns, so long pushed by the Women's Liberation Movement, touched something that was real for these thousands of women.

Unfortunately, our successes are not the whole story. The resurgence of reaction on the right testifies both to the continuing importance in people's daily lives of the issues we raised, and to the imbeddedness of male supremacy in the society. It shows us that reforms are not enough and that gains once made must still be struggled for, or we may lose them.

The current mobilization by the right on "personal" issues—the fight against the Equal Rights Amendment, medicaid abortions, and gay rights—reflects real insecurities that people experience around the tenuous nature of family and community, and real fears around sexuality, intimacy, and care. These anxieties are created by life in advanced capitalist society, but they are manipulated by the right into anti-woman positions. An example is the position that only if women stay in the home, providing nurturance and glueing the family together, can men and children expect stable, secure, and supportive living situations. If women don't act as emotional providers, they argue, who will?

When we in Bread and Roses and the Women's Liberation Movement first said that the personal is political, we meant to point to the political nature of what too many people still feel are "private" personal issues difficult or impossible to change. We meant too that there could be no personal or individual solutions to the pains of everyday life, generated as they are not only by the structures of government and economics but also by the structures of sexuality and gender. The fears that the right now plays upon—of isolation and worthlessness—are those we identified for women so many years ago. They still need to be addressed, by the Women's Movement and indeed by the left as a whole.

Women's rally in support of jailed Black Panther sisters, New Haven, Connecticut, 1969.   Photo by Barbara Rothkrug.

8

Something New Emerges:
The Growth of a Socialist Feminist

Leslie Cagan went into the streets for her first women's action when she was about five years old—though as she points out, in the early '50s no one knew that's what it was. Her particular personal/political history from that time to this is the history of one woman's participation in the movements of the New Left, and in particular of her path into the Women's Liberation Movement and her position today as a lesbian and a socialist-feminist.

The experiences which shape her consciousness range from cutting sugar cane in Cuba to womaning a national anti-war office in New York to living in a communal household in St. Louis. No person's history/herstory is "typical" of a movement, but each person's story captures some of the essence of any movement in a way that organizational chronicles cannot do. Leslie Cagan's story, especially, reflects in microcosm the ways in which the Women's Liberation Movement has been both a continuation of an existing left tradition and a break with it.

Leslie Cagan

Besides the activities she describes in this interview, Leslie Cagan has worked for HealthPAC (a radical organization doing research and education on the health care delivery system), and for the past several years has taught women's studies and gay literature at the University of Massachsetts in Boston. A formative experience was her personal interaction with the "criminal justice system" after indictment and arrest in 1969 for taking part in disruptive demonstrations against the Vietnam War and a pending Blue Cross/Blue Shield rate increase. She is a member of the national committee of the People's Alliance, an outgrowth of the July 4, 1976 counter-Bicentennial demonstrations, which is trying to make concrete links among different anti-imperialist constituencies and struggles.

I grew up in New York City, and had what I think is the good fortune to come from a "red diaper" family. My parents had once been in the Communist Party and had continued to be politically active. I had the added good fortune that my parents' ideas about politics continued to change through the 1950's and 1960's. So there was a lot of support not only for political activism, but for trying new things and breaking out of old ways of moving.

I have a series of memories of events that, with hindsight, I can see how each played a role in my coming to political maturity. At the time they were all isolated things that didn't necessarily hang together, but I can now see how they affected both my understanding and my emotional commitment to my politics.

I must have been in kindergarten, maybe even before, when I went on my first demonstration. We lived in a housing project and there were thousands of kids in the neighborhood, and one street corner where four or five streets converged without a stoplight. Kids kept getting hit by cars. So the mothers organized a demonstration which, looking back on it from the context of the Women's Movement, was a women's action, although I don't know that the women who organized it saw it that way. They went out on the street with their kids and blocked traffic, demanding a stoplight.

They never did win that light, unfortunately, just a stop sign. But what stuck with me was the notion that if you were upset about something, you could go out and say it to other people. You could tell total strangers you wanted something to change. I also learned that you could stop traffic, which was to come back later, in the '60s, as an important lesson.

There is also some recollection of the Rosenbergs.[1] I must have been six in 1953 so I don't recall the Rosenbergs very well. I do remember knowing that they were going to be killed, which was quite confusing, quite not-understandable. But that was very distant, and what I remember much more vividly was one meeting held in the project about a big demonstration that was going to happen in Washington, D.C., and all these adults were trying to figure out what to do with the kids. Should they take us along or leave us at home? They decided to leave us home, and they drew straws to see who would stay back and do the childcare. For some reason this stuck with me, that this issue of what was happening with the kids was important.

Later on I went with my family to ban-the-bomb demonstrations at the United Nations and Hiroshima Day commemorations. I remember this in combination with wearing dog tags we got at school. They gave us dog tags with our name and address on them, and the teachers told us the reason we wore these was that if an atom bomb ever fell on us, and we were burned beyond recognition, they would know who we were.

1. Julius and Ethel Rosenberg were executed on June 19, 1953. They were convicted of conspiring to commit espionage—specifically, of having passed the "secret" of the atomic bomb to the Russians—but were in fact the victims of the Cold War/McCarthy witchhunts of the '50s. Morton Sobell, their co-defendant, spent nineteen years in prison.

I think that for a whole generation of people around my age, growing up knowing that somebody—some Dr. Strangelove general or politician—could push the wrong button and you could just be blown away really shaped our consciousness about war. In part I now think it was this fear that pushed us to question the control politicians had over us and to take direct action, in the streets when necessary.

The next phase of my political growth came at the height of the Civil Rights Movement. I was young, but I knew that being Black in America meant a kind of oppression that no one else experiences. I remember going to a meeting that was held in a Black church in Brooklyn. Jim Peck had just come back from one of the Freedom Rides, and he had literally just gotten out of the hospital.[2] He had bandages on his head, his arm was in a sling, and he actually couldn't speak very well. I don't remember anything he said, but I remember what he looked like. It was a very emotional experience for me, that here was someone (a pacifist) riding on a bus because he believed Black people should be treated equally, and he had been severely beaten.

I was too young myself to go South, but there were people my older brother knew who went, and it was in the air. I wasn't too young to collect money for CORE (The Congress of Racial Equality) on the subway or to go to the Woolworth's picket lines in New York.[3] I went mostly with my brother, on cold winter mornings when we'd go and walk around for twenty minutes and then have to go in someplace to get warmed up, and then go back outside. And it was exciting,

2. Jim Peck, a member of the original CORE Freedom Ride of May 1961 (see p. 2), was beaten into unconsciousness with fists and pipes by six white men in Birmingham, Alabama.
3. The Woolworth's pickets—in support of the sit-ins at the chain's Southern lunch counters—were an attempt to bring civil rights work to the North.

being out on the street, even though it was freezing and I couldn't tell how people walking by responded. I also wasn't too young to go to the all-night vigils waiting for news of Goodman, Schwerner, and Chaney.[4]

Internationally, the revolution in Cuba and then the Cuban missile crisis were both real and important events for me. Finally, poor people on an island controlled by United States business had taken the matter into their own hands and were rebuilding their country. The revolution made sense to me. What didn't make sense was waking up one morning in 1962 to find our country on the brink of war—with the underlying threat of nuclear weapons being used. My younger sister and I came home from school at lunch-time every day and listened to the radio to see what was happening. I was scared and wondered why the U.S. was pushing this one so hard—it seemed crazy to me.

So, until the mid-sixties, those were the kinds of things that were shaping who I was and what I thought about. Of course, the other thing that was part of it—this is completely hindsight—was growing up in a family that, even though I was a girl, encouraged me to go to school, to think, to be active. Growing up in the '50s and being not only white but also in a family that was moving from a working class background into middle class comforts meant that certain expectations were raised. For sure, not all women who came out of that context ended up at the same place, but the combination of these facts of my life helped lead me to believe that I could do whatever I wanted to do. It was to become an issue later on, in the flowering of consciousness in the Women's Liberation Movement. But in the '50s and early '60s, for me there was no question about it. At one point I thought I would like to be a Senator. Being President seemed like too big a job, but I

4. Civil rights workers murdered in Mississippi (see p. 30).

thought I might someday run for the Senate or the House or something.

One other thing that happened, the summer I was seventeen, was that I had a sexual relationship with a woman. We were both seventeen, and the relationship was good and very loving and caring. We also knew that we shouldn't talk about it to anyone else, but I'll come back to all this later.

I graduated from high school in 1964, which put me in college from 1964 to 1968—very exciting and explosive political times. I was in New York City, at New York University, and very active. A group of us got together around a hodge-podge of issues; we were sort of a Friends of SNCC chapter, and sort of an SDS chapter. By the spring of 1966, we decided to focus in on the War in Vietnam. By then it was clear that thousands of American soldiers were fighting in Vietnam, and President Johnson had already begun bombing North Vietnam. It is hard to recall now just why everyone in that group was drawn to this issue, but I am sure that at least for myself there was a great sense of moral outrage pushing me.

In the main building of NYU our anti-war committee set up a literature table. This was unheard of. Everybody congregated in the lobby but nobody ever did anything political in that space. One day we just went and put out our literature, and from then on we were constantly discussing and arguing about the war. We did what in those days was a most outrageous thing. We put up pictures, posters actually of people who had been burned by napalm. Nobody had ever put anything on those walls, and there we were covering them with these posters. People were shocked and pushed into a great deal of discussion and debate. I think this was some of the best work we did, just pushing people to think about things.

This had a number of effects on me. One was that I never went to classes. I was always out there discussing. And so I was forced to become more articulate about what I was feeling. I couldn't just have feelings that the war was bad, which was how I started out. I had to explain why it was bad and why it happened in the first place. I slowly began to see that it wasn't some bad mistake of American foreign policy but rather it seemed to fit right in with our government's intervention policies throughout the world. Hadn't the Marines already landed in Santo Domingo? And didn't the U.S. really back up the Bay of Pigs invasion into Cuba? On top of that it became clearer that this country doesn't just fall into "bad mistakes;" there are people in Washington constantly projecting long-range policy. Finally, I also could see that the needs of big business in this country also had something to do with keeping this war going.

It was in that context that I developed an anti-imperialist consciousness. It wasn't just that war is bad but rather that the nature of U.S. capitalism and imperialism had created this war. It also became clearer to me that the Vietnamese people were fighting for the right to control their own lives, their own country. The principle of self-determination made a great deal of sense to me.

It's hard to chronicle the exact stages of that development, which of course didn't just happen to me as an individual. It all happened very quickly and there was always a lot going on. We talked about the war constantly. And we read articles in underground papers and left journals; there were teach-ins and speeches that filled in a lot of the factual information and drew out the more theoretical implications. I guess I really didn't take note of it at the time, but it was always the men writing the articles and making the speeches.

The next effect was that I was extremely busy. I was running around constantly: helping to fix the mimeo machine, doing the mailings, collecting bus money for trips to anti-war demonstrations in Washington, getting the posters, negotiating with the school administration. By the fall of 1967 I had become the chairman (and I purposely say chair*man* because that is just what it was at that point) of the NYU Committee to

End the War in Vietnam. There were lots of committees like that all over New York City, and we all came together for city-wide activities. Usuaully I was the representative to the city-wide group, and through that I also became active in the national Student Mobilization Committee, which at the time was still really a coalition.[5]

But there was another effect which I didn't understand at the time, and it was only through the insights of the Women's Movement that I later understood what those years meant to me on a social level. To a large degree, being a part of the leadership meant that I was seen as "one of the boys."

That meant that I was, I think, respected as a leader; in other words whenever there was a crisis or a decision that had to be made I would get called. I was pushed into leadership on the national level, and served for a while on the national coordinating committee of the Student Mobilization Committee. But I didn't get called to go out on dates. I had lots of friends, I was always with people, going to meetings or going to the movies, or eating out, but I was the third, or the fifth, or the seventh person in the group.

I think the women I was friends with also saw me as one of the boys. I don't know, because, not having that kind of feminist consciousness at that point, I didn't understand what was going on and I never talked to anyone about it. But I felt very lonely in a lot of ways, I felt bad about it. On some level I wanted to be normal.

I think I had some time before that put aside the notion that the most important thing to me would be to get married and settle down and have a family. I had enough of a flavor by then of what it meant to be an activist, to be an independent person, that I had things to do with my time and energy. That might mean at some point having a family, but it was not the

5. See footnote, p. 123.

primary thing that was motivating me. So I didn't want to be too normal, but at least I wanted what was normal in radical circles, which was to have a boyfriend.

I remember talking to a woman I knew at NYU who said, "Well maybe you shouldn't...maybe you should wear make-up." And the implication was, maybe you shouldn't be as aggressive and outspoken as you are. But whatever it was about my personality or the way I had grown up, or whatever, I just couldn't get into that kind of game playing. So I felt torn: on the one hand I said, "Well, fuck it, it's their problem. I have things to do, and I think I am an interesting person, and I'm going to go ahead and do them." And on the other hand I felt sad, and like I was being left out, and what would happen to me?

On an organizational level, I knew that the people I could count on in terms of getting leaflets distributed and getting the work done were women, and I also knew that men talked more at meetings, but I didn't think of this as a problem that we had to sort out. I wasn't tuned in enough to the dynamics of male-female relations in that political struggle to know what this was like for other women.

On top of that, at that time, was the immediacy of the war. Along with my sense that it was important to be building the Anti-War Movement, it was also a very emotional issue for me. Maybe just to say emotional doesn't really explain what I am trying to get at. Being active in the Anti-War Movement meant pulling together the old ban-the-bomb feelings, my outrage and disgust at what our government was doing to the Vietnamese people and their country, and also that very deep and strong feeling that only masses of people could exert the kind of force that it would take to make things change. It was always extremely moving to go to the big anti-war demonstrations, marching down Fifth Avenue in New York, seeing how they grew in size each six months.

I recall after the very big mobilization in New York in the

spring of 1967, at the end of the demonstration it started to
rain. I ran to my uncle's car where I was supposed to meet him
and my mother, and I got there first and just started to cry.
When they got there they thought something had happened,
that I had gotten beaten up by a policeman or something. I just
cried and cried and cried, and finally I calmed down and said
that here we'd just had 400,000 people marching in the streets,
and they are still dropping bombs in Vietnam. What are we
doing? We had spent six months organizing this demonstration, and in every respect it was a success. So many people,
more Black people than ever before. Martin Luther King
spoke at this rally. All that successful work still wasn't enough
to stop the horror. I learned at that very moment that it
wasn't enough to just have lots of people and that we might
really have to change our tactics. And for the next six months I
poured myself into work on the Pentagon demonstration.[6]

To a large degree I think it was this emotional connection
to the political work that kept me going. Compared to the
continued crises around the war, the question of who spoke up
at meetings didn't rise to the surface. At the same time though,
with the growth of the anti-draft movement, there were bitter
disagreements in our committee about whether women could
participate in discussing what men should do about the draft. I
remember one guy actually saying the women could come to
some meeting, but they shouldn't say anything. I thought that
was crazy. I knew that I was a hard worker, and other women
were hard workers. We weren't going to be drafted, but we

6. The demonstration at the Pentagon on October 21, 1967, was the
first national anti-war action to move to confrontation tactics. After
a march and speeches, several thousand of the demonstrators, as
planned, sat down on the Pentagon steps. They occupied the steps for
thirty-two hours, despite tear gas, systematic arrests and clubbings
by federal marshalls, and the deployment of troops with live
ammunition and fixed bayonets.

might have some ideas that could be useful! That was probably the first glimmering I had that something weird was going on, and that women were being slotted into a position of not being able to make important decisions.

There were other things going on during those years too. I almost got thrown out of school twice; once we took over the entire placement office at NYU to stop the work of a Dow recruiter (Dow Chemical produced the napalm being used in Vietnam), and at another time we sat-in at the campus bookstore. The store was privately owned and made a lot of money off of students. We wanted it turned into a co-op managed by the school. A good deal of what we did those years was tied to issues of control over our own lives on campus.

The spring of 1968 was the first time I heard about any women's meetings. I had gotten involved with a man. It was not great and I think I did it out of some sort of desperation. We had worked together on Stop the Draft Week that winter and he was nice enough to me, so I figured I would go with it. It lasted just a few months, but what was really interesting is the fact that he is the first person I remember telling me about the women's meetings. He was at Queens College and women there were starting to meet. I now wish that I remember more clearly just what he said to me, because I wonder how much of my reaction was just me, my own defenses, and how much it was the way he presented it. I felt very strongly, "I don't need that, that's for uptight women. I speak freely at meetings and I'm a big shot on campus; that's not for me." I didn't feel like it was wrong for women to get together, I just felt like it was a stage they had to go through and then they would be like me. You know it is embarrassing to admit this now.

By the time graduation came around that spring I was in real personal turmoil. What should I do? All that intense political work I had done the previous three years was tied up to being in school. On the one hand there was already talk about leaving the campuses and going out to organize the "working class"—although people meant all sorts of different things when they said that. My family background had already led me to believe that real change in America would come when the people who ran things day to day took control of their lives. There was a part of me drawn toward that and away from the university setting.

On the other hand it was scary to think about leaving school because that was the world I knew and all along I thought we were doing good things. I knew my role in that setting. I briefly even thought about going to graduate school in art history—I had actually gotten into it! But in the spring of 1968 I guess it just made more sense to think about going to museums as much as possible and figuring out ways to do political work for a living.

In the summer of 1968 I went to Europe. Aside from that being something you do when you graduate from college it was also a very important political experience for me. One thing was learning that I could go away for awhile and things wouldn't fall apart. Because I had been so central to so much of the political work at school, I had gotten into that kind of headset that you can never leave because everything will fall apart. And in the spring of 1968, things were happening real quick. But I went, and things didn't fall apart and I found out that I could go away and take vacations.

I went to the Ninth World Festival of Youth and Students in Bulgaria, which did wonders for my international conciousness.[7] There was a delegation from Spain, people who had had

7. Organized by Communist Parties (mostly Soviet-oriented) around the world, the Festival included a much wider variety of leftists and revolutionaries. Heated and lively discussions among participants covered not only the struggle against U.S. imperialism in Vietnam and elsewhere, but the recent student and worker uprising in France and the experiments of the Dubcek government in Czechoslovakia.

to smuggle themselves out of their country because there was a law in the books (and I am not sure if it's still there) that you couldn't travel to Eastern European countries without the possibility of five years' imprisonment. There were people from South Africa, who faced severe repression for having attended a communist youth festival, let alone for their own activities at home against apartheid. It was a very powerful experience, to be there with 20,000 young activists, exchanging our ideas and thoughts.

But the most important thing was meeting with the Vietnamese. It's ten years later but I remember every detail of it now. There were people from the North and South. Fighters with the National Liberation Front had taken almost six months to get there—walking through jungles, bicycling to the North, taking buses and trains. The whole Vietnamese delegation had taken a train across China and the Soviet Union to get to Bulgaria.

Most of us couldn't communicate in terms of talking to each other, but there was some powerful other level of connecting. It was incredibly moving. We would walk into a room, and these people that we were dropping bombs on and massacring would stand up and applaud us because they knew we were active in the Anti-War Movement. They had this incredible awareness that it was not the American people they were fighting against, but the U.S. government. Meeting the Vietnamese deepened the commitment I had already made to working to stop the war. Now the Vietnamese I had heard so much about were real people, not just an abstraction half-way around the world. And these people were taking *our* movement seriously—they wanted to know every detail of every organization and activity we were involved in. In a new way I understood how important our work at home was.

That fall I worked for the National Mobilization Committee to End the War in Vietnam, and basically me and another woman ran the New York office. We did tremendous national mailings, all the mimeoing and addressing, making sure necessary materials got sent out across the country, etc. It sometimes took weeks to do one mailing. We just worked night and day, while the men would sit in one of the offices making the decisions. Finally, here was a clear example of what women in the Women's Liberation Movement were speaking about: men making decisions and women carrying them out. I could see it happening to me.

It was during this time, in either December 1968 or January 1969, that my friend and co-worker told me about a women's meeting she had heard about. They were meeting that night and she asked me if I wanted to go. We didn't have any other plans, and I had never been to a women's meeting before, so we went.

It was a city-wide meeting that happened every week or every other week; people who came out of the New Left, the Anti-War Movement or SDS or Civil Rights work, and then people who had gotten into women's activities. Anyway, I don't even remember what the content of the discussion was that night, but it blew me away! Something had finally touched me about this women's stuff. Something began to click for me. When Ruthie and I left that meeting and walked home we decided we should get together some friends and start one of those small groups we had heard about. We called ten or twelve women and it was like the lid had been blown off. It was the most amazing six months that I think I have ever been through. We met every week, and I don't think anybody ever missed a meeting, unless they were sick or somethings dire had happened.

Looking back on it now I realize we just scratched the surface. It was a baby group compared to the ways our consciousness has changed over the past ten years. But we were talking about the most exciting things in the world—indeed, we were talking about ourselves and our lives. They were more personal, open group discussions than any of us had ever been in before. We talked about relationships, and political work, and social life. At the end of each meeting we would decide what to discuss the next week, and people would think about it during the week. One week, we would talk about growing up, or when we were little girls, another week we talked about working in the Anti-War Movement. We took a lot from the Civil Rights Movement too. I mean we made analogies between the ways Black people were oppressed and discriminated against and the ways we as women were. The fact that the Civil Rights Movement had torn apart assumptions about equality and freedom in America allowed us the space to question the reality of our own freedom as women.

It was all just terribly exciting and important. We even did some reading together. We read Engels (*The Origin of the Family, Private Property and the State*) and parts of Simone de Beauvoir's *The Second Sex*. I remember that we also read Reich's *The Sexual Revolution* which turned out to be real important for us and we discussed it for several weeks. In part it was because we were able to talk about sex in a way that I don't think any of us had ever done before. Again, I think it was just scratching the surface.

Meanwhile, after I went to that first meeting but before our small group had started, I went to the counter-inauguration demonstration in January 1969.[8] In fact, this was the big project that Ruthie and I had been working on at the Mobilization office. I recall quite vividly when Marilyn Webb and two other women got up to speak and the men yelled from the audience, "Get her off the stage. All she needs is a good fuck."

I was completely paralyzed by that. There was nothing I, or any individual, could do. It there had been a united women's presence, maybe something could have been done. It was disgusting, and it was another part of my understanding that what other women had been saying was true. It wasn't just a

8. See p. 198

question of some women having some hang-ups and not being able to talk at meetings. It was men who had the hang-ups. I began the see that there was a power dynamic between the group of people called men and the group of people called women. I was beginning to understand sexism. That demonstration was a shocking experience for me, and I didn't know what to do about it.

Some time later that spring there was a discussion at one of those city-wide meetings about whether or not we should go to an anti-war demonstration as a women's contingent with a banner saying something about women being against the war. The idea would be to try to introduce some kind of feminist presence into the march. There was a big fight about it, not because anyone there supported the war, but because some women said we shouldn't do something like that until the male-dominated left seriously took up our issues. Otherwise we would just get caught in the historical model of being a women's auxiliary and having our feminist issues get totally lost. I wanted to go and be part of a women's group. As I recall now, there were other women who thought we shouldn't make a decision as a group but individuals should decide for themselves. The fact that women were trying to figure out questions like this made a big impression on me.

I went to several national conferences that summer—SDS and the United Front Against Fascism which the Panthers were trying to form—where not only were there strong women playing active roles in the meetings, but also there were blow-ups around women's issues, and then women's caucuses trying to figure out what to do. The crux of the discussion was, should we as women, as feminists, be involved in the male-dominated left which isn't taking our issues seriously and wasn't responding to our demands? Should we pull out, or should we hang in there and push them?

This was very confusing for me personally. On the one hand I felt like it was true, men weren't taking what I said and felt about Women's Liberation seriously. For all of my anti-war activities, they weren't going to take me seriously as a feminist. That's what it meant to be one of the boys, right? I started to understand things much better. It became clear that as women we needed to find ways and forms for talking to each other—we would have to meet separately and probably form our own organizations.

At the same time, deep in my heart of hearts I felt that we couldn't separate ourselves totally. We had to deal with the fact that Panthers were being shot down, we couldn't ignore the war in Vietnam. I didn't know how to do it, how to pull it all together. So I felt and acted as if I were several different people all at once; I was an anti-war activist; I was a Panther support person; I was a feminist and my women's group probably had the biggest impact on me.

Within the Women's Movement there was a tension between the "politicos" and the "feminists," and I felt torn apart by that distinction. For sure, there were clearly different perspectives that women came into the Women's Movement with. Some people came as feminists first; this was their first political work and the identity they had taken on. At one end of the spectrum of women calling themselves feminists were women who believed that the oppression of women by men, sexism, was the base from which all other forms of oppression and hierarchy grew. Other people came out of the New Left, out of other different political activities, and then became feminists. It felt like the "politico-feminist" distinction was not quite accurate, and it certainly did not give people space to really find ways to pull it together. After all, we were all exploring lots of new ideas.

I knew personally the insights of the radical-feminists were blowing my mind open. I wanted to learn more about sexism and how we could fight against it. No, it wasn't a secondary issue but, in fact, was quite central to who I am as a woman. Personally I felt I was a "politico" *and* a "feminist."

Did this mean that nobody would have me in their camp?

By the fall of 1969, I had become active with the Venceremos Brigade organizing efforts.[9] Here was an opportunity to go to Cuba—a place I had heard so much about and which had been such a strong part of my own political growth. Not only would I be able to see this island but in fact I would be able to actively participate in their sugar harvest. Going to Cuba turned out to be another one of these intense critical experiences for me.

In part it was similar to something I referred to before when I talked about meeting the Vietnamese people in Bulgaria. Here was a real, concrete example of real people making changes. It was not an abstract idea of socialism or revolution. It was real people, real land, real mountains, real sugar cane. And very concrete changes were already visible in everything from housing, health care and education to a kind of honesty in the daily give and take between people. There was a feeling that it was important for people to speak openly with each other and to respect one another. A kind of respect that I had never witnessed in this country. That possibility of a more humane interaction among people based on a profound respect for each other as human beings was just mind blowing. And in a way it seemed to me to fit in with what the Women's Liberation Movement was also saying.

Of course, there were also obvious and critical problems. It was true that more women were getting into more varied types of jobs and higher levels of responsibility. But the machismo of Cuban men still seemed very much intact. And

9. The Venceremos Brigade is a continuing program in which Northamericans of all ages go to Cuba for one or two months to work and travel in Cuba. At the time the Brigades began, U.S. citizens were forbidden by our government to travel to Cuba, although the penalties came in the form of FBI harassment rather than prosecution.

the anti-gay attitudes on the part of the Cuban government left me feeling uneasy—even though I myself was not yet out.

The experience of those two-and-a-half months in Cuba pushed my feminist consciousness in a way that wasn't really in the Cubans' game plan. Part of that had to do with a struggle in the Brigade about whether or not women were going to cut cane. In the first big meeting they announced that the men would cut cane, and the women would stack it. There was a collective gasp, because we had very clearly been told back home that everyone would do the same work. This announcement from the Cubans sent us all into three days of intense discussions and meetings. Meetings between the Northamerican women and the Cuban women, between the Northamerican men and women, big groups and small groups, everyone talking about this issue of whether or not women would be allowed to cut cane.[10]

The decision the Northamerican women finally made was that we had come to Cuba to help them in their harvest, so we were not going to tell them how to collect their sugar cane. We would agree to do whatever jobs they gave us, on the condition that we would continue to talk about the issues, and that we would push them as time went on. Also, a few women insisted on being allowed to cut cane, and they did.

10. The process of harvesting cane involved chopping the stalks at their base with a machete, and then chopping them again to remove leaves and debris. The cleaned stalks were then picked up by mechanical lifters and placed in tractor-drawn carts for transport to a sugar mill. In order to lose as little cane as possible during the lifting, either the cutter or someone else had to leave it in relatively neat piles of parallel stalks.

The 216 Northamericans and approximately 60 Cubans of the first Venceremos Brigade did their cane cutting in nine small work brigades. The process by which the women came to cut cane varied from group to group according to decisions reached in weekly meetings, but the outcomes were the same.

What happened on my small work brigade is that we did keep bringing it up whenever there was an opportunity, without hounding the Cubans about it. We pointed out that the Northamerican men were just learning how to do it, so why shouldn't we also be taught to cut cane? Also, near the end of the time we were there, the men had become better cutters and so were leaving neater piles that needed less stacking, and the women had gotten stronger and worked faster too. This meant we ended up having a lot of free time, a lot of wasted time, with no work to do. When we pointed this out to the Cubans, they agreed and allowed us to cut cane. And on the later Brigades to come down, the women cut right from the beginning.

So this worked in a way that I think was better, maybe, then pushing too hard initially, in terms of getting the Cubans to understand it. The reason why I think this was real important as a process was the way it affected the Cuban women. One of the Cuban women with whom I became pretty good friends had worked in ten harvests and had never cut cane before and when she did it she said she would never stack cane again. But if we had been really pushy at the very beginning, she would have backed off and wouldn't have gone through those changes slowly with us.

It was really important to feel that just as we were being affected by the Cubans, we had something to offer them. They were taking our movement back home, the left, very seriously, and we should take it seriously too, because we did have important business to take care of. I came back from Cuba feeling it was real important to push our feminist movement, to be clearer about what our demands were, what we were struggling for. And feeling that there was a place for us in the continual development of a left perspective.

In the spring of 1970, after I had returned from Cuba, I became active in an effort to raise the bail money for Joan Bird, one of the defendants in the Panther 21 case. Joan was one of two women in the case, and the only one in jail at that time. With the slogan "100,000 women will free Joan Bird" we began the work of raising her bail.[11] We figured we could get a dollar each from 100,000 women. We didn't get a dollar from 100,000 women, but we did raise the bail money for her. (In fact we didn't have to raise the whole amount in cash; I think it actually took $40,000 to get her out.) One of the most successful things about this campaign was our ability to go to the Panthers and say that we were feminists and our concern around this issue was both that she was an activist with the Black Panthers fighting against racism, and also that she was a woman, and that we wanted to raise the women's issues connected to this case.

It was scary. I remember that once I and somebody else went to the Panther office in Harlem to show them the text of the brochure we were writing and to defend the women's consciousness in it. Going up on the subway, I was scared: What if they don't like it? Are we going to have a fight with the Panthers?

As it turned out we didn't have to have a big fight. Us figuring out our ideas and being fairly sure what we wanted to say before we went up there made it a lot easier. There was a beginning of what seemed to be some mutual respect. We weren't just coming as some sort of guilty white people who wanted to help the poor Panthers. We were saying that we had a struggle too and we thought there was some way to connect the two.

11. Twenty-one members of the Black Panther Party in New York were charged on April 2, 1969, with conspiracy to blow up five midtown Manhattan department stores and the Bronx Botanical Gardens. The preposterous charge was part of the nationwide police-and-FBI campaign to disrupt and if possible destroy the BPP. Thirteen of the 21 eventually stood trial, and all were acquitted on all counts on May 13, 1971, after only two hours of deliberation by the jury. Joan Bird, a student nurse, was nineteen at the time of her arrest.

This wasn't a conscious attempt to pull these two worlds together. It was just that she was in jail and we thought it would be good to raise the money, and it just flowed. There was something organic about the way it was coming together, which felt real good.

One thing about using the word organic is that I think it touches on the issue of how we each individually connect to political work and struggle. For instance, I know that my own deep connection with the Women's Liberation Movement has to do with it being *my* struggle, with it addressing the reality of my own day-to-day experiences.

The issues of process and not only how we made decisions about our individual political work but also how we worked together as a group of women had also become important to me. One of the great lessons from the Women's Movement is that the process of the work you do is critical. I think it comes from the basic feminist understanding that each of us is important and has something to offer. Groups that seem to be caught in their own hierarchies and don't develop ways for people to explore and grow seem to lose touch with the fact that activists aren't cogs in the machine of revolution but we are real, living people with honest and important needs.

By June of 1970 I knew that I wanted to make some changes in my life. I wanted to leave New York and I wanted to live collectively. So that summer I put some energy into figuring that all out.

Wanting to live collectively (and not just with roommates) was brought on by a number of things. The Women's Movement challenged the isolation of how people usually lived, in the traditional nuclear family. Weatherman and other leftists were pushing people to think about how we led our daily lives. My limited but, I think, important contact with youth culture (rock music, be-ins, drugs) also affected me. It was another level of saying that the traditional American middle-class values were all up for questioning, including my own living situation.

The experience in Cuba also left me not wanting to live alone in my own little apartment. I came back feeling that I didn't need half the things I had; one way to deal with that would be to live and share with other people.

Living collectively in New York was not impossible, but it was practically and financially real hard to pull off. And somewhere, maybe in Cuba also, I realized that I wanted to experience living in other parts of this country. On top of that, though I know I didn't lay it out like this back then, I needed to pull back a bit. I had been hot and heavy in the thick of political activity for a good five years and I needed some way to get a new perspective on the work I was doing and the ways I led my life. Maybe if I had some space I could try to figure out something about the fragmented pieces of my political identity. It was still real confusing being an anti-war activist on Tuesday, a Black Panther support on Thursday, organizer for the Venceremos Brigades on Friday and a feminist on Saturday.

In September of 1970 I moved to St. Louis and spent two years there. There we were on the Mississippi River living collectively in a great big house. I think the most important thing about those two years was the experience inside the house. We could have lived, really, in almost any city in the United States.

There were various political projects that I was involved with in St. Louis. There was anti-war work. I was active with something called the McDonnell-Douglas project and we tried to organize around the fact that this was the company making the Phantom jets dropping bombs in Vietnam, and it was also the largest private employer in the state of Missouri. We made a fairly decent film about the company and raised issues of unemployment, racism and sexism at the plant, and the war. And then in the spring of 1972, when Nixon announced the mining of the harbors of North Vietnam, we seized a former U.S. Navy minesweeper that was sitting on the river. We put out a call for Vietnam veterans to help put it into working order so we could sent it to Vietnam and sweep mines. We knew we would never really do that but we got a good deal of press out of it and left before we got arrested.

I also worked on a lead-poisoning screening program in a poor white neighborhood in coordination with Black people working on the same issue in the Black ghetto. And at one point a group of women got together and learned some radio skills and we produced a regular women's show for a local FM station. I was also in another consciousness raising group out there; this was actually my third one since I had been in a second group in New York after I got back from Cuba. So in lots of ways the political work I did in St. Louis was a continuation of the activities I had been connected to before. But it was different to move in a new setting and a city that didn't have either the recent history of extensive movement activity or the more general left-liberal support I was used to back in New York City.

The combination of the Women's Movement activity, my own reading and thinking, and the collective living experience meant that the greatest part of my time and energy and interest was tied to women's issues and feminist concerns.

The house was mixed—men, women, and children. I had never really lived with kids before and here came two years of living with them and taking on some pretty primary responsibility. It wasn't just that I babysat while their mother went out, but all of us shared the responsibilities of childcare, and it became more than a chore. We developed independent relationships with the kids, which turned out to be very important to me.

This clarified some things for me about my own relationship to family and children. Ever since, I have felt that I don't necessarily need to have my own kids, but that part of what it means to be human being is to have relationships with kids, who are other human beings. They're different from adults, and there's something sometimes harder about being with them, but there's something you get from them that you don't get from adults. This issue of adults relating to children has been something that the Women's Movement has tried to talk about. But again, here it became a real concrete experience for me, with real children.

The other thing that happened in the house was that I began to understand sexism in a new way. The women who lived there were all active in the Women's Movement, and the men were very tuned in. There was no problem about whether the men would do dishes and childcare. Yet there was still something wrong; we weren't all equals in the house. There is a way that men are able to integrate the surface changes like doing dishes and cooking and laundry, but there is another level of what it means to be a man and what it means to be a women that we still haven't changed.

There is a deep psychic kind of thing, and it has to do with where our own identities are centered. In this culture, most women still are identified through their relationships with other people, and often that is men and/or children. That is not to say you have to be in a relationship with a man or that you have to have children. It has more to do with how the world defines what it means to be a woman; you serve others. And men's identities come much more from themselves, or other men. Maybe I should give a concrete example of what I mean, which is not to say those individual men are bad or evil, but to highlight the intense socialization we all go through. The men in the house would assume something about the primacy of their needs. For instance, two or three of the women would be sitting in a room talking, and one of the men would come in because something important had happened to him, or he needed something, and he would take the space to put forth his needs. Whereas women either try to gradually shift the conversation, or they wait until there's a whole new conversation. This is a very different sense of how you take your space.

But emotional needs didn't always get so clearly expressed by the men—they came out more indirectly. In other words, they would set up situations where the women had to figure out what was going on and what sorts of things were needed. This is a very traditional thing. Women are constantly having to figure out how to meet men's needs, and it would be a lot easier if men would just say, "I don't feel good today," or "I'm in a bad mood," or "I need this." One of the things the Women's Movement has tried to do is to push not only women but men too to speak more honestly about feelings, what needs are real needs, and what needs you only think are there. This all helped lay the groundwork for my understanding that our work as feminists was going to have to go deeper than we had maybe first understood or appreciated. As a movement we would need to find ways to dig in deeper to grasp what made us all tick and what would have to be called forth to try to change things.

Living collectively in that house was a really powerful and intense experience in which I began to understand that kind of stuff. It was also part of my process of coming out. This was basically because I fell in love with one of the women in the house. By that time, early 1971, falling in love with a woman may not have been totally okay in all parts of the Women's Movement, but there were enough people talking about it that it was not a weird, foreign thing. This was very different than anything I had known before.

As I said earlier, I had actually had a relationship with a woman when I was seventeen. When I was sixteen I spent the summer at a work camp in North Carolina and became very good friends with a woman from California. The next year I went out there to spend the summer with her, and we had a sexual relationship. I was always glad about that, and never felt that it was bad or wrong, and we've been friends ever since. The fact that it was such a good experience has always stayed with me, and I'm sure it became a positive force in helping to shape my sexuality. While it was a great summer, both of us knew instinctively that it was *not* something you tell people about.

For a long time I thought it was just my "typical adolescent experience"—something that you grow out of, and then you go out with men.[12] But when I wasn't going out with men, I thought that maybe this was why, maybe they could tell. When I first got involved in the Women's Movement I knew in my head and in my gut that this was going to open up the space for me to really get in touch with who I was, and this could certainly be a part of it. Of course, in those early days I still didn't talk to anyone about it—not even my consciousness raising group. After all, it wasn't all that accepted!

Falling in love with the woman in the house sort of crystallized what I was all about. At least I knew that I was open to and interested in being involved with women.

I came back and forth to the East Coast a lot while I was living in St. Louis, and I got involved with a woman in Boston who I had been friends with. Mostly the relationship was a series of incredibly intense letters, which, as I now look back on them, were a crucial part of my coming out. She kept saying, "You're a lesbian." And I kept saying, "No, I'm bisexual," and "What difference does it make who I sleep with, it's not essential to who I am or what my politics are," and "Why do I have to take on that label?" She pushed me to think about what it meant to not take on the label. After all, to not say you are gay allows people the option of assuming that you are straight, so you've got a label anyway. And of course it is more than just a question of a label. It has to do with your own identity and self-acceptance—to say nothing of the ways others will interact with you.

12. I had read parts of *The Second Sex* by Simone de Beauvoir in which she discusses adolescent sexuality, including young women going through a "phase" with each other. —Leslie Cagan

I did come to see myself as a lesbian, and I came out. (Actually, I think that while you can remember the first time you came out, it is something that doesn't ever really stop. You just keep doing it in different forms with different people throughout your life.) Although I had support from people in my house, no one else was a lesbian. I knew only one or two other lesbians in St. Louis and I needed to go some place where this was more than accepted by straight people, where it was a part of peoples' lives.

So, in September of 1972 I moved to Boston, which not only had a large, active, and militant women's community, but also a lesbian community. One of the things I jumped into right away, and have continued to do, is public speaking about being a lesbian. Over and over again people ask, "What made you a lesbian?" The truth of the matter is that I don't totally know, lots of things must have gone into it. But one thing is crystal clear. My love for women is a strong and healthy set of emotional, political, social, and maybe even spiritual connections. Being a lesbian isn't a negative reaction to men but comes from the positive experiences and connections I have always, throughout my life, made with women. Anyway, in the course of what has felt like a long time I came to understand that not only my sexuality, but in fact everybody's sexuality, is a political issue.

I think people have come to see that gay and lesbian oppression has made being gay a political issue. But sexuality is an important part of everyone's life, and the ability to express yourself sexually can be an important part of everyone's life, and the ability to express yourself sexually can be an important component in self-awareness and each of our own abilities not only to interact with others but also to engage in struggles of all kinds.

Early on the Women's Liberation Movement developed the notion that the "personal is political." Part of the New Left critique and understanding of alienation in the U.S. also pushed out the idea that how we are able to lead our lives has political implications and is in the first place created by social, economic, and political forces. But the Women's Movement pushed that understanding to a much deeper level, especially around the question of sexuality. We began to see that sex between men and women, for instance, is often the arena where the power relations between the sexes is played out.

On top of that the Gay Liberation Movement and lesbians in the Women's Movement began to challenge this culture's assumptions about "normal sexuality," which is supposed to be both heterosexual and also the long-term monogamous couple. We began to say that maybe there isn't any one normal sexuality, maybe there are lots of ways to express our sexuality. And all those fine lines that are drawn about what is "normal" and what's okay are in fact a form of sexual repression.

I think we still don't know a lot of what we're talking about when we say that sexuality is a political issue, or how it is used to control people, but whatever sexuality is, people still don't talk about it openly and freely. It's still an area where people are very much afraid to step out of line. It is a kind of repression that makes people afraid to assert their own needs and desires.

A corollary is that when people do start to demand space in their lives to express their sexuality, that opens up the possibility of challenging other restrictions that have been placed on us. For someone to say, for instance, "No, I'm not going to be monogamous, I'm going to related to as many people as I want because that's important to me," I think it helps them to make other kinds of jumps like, "Why should all my friends be white? Why can't I have friends that are also Black or Spanish-speaking?" Once you make a jump and question one heavy norm, there's no guarantee that you'll make other jumps, but it's easier.

The other way that sexuality is a political issue is indicated by what we've seen in terms of the backlash against the Women's Movement and the Gay Movement. There is a real anti-sex attitude that comes out around the anti-ERA, anti-abortion and anti-gay campaigns. I think the anti-abortion campaign is at its core anti-female-sexuality—if women play, they have to pay. Somehow the New Right has seen that sexual conflicts are very powerful and motivating forces in people's lives.

The left has to take up these issues too. There's a crazy notion that the "working class" is only interested in bread and butter issues. But all people, whether you work in a factory or an office or are a teacher or whatever, are concerned about sex. And the left, if we are ever to be a more cohesive body than we are now, might find that it makes sense to put some energy into thinking about creative ways to raise issues of sexual politics. The Women's Movement has already shown that for a lot of women becoming a political activist doesn't happen only on the job. Women have engaged in struggle in relation to their children, their sexuality, and their communities.

So, I have come to understand some things about sexuality and politics. And I have also gone through some changes in the ways I think about the relation between the Women's Movement and other parts of the left. I believe very strongly in the need to build the autonomous Women's Liberation Movement. By autonomous I mean taking our struggles, our issues, seriously enough to give ourselves the time and space away from men not only to articulate what the problems are but also develop strategies for change. I honestly believe that it will only be out of the strength we gather in our autonomy that we will be able to work side by side with other groups of people struggling around their issues.

Since I have been in Boston, my primary arena of political work has been the Women's Liberation Movement. I have done other things, including anti-war work up until the peace treaty was signed, but the Women's Movement has been primary. I worked with the Cambridge Women's School, where women teach other women everything from skills like auto mechanics to women's history to Marxism. And for several years I was very involved with the Boston Women's Union, an attempt to build a city-wide socialist-feminist organization. For sure there were many problems in that organization, but I feel like I learned a great deal about the question of organization, things that I hope will someday be useful for thinking again about building socialist-feminist organizations.

I also spent two years working on the Susan Saxe Defense Committee. Susan was arrested in the spring of 1975 after having been undergound for four-and-a-half-years. She was brought to trial in Boston on charges of armed robbery and murder stemming from anti-war activities she had been involved in back in 1970. When she was arrested, she said that she was a lesbian. In a flash I felt connected to her. Our past experiences were different, but there were changes we each had obviously gone through that tied me to her defense. Taking up that work also provided me with some form for once again discussing what the war in Vietnam and the Anti-War Movement had been all about. In those few short years so many people seemed to forget, seemed to even want to forget.[13]

And then, since last summer, as it became clearer and clearer that the right to abortion was being systematically chopped away at, I became active with the Abortion Action

---

13. In October 1976, Susan Saxe's Boston trial ended in a hung jury. That in and of itself was a major victory. It also helped lay the groundwork for negotiations with the District Attorney. On January 17, 1977, Susan Saxe pled guilty to armed robbery and manslaughter and in return was sentenced to 12-14 years in state prison, a significant reduction from the original two natural life sentences she faced. She is now eligible for parole in 4 1/2 years.

Coalition. I've been working around the abortion issue for this past year-and-a-half now and actually think I will be doing it for some time to come. It is one of those arenas that the New Right has focused in on. It is one area of struggle where we are basically trying very hard to hold onto a minimal but important reform won out of the struggles of the 1960s and early 1970s.

Somewhere in all of this I started to think of myself as a socialist-feminist. I don't know where I first picked up the term, but I do know that for me the primary word is feminist. It's not just a question of being a socialist and being a feminist and putting them together. It involves trying to go one step further and seeing if we can understand how each type of consciousness has shaped the other. Hopefully in that process something new emerges, something which speaks to ways that sex and race and class all interweave with each other.

For instance, I believe that in contemporary America the reality is that sexism cannot be pulled out from the nature of capitalist hierarchy, and that the nature of class distinctions and things like conditions on the job are so affected by sexism (and vice versa) that you cannot say, "First we will work on one and then we will get around to dealing with the other." You can't leave race or sex or class at the door, and you can't simply say that for all situations and for all people there is one thing that is more important than anything else. That is an idea. Hopefully I and other socialist-feminists can test that one out with more practice in organizing, more talking to each other, and lots more hard thinking.

There are some other things that go into defining the outlines of my politics these days. One is my constant concern about building mass movements of people—which of course goes way far back in terms of my own political history. And another thing is my continual desire to be as public as possible about my politics. Often that translates into getting involved in the planning of street demonstrations and rallies. There has been lots of criticism of that form of political work, and while I think much of it makes sense I also still believe that—since our options for reaching masses of people are often limited or totally cut off—there are times we have to just walk down the street with our message.

You know, in some way, the hardest part of laying my own history out here has been the last five years. During that time there have been hundreds, maybe thousands, of women like me who have been going through a tremendous process, both as individuals and as a community/movement. It is a process that I believe has had, and will continue to have, profound impact on how we lead our lives and how we all think and act politically. The Women's Liberation Movement, along with the Lesbian and Gay Liberation Movement, has begun to open up our concepts of what politics are and what being an activist means. For instance, many of us struggle, and I mean struggle in the deepest sense of the word, with relationships, with questions of how we can earn a living, with issues of family and community. I guess it is more complicated to talk about something you are in the middle of than things that happened ten or fifteen years ago. I just hope that we can use that past to help us think about what we do today.

Probably one of the most important things for me about working in the Women's Movement is that it has been a space to begin to think in new ways. We have tried to encourage each other to break out of old patterns. Sometimes that means taking risks, and it isn't always so easy, but it also seems to me to be absolutely critical if we are ever going to be able to turn the monster around.

I have a feeling that even if it weren't for all those movements of the 1960's, eventually there would have been a Women's Liberation Movement. There are certain material, objective conditions that women would have gotten more and more upset about, and it would have exploded at some point. But the fact of the Civil Rights Movement, and the Black

Power Movement and the Anti-War Movement and the New Left, all made that happen much faster and helped shape the way it happened. It is hard to say for sure, but my own guess is that the Civil Rights Movement probably had the most profound impact on us. It began to crack the myth of the American Dream and the promise of equality for all. Whether directly or not, it all had a tremendous effect on the early consciousness of the Women's Movement.

There is a social and political history to who we are. We need to share that history and those experiences with other people who were either too young to be involved at the time or, for whatever reasons, were just not touched by those movements. There are things buried in that past that will help us better understand the present, to say nothing of possibly shedding some light on the future. There is a tremendous amount that we have yet to know about the links that have existed between different struggles. It is going to take the pooling of many people's different experiences and insights to see what those links are and can be. And part of that process is writing our own history. We know that "they" are never going to write our history the way it really happened. We have to do that one ourselves.

So What?
A Conclusion

Well, so what? That was the age of the New Frontier, prosperity, Martin Luther King, and Bob Dylan. This is the age of Born-Again Plastic, recession, Andy Young, and Anita Bryant. What has all this got to do with the price of gas?

Well, you show me any difference between the policies of Jimmy Carter and John Kennedy and I'll give you my entire collection of JFK's speeches on the "missile gap." The problems confronting the people of this country are the same, and the answers out of Washington are as empty as ever. The question is, what hopes or lessons does our recent history hold out for a change in this picture?

I'm going to sketch, briefly, four points about the New Left that I believe deserve to be considered by anyone who's trying to move us on from here.

Socialism is no longer a dirty word. I don't think most Americans yet find it realistic, or even relevant, but so many people and movements came to see socialism as the only way out during the 1960s that it is back in the American political spectrum. "Revolution" got to be such a catchy idea that it was used to sell everything from cigarettes to insurance.

In a negative sense, this has a number of advantages. Anti-communism can no longer be used as the glue to hold a splintering society together. This is true both internationally and domestically. Internationally, the commies are not so scary any more, so adventures like Vietnam are not so easy to justify. This is not to say there is no need for a movement against (for example) U.S. intervention to put down revolutions in Southern Africa; just that there are some ways building that movement will be easier now. Domestically, it is no longer so easy for our rulers to split and intimidate protest movements by red-baiting them.

In a positive sense, the return of socialism from the regions of hell-fire is only an opportunity, nothing more. The fact that academics can now debate the fine points of Marxism or that socialist papers are sold openly at factory gates does not mean that there is a vision of socialism which can become real to the millions of working Americans or respond to their needs as paid producers, childrearers, and citizens. More struggles must go on in which participants will see the necessity for a change in the class structure and will develop an idea of a different one. Also, somehow, Americans must become more able to extend solidarity to other peoples and learn from their struggles.

Mass struggle produces reforms. In response to mass struggle, mass disaffection, and mass doubt that the existing system can deliver what is needed, the ruling class concedes certain reforms. The reforms are made in such a way as to change as little as possible about the structure of the society, but they are made.

There are many examples of reforms won by recent movements: the extension of new legal rights to Third World people, women, and gay people; the diversion of some funds from private investment to public community services; the requirement that corporations and other institutions make up for past discrimination through effective affirmative action; the creation of open admission programs in some colleges, broadened admissions in most, and more relevant, critical, and less rigid curriculum in many; the withdrawal from Vietnam and the creation of legal checks on the warmaking power of the ✓IRAN? President; environmental and workers' health and safety restrictions on corporations, some legal and social recognition of living arrangements other than the traditional male-dominated nuclear family.

None of these reforms really transfer power to the people who demanded them. It is still, for example, up to private corporations to hire and fire; the government to send people to war; school officials to determine curriculum; and police departments to operate without community control. But some new limits have been placed on what the owners of wealth can do with their private property, and what barriers government and corporations can set up to divide people into more and less privileged groups or to bolster safe living patterns and authorties which function to keep things as they are.

Because these reforms do not involve a transfer of power, they can be taken away when the mass pressure subsides—just as they were granted when the pressure was great. Without exception, the reforms I just cited are under attack. Some examples: abortions for poor women and state employees are threatened by fund cut-offs; in the wake of the Supreme Court decision in the Bakke case, some corporations are trying to scuttle their affirmative action programs; more colleges and high schools are trying to cut bilingual programs and innovative courses.

The spearhead of the recent attack is a right-wing movement to restore certain traditions—forced heterosexuality and forced childbearing, a head start for white males in unregulated economic competition, and education which encourages conformity rather than experimentation. That movement no doubt springs out of real fears and real needs for traditions to hang on to. But in many cases this "New Right" is enthusiastically seconded (and financed) by the class and the institutions whose power would be enhanced by a rollback of the reforms.

Defending these reforms is important, but movements are not built around defending reforms. Movements are built around going forward (or going backward). I say this without any more idea that anyone else about how to create new forward motion. But as a lesson of the '60s, it seems to me that progress is made by offensive, radical mass movements which gain the political and cultural initiative.

The left must take a broad view of politics. Most of the movements of the New Left came to regard the class structure of capitalism as a (not necessarily *the*) major source of the evils and oppressions which they were trying to end. But the issues that created a New Left in the 1960s were not what American leftists have traditionally thought of as the key issues of the class conflict between those who work and those who own. The participants did not usually identify themselves as "workers," and to the extent to which the different movements saw each other as allies, it was because they had common enemies, not because they were members of a common class.

In the '70s, there has been significantly more political motion in the workplace—for union reform and for control over such aspects of work as safety, layoffs, and overtime. There had also been an increasing tendency for former participants in New Left movements to see class issues as the overriding ones, and to look for ways of uniting Blacks, other minorities, whites (and sometimes men and women) around the aspects of their experience which are the same

But it remains true that many major issues which cause crises in American society are not directly economic ones: race, sexual roles, foreign policy, resources and environment, culture. Even the economic issues causing the greatest uproar today—taxes and inflation—are not directly part of the conflict between owner and worker.

It is also true that in those revolutions elsewhere in the world which have resulted in attempts to establish socialism, issues other than the issue of class-against-class have played an important role in mobilizing the revolutionary sentiment. (These issues have been war and dictatorship in Russia; colonialism in Vietnam, Angola, Mozambique, and Guinea-Bissau; dictatorship and foreign domination in Cuba; and foreign invasion in China.) These societies were all less capitalist and much different than our own, but this lesson might apply as well as others that have been drawn.

So—the New Left certainly did not solve the question of the relationship of the class conflict to other conflicts in the society. The sudden, almost shocking emergence of a class analysis in the late '60s drove home some important basic points, but it did not lend itself to much new, clear thinking. The newer lefts which will be built in the future will benefit by being more class conscious than the New Left was in its beginnings. But these newer lefts will also have to be built around a clear understanding of what conflicts are actually moving people and a clear analysis of the sources of those conflicts both in class relations and in other structures.

Among the reasons why people join movements are personal reasons. If you look through the statements that make up this book, you see this over and over again: to become empowered, to not be afraid any more, to revolutionize themselves, for purpose and community, for survival, friends, and ethics, for the excitement and relief that come with the act of sharing, because "something began to click for me."

I doubt that this process is unique to the New Left. It is possible that the New Left paid more attention to it than previous movements. But it is also possible that previous movements did so in their own particular ways, and the fact that I, or we, don't know this only testifies to how much of this history has been suppressed or lost.

In line with this point, and because so much of this book is devoted to personal views of our recent history, I'd like to close by saying what participation in the New Left did for me. It is hard for me to understand how I could have developed however much confidence, discipline, respect for other people, patience, and respect for myself I possess if I had not gone through that experience of struggling together with other people against the system under which we live, and for a better one. It goes almost without saying, I hope, that what I "owe" in return is to try to put those qualities to work in pushing that struggle forward.

Appendix

These books and articles describe in greater depth the movements and organizations represented in this book. Most are by participants. A number are out of print or difficult to find in stores, but they can be found in libraries.

Chapter 1: On the origins of the Greensboro sit-in, William Chafe, "The Greensboro Sit-Ins," in *Southern Exposure* magazine, Fall 1978 ($3.00, PO Box 230, Chapel Hill, NC 27514). On SNCC, two memoirs: Cleveland Sellers, *River of No Return* (Morrow, 1973, hardback only), and James Forman, *The Making of Black Revolutionaries* (MacMillan, 1972, hardback only); and one sympathetic outside account: Howard Zinn, *SNCC: The New Abolitionists* (Beacon, 1965, out of print).

Chapter 2: Two memoirs: Bobby Seale, *Seize the Time* (Vintage, 1970, out of print), and Huey Newton, *Revolutionary Suicide* (Ballantine, 1974). A sympathetic but critical outside account: Gilbert Moore, *A Special Rage* (Harper & Row, 1971, out of print). And Huey Newton's political writings, *To Die for the People* (Vintage, 1972).

Chapter 3: The essay is based partly on notes taken by Shola Akintolaya and the author in 1970-71, as well as recent interviews by the author with Luke Tripp and former ELRUM member Sylvester Hyman. Two books on the LRBW are Dan Georgakas & Marvin Surkin, *Detroit: I Do Mind Dying* (St. Martins, 1975) and James Geschwender, *Class, Race, and Worker Insurgency: The LRBW* (Cambridge University, 1977); the author reviews the first *Radical America,* Jan.-Feb. 1977 (PO Box B, N. Cambridge, MA 02140) and *Journal of Ethnic Studies,* forthcoming, respectively. Also *Radical America,* March-April 1971; and the following interviews: John Watson, *Radical America* July-August 1968, *The Fifth Estate* May 1 & May 15, 1969; Mike Hamlin, *Guardian* Feb. 28,1973; and Hamlin & Cockrel, *Leviathan*, June 1970.

Chapter 4: Kirkpatrick Sales, *SDS* (Vintage 1973, out of print); *Radical America* issue on the New Left, July-August 1972. On the formative experience of white volunteers in the South, Elizabeth

Sutherland, *Letters from Mississippi* (Signet, 1965, out of print). On international context, Barbara and John Ehrenreich, *Long March, Short Spring: The Student Uprising at Home & Abroad* (Monthly Review Press, 1969). On youth culture, Abbie Hoffman, *Woodstock Nation* (Vintage, 1969, out of print).

Chapter 5: Thomas Powers, *The War at Home* (Grossman, 1973, out of print) is a liberal but sympathetic account. Dave Dellinger, *More Power Than We Know* (Anchor, 1975). James O'Brian, "The Anti-War Movement and the War," *Radical America* May-June 1974.

Chapter 6: David Cortright, *Soldiers in Revolt* (Doubleday, 1975, hardback only), is an excellently researched history by a participant. Matthew Rinaldi, "Olive Drab Rebels," *Radical America* May-June 1974, and Alband, Rees, & Woodmansee, "The GI Movement Today," *Radical America,* 1977.

Chapter 7 & 8: Robin Morgan, ed., *Sisterhood is Powerful: An Anthology of Writings From the Women's Libertion Movement* (Vintage, 1970) is already a classic. Sara Evans, *Personal Politics: The Roots of Women's Liberation in the Civil Rights Movement and the New Left* (Knopf, 1979) is a study by a participant. Also Edith Hoshino Altbach, ed., *From Feminism to Liberation*)Schenkman, 1971, out of print) and Judith Hole & Ellen Levine, *Rebirth of Feminism* (Quadrangle 1973).

SOUTH END PRESS TITLES

ABOUT SOUTH END PRESS

South End Press is committed to publishing books which can aid people's day-to-day struggles to control their own lives.

Our primary emphasis is on the United States—its political and economic systems, its history and its culture—and on strategies for its transformation.

We aim to reach a broad audience through a balanced offering of books of all kinds—fiction and non-fiction, theoretical and cultural, for all ages and in all styles and formats.

South End Press, Box 68, Astor Station, Boston, MA 02123